Catholic
Social Teaching
1891–Present

A Historical, Theological, and Ethical Analysis

Moral Traditions Series

A series edited by James F. Keenan, S.J.

Catholic Social Teaching

1891–Present

A Historical, Theological, and Ethical Analysis

CHARLES E. CURRAN

Georgetown University Press
Washington, D.C.

Georgetown University Press, Washington, D.C.
© 2002 by Georgetown University Press. All rights reserved.
Printed in the United States of America

10 9 8 7 6 5 4 3   2002

This volume is printed on acid-free offset book paper.

Library of Congress Cataloging-in-Publication Data

Curran, Charles E.
    Catholic social teaching, 1891–present : a historical, theological, and ethical analysis /
Charles E. Curran.
        p.cm. — (Moral traditions series)
    Includes bibliographical references and index.
    ISBN 0-87840-880-0 (alk. paper) — ISBN 0-87840-881-9 (pbk. : alk. paper)
        1. Sociology, Christian (Catholic) 2. Catholic Church—Doctrines. I. Title. II. Series.

BX1753 .C865 2001
261.8'088'22—dc21

                                                                    2001040803

to BILL DONNELLY

Contents

Acknowledgments

Citations of the documents of Catholic social teaching are taken with permission from David J. O'Brien and Thomas A. Shannon, eds., *Catholic Social Thought: The Documentary Heritage* (Maryknoll, N.Y.: Orbis, 1992). I have changed the language to be inclusive, however.

I am especially grateful to my institution, Southern Methodist University, for providing me the opportunity and support for my research. I am privileged to hold the Elizabeth Scurlock University Professorship of Human Values established by Jack and Laura Lee Blanton in memory of Laura Lee Blanton's mother. Laura Lee Blanton died in 1999, but her memory and good deeds live on. The librarians and holdings of the Bridwell Library continue to facilitate my work. My associate Carol Swartz, a most congenial officemate, skillfully prepared this manuscript for publication, and Rosemarie Gorman prepared the index.

Introduction

This book deals with the contemporary body of Catholic social teaching as found in papal and hierarchical documents, beginning with the 1891 encyclical of Pope Leo XIII, *Rerum novarum,* and continuing to the present. In addition, the letters of the U.S. Catholic bishops on peace and the economy in the 1980s constitute a fuller development of the primary source. These documents constitute what has often been called Catholic social teaching. Obviously, although Catholic social teaching is broader than these documents, in the context of Catholic ecclesiology these official documents have been identified with Catholic social teaching. This volume uses the commonly accepted terminology of Catholic social teaching to refer to this body of documents; it also shows the diversity and differences among these documents, however.

Many excellent books and articles have been written about this body of Catholic social teaching. Three different perspectives or ways of treating these documents are possible, although there will always be some overlap. The first perspective considers these documents from the viewpoint of Catholic social teaching, with the emphasis on the "teaching" aspect. What positions have been proposed?[1] The second perspective, often in conjunction with the first, considers the historical development of these teachings in light of the circumstances and times in which the various documents were written.[2] The third perspective comes from the discipline of Catholic ethics and is the approach followed here. Catholic social ethics, as a second-order discourse, endeavors to study the social teachings in a thematic, systematic, and scientific way. Systematic and scientific study of these documents gives great importance to methodological aspects. Although these documents themselves do not explicitly develop their methodology at length, methodological approaches play a very significant role in all of them. The discipline of social ethics also is concerned with the major themes and positions taken, but it tries to put all the aspects together in a logical, thematic, and systematic manner. Because this body of teaching developed over many years, this book considers the historical development with regard to methodology and to a systematic understanding of the positions taken in Catholic social teaching.

BROADER CONTEXT OF THE DOCUMENTS

Catholic hierarchical social teaching and Catholic social ethics today build on a long tradition of social teaching originating in the Scripture and various attempts to propose a more systematic ethic down through the years. This introductory section briefly describes the historical antecedents of Catholic social teaching.

Early Historical Development

A primary source for Catholic social ethics is the social teaching in the Bible. The Hebrew Bible contains much social teaching—including the Ten Commandments, which traditionally have played a major role in Catholic teaching. Some Scripture scholars maintain that the commandments themselves probably arose in light of the experience of the community and the need for some norms and guidelines to promote and safeguard the life of the community and of its members.[3] The Hebrew Bible regards the individual as belonging to a community and working for justice within that community. The prophetic books of the Hebrew Bible emphasize, in a special way, concern for poor people and often single out the need to take care of widows, orphans, and strangers. Usury or interest-taking on loans was forbidden, at least within the community. The very first pages of Genesis discuss the role of work in human affairs.

The New Testament contains many of the same themes—especially the dangers connected with wealth. Subsequent Christians often have pointed to the saying of Jesus about giving to God what is God's and to Caesar what is Caesar's to recognize different roles as well as potential tensions between one's obligation to the state and one's obligation to God. The biblical teaching on slavery and the role of women in society raises significant problems for contemporary Christians. At the very minimum, many Christians today employ a historical hermeneutic to explain that these positions cannot be maintained in different historical and cultural circumstances. One of the functions of Christian ethics entails proper interpretation of the sources in Scripture.[4] The Scriptures constitute an important source for Catholic social ethics, but they deal especially with specific teachings and are not primarily interested in methodological or systematic concerns.

In its first thousand years, the Christian Church and its leaders had to deal with all the issues impinging on life in the world. Augustine's *City of God* is a move toward a somewhat systematic and more scientific understanding of the relationship between the secular and the sacred: between the state and the church.[5] These tensions have been perennial questions for Christians. Issues of politics, commerce, and family were discussed in great detail. Concerns of justice and care for people in need always constituted an important concern for the church throughout its history. These themes of life in the world continue to be discussed in the beginning of the third Christian millennium.

The early part of the second millennium saw the origin of universities and attempts at more systematic and scientific knowledge, especially concerning theology and law. Medieval scholasticism in a university context fostered such more systematic approaches. The best example of systematic theology in this period (which became most important for the future development of Catholic theology in general and social ethics in particular) was the work of Thomas Aquinas (1225–1274). Aquinas's *Summa theologiae* tried to systematically present all theology in a unified whole, with moral theology or ethics as a part of this whole.[6] At this time, an explicitly systematic and scientific discussion began and flourished.

Aquinas provided a lasting orientation for Catholic social teaching through his dialogue with and incorporation of many Aristotelian perspectives, especially the anthropological basis for social ethics. The Christian tradition understands the person not as an isolated monad but as existing in multiple relationships and called to live and work with others in the basic communities of the family, the church, broader human social communities, and the state. In light of the Christian understanding of anthropology, Aquinas adopted Aristotle's notion that the human being is social and political by nature. As a result, the state is something natural, necessary, and basically good, to which the individual is called by one's very nature to belong to achieve one's own happiness and fulfillment. Aquinas also took from Aristotle the understanding of justice that—in keeping with the social nature of human beings—involves not only one-on-one relationships but also the relationship of the individual to society and society to the individual. The Dominican friar gave more space to justice than to any of the three theological virtues or the other three cardinal virtues.[7] These fundamental ideas have exerted a lasting influence on Catholic social ethics and social teaching.

Catholic scholars did not universally accept Thomism in the thirteenth and subsequent centuries, but a Thomistic revival occurred near the beginning of the sixteenth century simultaneously in Germany, Italy, and France. Thomistic moral theology (a term Aquinas did not use) flourished especially in Spain at the University of Salamanca. Francisco de Vitoria (1492–1546), often called the founder of international law, studied the political problems of his time in light of Thomistic methodology and principles. The authors of the School of Salamanca (e.g., Domenico Soto, 1495–1560) wrote learned commentaries on the justice treatise in Aquinas and dealt with many of the new political and economic problems facing Spain at that time, including maritime trade and colonization in the Americas.[8]

Following the Protestant Reformation and the Council of Trent, Catholic moral theology in general became more involved with the internal life of the church and often engaged in polemical apologetics with Protestantism. Catholic moral theology concentrated on preparing confessors for the sacrament of penance; in this context, the *Institutiones Theologiae Moralis* appeared as textbooks for the discipline. The emphasis of these textbooks on discerning sinful acts and the degree of their sinfulness was not conducive to developing a Catholic social ethics.[9]

Eighteenth and Nineteenth Centuries

The eighteenth century witnessed the growth of the Enlightenment, with its emphasis on the individual and human freedom. The Enlightenment affected Catholic social teaching and social life above all in its political theory and practice. There were some attempts in the eighteenth and nineteenth centuries to dialogue with political liberalism, but in the end the Catholic Church found itself in opposition to the Enlightenment. In theory, the Catholic approach strongly disagreed with the Enlightenment's emphasis on the individual, human freedom, and human reason totally cut off from any relationship to God and God's law. Catholicism often saw a connection between Protestantism and the Enlightenment because Protestantism first initiated the emphasis on the freedom of the believer and cut the individual off from the important relationship to the church and its teachings. Thus, the Reformation personified religious liberalism by extolling the conscience and freedom of the individual believer. Philosophical liberalism stressed the freedom of the individual and the power of human reason—both of which, however, were divorced from any relationship to God and God's law. Political liberalism stressed the role of the individual citizen, with decisions being made by majority vote and no consideration given to God's law. Roman Catholicism reacted very negatively to the abuses of the French Revolution: its atheism, its rationalism, the seizure of church property, and the imposition of the Civil Constitution of the Clergy. The Catholic Church became an opponent of democracy and a strong supporter of the *ancien régime*. The *Syllabus of Errors* promulgated by Pope Pius IX in 1864 well illustrates the Catholic opposition to the Enlightenment in general and democracy in particular.[10]

In the second half of the nineteenth century, economic questions came to the fore with the rise of the Industrial Revolution, with its capitalistic underpinnings and exploitation of workers. Several factors influenced the reaction of the church to these economic developments. On the pastoral scene, the plight of workers became an important practical concern. In European countries and in the United States, many Catholics were among the new workers who came to the cities to find employment and wealth. These workers had no real rights, however, and were subject to the voracious appetite of the marketplace. Minimum wage laws, limited working hours, the right to organize, disability insurance, and protection against unemployment did not exist. Many pastors identified with the plight of the urban poor.[11]

Competing ideas and approaches swirled in the intellectual realm. Catholics often regarded capitalism as another illustration of the excesses of the Enlightenment. Economic liberalism allowed the individual or entrepreneur to do whatever he or she wanted in the pursuit of profit, with no concern for others involved in the enterprise. In light of these contemporary problems, some Catholics reminisced in a nostalgic and romantic way about what had existed during the Middle Ages. The Middle Ages seemed to be the golden period of human existence; ever since, thanks to the Reformation and the Enlightenment, the world had been going downhill. The title of a famous book published in the United States at the beginning of the twentieth century by well-known writer and layperson James J. Walsh illustrates this approach: *The Thirteenth Greatest of Centuries*.[12]

Catholic fascination with the Middle Ages continued well into the twentieth century and often was regarded as existing in opposition to the inequalities and injustices of the modern world. The Middle Ages epitomized the Christian ideal: the social person in an organic society. Liberalism, individualism, and selfishness did not exist at that time. All Christians were united in the one true Christian religion, which permeated the lives of everyone and the culture of the times. Kings and rulers recognized their obligation to God and to natural law. They served as defenders of the poor, the downtrodden, widows, and orphans. Social solidarity, as illustrated in the guild system, marked the economic organization of society. The guilds brought together everyone in a particular craft and worked for the good of all. The individualistic quest for wealth and personal gain did not exist; labor and work aimed primarily not at acquiring a personal fortune but at earning a comfortable living. The ideal was the small town surrounded by farm areas and presided over by the steeple of the church in the center of the town. There were none of the problems that the Industrial Revolution brought to the burgeoning cities of the late nineteenth century. Yes, such a society was hierarchical, static, and heavily agrarian, but in the eyes of many Catholics this was the Christian ideal.[13]

On the other hand, socialism provided a competing worldview and philosophy. Earlier than most people, Karl Marx recognized the horrendous problems of the urban poor and workers brought about by the Industrial Revolution. Catholics at that time totally rejected the atheism, materialism, and determinism associated with socialism. They also recognized the danger of subordinating the individual to the totalitarian state.[14] The Enlightenment and socialism were polar opposites, a kind of Scylla and Charybdis; the Catholic approach was trying to find a middle ground. The use of neoscholasticism in the nineteenth century presented Catholic thought with the theology and philosophy of Thomas Aquinas.[15] Aquinas's anthropology—with its insistence on the human being as social and political—provided a firm basis for avoiding the dangers of liberalism and socialism. This middle position, opposed both to liberalism and to socialism, continues to have a great influence on Catholic social teaching to this day.

The term "Catholic social teaching" today describes the hierarchical documents of the Catholic Church that deal with social issues, beginning with the encyclical *Rerum novarum* of Pope Leo XIII in 1891—although Catholic social teaching involves much more than just these papal documents. There is no official canon or list of Catholic social teaching, but commentators generally agree on the items that belong to this group. Earlier nineteenth-century popes also wrote some encyclicals on social issues,[16] but these documents usually are not considered a part of Catholic social teaching. From the perspective of this book, beginning with Leo XIII makes even more sense because he made neoscholasticism the Catholic approach to philosophy and theology and used this philosophical approach in developing his social teaching.[17] Subsequent popes continued to use the neoscholastic approach, but with some significant modifications. Because this book deals primarily with ethics as a systematic discipline, neoscholasticism and its basis in Thomistic philosophy are discussed in great detail in subsequent pages.

By the time of Leo XIII, many factors influenced a Catholic response to the economic and political questions of the day brought to the fore by the Industrial Revolution: teachings in Scripture and church tradition, the pastoral response to the needs of workers and poor people, Catholic attitudes toward socialism and the Enlightenment, a Catholic tendency to look on the Middle Ages as the golden period of human existence, and revived interest in the philosophy and theology of Thomas Aquinas.

DOCUMENTS OF CATHOLIC SOCIAL TEACHING

There is no official canon of these papal documents. Generally, however, the following documents are included:

- *Rerum novarum*, "The Condition of Labor" (1891), Pope Leo XIII

- *Quadragesimo anno*, "After Forty Years" (1931), Pope Pius XI

- *Mater et magistra*, "Christianity and Social Progress" (1961), Pope John XXIII

- *Pacem in terris*, "Peace on Earth" (1963), Pope John XXIII

- *Gaudium et spes*, "Pastoral Constitution on the Church in the Modern World" (1965), Second Vatican Council

- *Dignitatis humanae*, "Declaration on Religious Freedom" (1965), Second Vatican Council

- *Populorum progressio*, "On the Development of Peoples" (1967), Pope Paul VI

- *Octogesima adveniens*, "A Call to Action on the Eightieth Anniversary of *Rerum novarum*" (1971), Pope Paul VI

- *Justitia in mundo*, "Justice in the World" (1971), Roman Synod

- *Evangelii nuntiandi*, "Evangelization in the Modern World" (1975), Pope Paul VI

- *Laborem exercens*, "On Human Work" (1981), Pope John Paul II

- *Sollicitudo rei socialis*, "On Social Concern" (1987), Pope John Paul II

- *Centesimus annus*, "On the Hundredth Anniversary of *Rerum novarum*" (1991), Pope John Paul II

In addition, two documents of the U.S. Catholic bishops are included in "the canon" in the United States:

- *The Challenge of Peace: God's Promise and Our Response* (1983)

- *Economic Justice for All* (1986).[18]

The papal documents began with Leo XIII's *Rerum novarum* in 1891; subsequent papal documents often were issued on the occasion of anniversaries of this encyclical. Many of these papal documents took the form of encyclicals, which are formal teaching documents of the pope addressed primarily as circular letters to all bishops around the world and later addressed as well to all people of good will. Some of these documents, however, are less authoritative papal writings or come from other sources (e.g., the Second Vatican Council).

The continued significance of these documents today undoubtedly owes much to their origins in the hierarchical teaching office of the Roman Catholic Church. Another very important factor is at work, however. Many other papal encyclicals and documents from the time of Leo XIII to the present are no longer cited or even remembered in the Catholic tradition. Why are the documents in the foregoing list still regarded as important and significant? Catholic theology has always recognized the role of reception played by the whole church with regard to hierarchical documents.[19] These documents remain important because the contemporary church has received them as such.

My focus here involves an ethical study that emphasizes methodology and systematic understanding of the various teachings proposed in the context of historical developments that have occurred in this body of teaching. This book deals with the more important issues that have been developed in these documents; it explores these issues in light of broader methodological approaches and systematic relationships with other aspects of the teaching. A brief summary of each individual document and its historical context will be helpful for our purposes.

Leo XIII: *Rerum novarum,* 1891

The first modern use of the encyclical occurred with Pope Benedict XIV in 1740. Only with Pius IX in the nineteenth century, however, did the encyclical form become more frequently employed. Pius IX also used encyclicals to address questions of the political order (e.g., *Quanta cura,* 1864) in his condemnation of liberalism and secularism as well as socialism. Thus, Leo was not the first to use encyclicals or to address the political order.[20]

History holds a special place for Leo XIII not only for his encyclicals and other teachings on the social, political, and economic orders but also for his official imposition of the approach of Thomas Aquinas in Catholic theology and philosophy.[21] It is no surprise, then, that Leo used Thomistic approaches in his discussion of the political and economic issues of his day.[22] Many commentators have praised the Leonine imposition of Thomism on Catholic theology and philosophy as a positive factor that enabled Leo to speak effectively to the modern world. Without doubt, the Thomistic approach enables one to dialogue with all other human beings on the basis of human reason to determine what is the moral good for society.[23] However, the authoritative imposition of Aquinas also was a way to prevent dialogue with modern philosophical thought. The Catholic Church opposed many of the philosophical and political developments in the seventeenth and eighteenth centuries associated with the Enlightenment. This harking back to the teaching of Thomas Aquinas reflects the tendency to regard the Middle Ages as a golden period.

In responding to the problems raised by the Industrial Revolution, Leo learned much from Catholic thinkers who had been dealing with the issues for several decades. As might be expected, Catholic approaches condemned not only the one-sided individualism associated with liberalism and the Enlightenment but also the socialist alternative with its subordination of the individual to society. In retrospect, three generic approaches had been discussed. A more conservative approach associated with the school of Angers and the Belgian Charles Périn (1815–1905) opposed any state intervention but insisted on the Catholic obligation of charity to help poor workers. At the other extreme was the corporatism associated with the Austrian Karl von Vogelsang (1818–1890) and with the Fribourg Union, which espoused a more radical reconstruction of the social order along corporate lines—bringing together capital, owners, workers, and "consumers" into occupational groups that would work together for the good of the industry under the direction of a broader corporation and thus overcome the division between capital and labor. Notice a resemblance to the guild system of the Middle Ages. A third or middle approach associated with the Germans Wilhelm Emmanuel von Kettler (1811–1877) and Paul Hitze (1851–1921) advocated a more reforming approach involving the right of workers to organize to protect themselves and endorsing some state intervention to defend workers and the weak. [24]

In *Rerum novarum*, using a Thomistic method and anthropology, Leo XIII strongly attacked socialism; recognized the legitimacy of and need for greater participation by all people in private property; and defended the just wage, the right of workers to organize, and the need for limited state intervention to help groups in trouble. "Whenever the general interest of any particular class suffers, or is threatened with, evils which can in no other way be met, the public authority must step in to meet them. . . . [T]he law must not undertake more, nor go further, than is required for the remedy of the evil or the removal of the danger" (nn. 28–29, O-S, p. 28). Thus, the beginning of modern Catholic social teaching insisted on what might be called today a relational anthropology that avoided the opposite extremes of individualism and collectivism. Historical circumstances would influence and shape this trajectory.

Pope Pius XI: *Quadragesimo anno,* 1931

Quadragesimo anno addresses the continuing problems of the industrial revolution and its impact on workers as exacerbated by the Great Depression at the end of the 1920s. Pius XI continued the basic defense of workers and their rights—calling for some state intervention; the qualified right to private property, which also retains its social dimension; and the condemnation of the extremes of socialism and capitalistic individualism. In a long final section, however, Pius proposes a reconstruction of the social order, based on corporatist principles as an alternative to both capitalism and socialism. Thus, this document puts forth a more radical solution, at least in the long term, than did *Rerum novarum*. Such an approach served as the basis for understanding Catholic teaching as a third and distinctive model, but subsequent popes abandoned this concept without ever explicitly disagreeing with the proposal.

Pope John XXIII: *Mater et magistra,* 1961

This document builds on the earlier teaching in light of the many significant developments that occurred after World War II. This encyclical is best remembered for its insistence on socialization: the more complex interdependence of citizens that calls for growing state intervention because only the state can deal with such all-embracing issues. This emphasis exists in tension, however, with the older principle of subsidiarity. John XXIII recognizes the right to private property but insists on the social dimension of property and condemns the inequalities that exist in our world. The encyclical develops the understanding of the just wage in this new context, calls for wider participation of workers in industry, and deals with contemporary problems in agriculture.

John XXIII: *Pacem in terris,* 1963

This encyclical on the basis of the natural law written in the human heart develops the moral order that guides human life in four areas: order between human beings, relations between individuals and the state, relations between states, and the world community. Three new developments stand out in this encyclical. For the first time one finds a somewhat developed discussion of human rights. By distinguishing between false ideological teachings and movements that address social and economic questions, John opens the door for dialogue between East and West. A few paragraphs deal with the disastrous arms race and war; an official but erroneous translation of one sentence gave the false impression that the pope had adopted a pacifist position.[25]

Vatican Council II: *Gaudium et spes,* 1965

The Pastoral Constitution on the Church in the Modern World incorporates many of the methodological shifts associated with the Second Vatican Council. This document from Vatican II deals with the church's relationship to the world and laments the split between faith and daily life. The first part consists of four chapters dealing with the dignity of the human person, human community, human activity in the world, and the role of the church in the modern world. The second part considers five problems of special urgency: marriage and family, culture, socioeconomic life, the political community, and the fostering of peace.

Vatican Council II: *Dignitatis humanae,* 1965

This Declaration on Religious Freedom for the first time officially accepts religious freedom that is based on the right of all citizens to be free from external coercion to act against their conscience or preventing them from acting in accord with their conscience in religious matters. This teaching is based on the dignity of the human person that has been impressing itself more and more deeply on contemporary consciousness. John Courtney Murray, the American Jesuit, exerted great influence on this document, which was of major concern for the American bishops at the council.

Paul VI: *Populorum progressio,* 1967

This encyclical maintains that development is the new name for peace and insists on personal and social development in the context of a transcendent humanism. Paul stresses the destiny of the goods of creation to serve the needs of all, the growing gap between rich nations and poor nations, and the need for social justice to govern world trade. This letter emphasizes that the social question has become worldwide and underscores the needs of the developing world.

Paul VI: *Octogesima adveniens,* 1971

This document is not an encyclical but an apostolic letter of the pope to Cardinal Maurice Roy, president of the Council of the Laity and of the Pontifical Justice and Peace Commission. (Paul VI never wrote another encyclical after the 1968 encyclical *Humanae vitae,* which condemned artificial contraception.) In *Octogesima adveniens,* Paul issues a call to action to Christians to participate and contribute to solving the many problems facing individual countries and the world. The first step involves analyzing the particular situations in which they find themselves. This document emphasizes the human aspirations to equality and participation; recognizes some legitimate aspects in Marxism, especially as a tool of sociological analysis; condemns liberal ideology; discusses urbanization; and mentions the environment for the first time.

Roman Synod: *Justitia in mundo,* 1971

The 1971 international synod published this document on justice, which contains the most commonly quoted sentence from Catholic social teaching: "Action on behalf of justice and participation in the transformation of the world fully appear to us as a constitutive dimension of the preaching of the Gospel" (O-S, p. 289). The bishops call for significant structural change in our world, based on justice and universal solidarity. For the first time, this document recognizes the need for the church to bear witness to justice in its own life if its call for justice in the world is to be credible.

Paul VI: *Evangelii nuntiandi,* 1975

This apostolic exhortation deals with the broader question of evangelization but continues the insistence that working for social justice is an essential part of the meaning of the Gospel. "[E]vangelization involves an explicit message, adapted to the different situations constantly being realized, about the rights and duties of every human being, about family life without which personal growth and development is hardly possible, about life in society, about international life, peace, justice and development—a message especially energetic today about liberation" (n. 29, O-S, p. 313). Notice the influence of liberation theology.

John Paul II: *Laborem exercens,* 1981

The first social encyclical of Pope John Paul II is a more theological and philosophical reflection on human work, written on the ninetieth anniversary of *Rerum novarum.* As is his wont, John Paul II appeals to certain scriptural passages—in this case, in Genesis—as the starting point for his consideration. In a personalist perspective, this document insists on the subjective aspect of work (the person who does it) as being superior to the objective aspect, thus grounding the priority of labor over capital. The encyclical develops a theology and philosophy of work and the rights of workers. John Paul II introduces the concept of the indirect employer involving other institutions, including the state, to help overcome the structural injustices that affect workers. The priority of labor is the basis for criticizing the ideology of rigid capitalism and the ideology of scientific socialism and communism. The principle of the common use of the goods of creation constitutes the first principle of the whole ethical and social order and grounds the call for socialization of certain means of production. The insistence on solidarity and human rights indicates a significant emphasis that was to become central in the social teaching of John Paul II. Solidarity obviously also alludes to the Polish labor movement that was active at this time in Poland.

John Paul II: *Sollicitudo rei socialis,* 1987

This encyclical commemorates the twentieth anniversary of *Populorum progressio* and builds on its notion of development, with special emphasis on the emerging world of the South. Catholic social teaching criticizes the opposing blocks of liberal capitalism in the West and Marxist collectivism in the East, which by their rivalry have contributed to the lack of development in the South or the Third World and Fourth World. John Paul II again stresses solidarity and incorporates, to a degree, two significant emphases of liberation theology: structural sin and the preferential option for the poor. This encyclical continues to attack economism and materialism, calls attention to some demographic problems first discussed in *Populorum progressio,* and recognizes some ecological concerns mentioned in *Octogesima adveniens.*

John Paul II: *Centesimus annus,* 1991

The entire Catholic world expected this encyclical on the hundredth anniversary of *Rerum novarum.* The document begins by summarizing the teaching of *Rerum novarum* and emphasizing events and ideas that developed in the meantime. John Paul strongly argues against atheism and socialism. One chapter discusses the momentous changes of 1989 (i.e., the fall of Communism). All commentators agree that the pope played a significant role with regard to the fall of Communism in Poland and in other areas of the East. Chapter 4 insists on the universal destiny of the goods of creation to serve the needs of all people. The failure of Communism does not mean that John Paul uncritically embraces capitalism and free markets. He accepts the market economy, but only within a strong juridical framework to protect the rights of all people, especially those who are poor and needy. He criticizes the welfare state by name, although commentators have disagreed about the true meaning of this condemnation. George Weigel calls this statement the most striking papal endorsement of the free economy.[26] Donal Dorr suggests that the condemnation refers to the fact that the welfare state treats poor people as objects rather than as subjects who are actively participating in their own political and economic life.[27] The pope insists again that the church has no precise models to propose for socioeconomic life and recognizes the need to bear witness to justice and the preferential option for the poor in the life of the church.

U.S. Catholic Bishops:
The Challenge of Peace: God's Promise and Our Response, 1983

This pastoral letter, while recognizing the legitimate call of individuals to pacifism and nonviolence, develops the "just war" theory for the guidance of states. In light of the cold war debate over U.S. deterrence policy, the letter concentrates on this aspect. The bishops oppose countercity weapons and first use of even counterforce nuclear weapons but leave some ambiguity about retaliatory counterforce weapons. In the context of this understanding of the use of nuclear weapons, the pastoral letter calls for a strictly conditioned moral acceptance of some limited counterforce deterrence.

U.S. Catholic Bishops: Economic Justice for All, 1986

This pastoral letter proposes a Christian view of economic life that is based on biblical perspectives and traditionally accepted natural law principles of Catholic social teaching. The document recognizes our relationship with all other human beings and develops the guiding principles of love, solidarity, and justice. These principles call for an option for the poor, minimal levels of participation in the life of the human community for all, and securing the economic rights of all. A "new American experiment" of partnership for the common good insists on the cooperation of all, including the state, to secure the basic rights of everyone in the American economy. The letter applies the general teaching to four specific areas: employment, poverty, food and agriculture, and developing nations.

Focus of This Volume

The subject matter of this book is the body of Catholic social teaching beginning in 1891. Because this teaching spans 110 years, I pay special attention to historical developments and changes. I intend to examine the body of Catholic social teaching from the perspective of Catholic social ethics that involves a thematic, reflexive, and systematic study of morality. Within Catholic social ethics, there can and should be many different ways of systematically and scientifically understanding and approaching this discipline. In a sense, "Catholic ethics" is a generic term; it can include many different approaches that share characteristics that have been developed in Catholic social teaching and ethics over the years and centuries. I do not claim that my approach is the only possible approach; the reader should recognize that my analysis and criticism of Catholic social teaching is based on my own systematic understanding.

This study discusses the major issues developed in Catholic social teaching. The documents of Catholic social teaching deal primarily with social, economic, and political issues. Some topics—such as the family, the role of women, and the environment—are mentioned in these documents but are developed in greater detail in other papal and hierarchical writings. This book does not deal in depth with these issues precisely because they lie outside the scope of Catholic social teaching. The major issues discussed here are considered in terms of their relationship to the thematic understanding of Catholic social teaching and its various parts.

The first part of this book examines the ethical methodology in Catholic social teaching. The methodology section has three distinct aspects: the theological aspect (chapter 1), the ethical aspect (chapter 2), and the ecclesial or church aspect (chapter 3). The second part of the book examines the content of or substantive positions taken in Catholic social teaching, with an emphasis on a systematic understanding that tries to relate particular teachings to one another and to the whole in a coherent and consistent way. Chapter 4 discusses the anthropology of Catholic social teaching as the primary synthesizing aspect of the various issues considered. Chapters 5, 6, and 7 develop the economic and political teachings in these writings and emphasize how they fit together. Both parts of this book explore significant historical developments that have occurred within Catholic social teaching over the years. The documents themselves downplay change and development; they frequently cite earlier documents, insist on continuity within the tradition, and never explicitly disagree with previous documents. Finally, I believe that social location affects one's perspective. I have written this book in the United States, and I engage in dialogue with that context.

NOTES ────────────────

1. Peter J. Henriot, Edward P. DeBerri, and Michael J. Schulteis, *Catholic Social Teaching: Our Best Kept Secret* (Maryknoll, N.Y.: Orbis, 1992).

2. Two excellent illustrations of this approach are Donal Dorr, *Option for the Poor: A Hundred Years of Catholic Social Teaching*, rev. ed. (Maryknoll, N.Y.: Orbis, 1992), and Marvin L. Krier Mich, *Catholic Social Teaching and Movements* (Mystic, Conn.: Twenty-Third, 1998). The former emphasizes the broader global context; the latter relates papal social teaching to various movements in the United States.

3. A. D. H. Mayes, "The Decalogue of Moses, An Enduring Ethical Program?" in *Ethics and the Christian*, ed. Sean Freyne (Dublin: Columba, 1991), pp. 25–40; Johann Jakob Stamm, with Maurice Edward Andrew, *The Ten Commandments in Recent Research*, Studies in Biblical Theology, Second Series, no. 5 (Naperville, Ill.: Alec R. Allenson, 1968), pp. 66–75.

4. Carolyn Osiek, "Jesus and Cultural Values: Family Life as an Example," *Hervormde Teologiese Studies* 53 (1997): 800–814; James D. G. Dunn, "The Household Rules in the New Testament," in *The Family in Theological Perspective*, ed. Stephen C. Barton (Edinburgh: T and T Clark, 1996), pp. 43–63; Jeffrey S. Siker, *Scripture and Ethics: Twentieth Century Portraits* (New York: Oxford University Press, 1997).

5. William S. Babcock, ed., *The Ethics of St. Augustine* (Atlanta: Scholars, 1991).

6. Thomas Aquinas, *Summa theologiae*, 4 vols. (Rome: Marietti, 1952).

7. Aquinas, *IIaIIae*, q. 57–122.

8. Louis Vereecke, *Storia della teologia morale in Spagna nel XVIo secolo e origine delle "Insti-*

tutiones Morales" (Rome: Accademia Alfonsiana, 1980), 17–98.

9. Ibid., 99–124

10. Wolfgang Muller et al., *The Church in the Age of Absolutism and Enlightenment*, vol. 6 of *History of the Church*, ed. Herbert Jedin and John Dolan (New York: Crossroad, 1981); Roger Aubert et al., *The Church in the Age of Liberalism*, vol. 8 of *History of the Church*, ed. Herbert Jedin and John Dolan (New York: Crossroad, 1981).

11. Paul Misner, *Social Catholicism in Europe: From the Onset of Industrialization to the First World War* (New York: Crossroad, 1991), 1–168.

12. James J. Walsh, *The Thirteenth Greatest of Centuries* (New York: Catholic Summer School, 1907).

13. William J. Engelen, "Social Observations IX: Medieval Social Ideal," *Central-Blatt and Social Justice* (July 1923): 111–13. See also Philip Gleason, "American Catholics and the Mythic Middle Ages," in *Keeping the Faith: American Catholicism Past and Present* (Notre Dame, Ind.: University of Notre Dame Press, 1987), 11–34.

14. Misner, *Social Catholicism in Europe*, 101–212.

15. Gerald A. McCool, *Catholic Theology in the Nineteenth Century: The Quest for a Unitary Method* (New York: Seabury, 1997).

16. Michael J. Schuck, *That They May Be One: The Social Teaching of the Papal Encyclicals, 1740–1989* (Washington, D.C.: Georgetown University Press, 1991).

17. McCool, *Catholic Theology in the Nineteenth Century*, 226–40.

18. For a collection of these documents, see David J. O'Brien and Thomas J. Shannon, eds., *Catholic Social Thought: The Documentary Heritage* (Maryknoll, N.Y.: Orbis, 1992). For a similar collection from England containing all of the documents in O'Brien-Shannon except the pastoral letters of the U.S. bishops, see Michael Walsh and Brian Davies, eds., *Proclaiming Justice and Peace: Papal Documents from Rerum Novarum through Centesimus Annus* (Mystic, Conn.: Twenty-Third, 1991). This collection also includes two other earlier encyclicals of John Paul II—*Redemptor hominis* (1979) and *Dives in misericordia* (1980). References to these documents in the text include the paragraph number (n.) from the document itself and the page number (p.) from O'Brien-Shannon (O-S). The English translations in O'Brien-Shannon use exclusive language; I use inclusive language.

19. Richard B. Gaillardetz, *Teaching with Authority: A Theology for the Magisterium in the Church* (Collegeville, Minn.: Liturgical, 1997), 227–73; Hermann J. Pottmeyer, "Reception and Submission," *Jurist* 51 (1991): 262–92.

20. Schuck, *That They May Be One.*

21. Pope Leo XIII, *Aeterni Patris*, in *The Papal Encyclicals 1878–1903*, ed. Claudia Carlen (Wilmington, N.C.: McGrath, 1981), 17–27.

22. Leo consigned the first draft of *Rerum novarum* to the neoscholastic Jesuit, Matteo Liberatore. See Misner, *Social Catholicism in Europe,* 214.

23. Note the title of one collection of Leo XIII's encyclicals: Etienne Gilson, ed., *The Church Speaks to the Modern World: The Social Teachings of Leo XIII* (Garden City, N.Y.: Doubleday Image, 1954).

24. Misner, *Social Catholicism in Europe,* 101–212.

25. Paul Ramsey, "*Pacem in terris,*" in *The Just War: Force and Political Responsibility* (New York: Charles Scribner's Sons, 1963), 70–90.

26. George Weigel, "The New 'New Things,'" in *John Paul II and Moral Theology: Readings in Moral Theology, No. 10*, ed. Charles E. Curran and Richard A. McCormick (New York: Paulist, 1998), 319–20.

27. Dorr, *Option for the Poor,* 346.

PART I

Methodology

CHAPTER 1

Theological Methodology

Three overlapping and interrelated methodological approaches rooted in theology have greatly influenced Catholic social teaching and Catholic social ethics: catholicity or universality, the goodness of creation, and mediation.

CHARACTERISTICS OF CATHOLIC THEOLOGY

The Catholic tradition is catholic with a small "c"—meaning universal, embracing and touching all reality. This emphasis on catholicity and universality argues against any reductionistic approaches. Because the Catholic approach strives for universality, it tends to be inclusive rather than exclusive. Thus, Catholic theology has insisted on "both-and" rather than "either-or" approaches. The most distinctive aspect of Catholic theology is the Catholic "and." Catholicism has insisted on the Scripture and tradition, not the Scripture alone; grace and works, not grace alone; faith and reason, not faith alone; Jesus and the church and Mary and the saints, not just Jesus alone. The Catholic tradition's problem comes from a tendency to give too much importance to the element after the "and" at the expense of the elements before the "and." For example, at times Catholicism has given more importance to tradition than to Scripture, to Mary than to Jesus, to works rather than to grace. The "both-and" aspect is characteristic, however, of an all-embracing universality that is wary of "either-or" approaches. The church catholic is concerned about the church *and* the world.

An important foundation for the insistence on universality in the Catholic approach, especially with regard to the area of social ethics, comes from acceptance of the fundamental goodness of creation. Creation and the world are not inherently evil (and therefore opposed to the Christian). God created the world and saw that it was good. A danger in the Catholic emphasis on the basic goodness of all that God has made has been a failure to give enough recognition to the presence of sin; nevertheless, humans and creation are not opposed to the divine and the Creator.

Presupposing catholic universality with its "both-and" approach and acceptance of the goodness of creation and the human, how should we understand the relationship between the divine and the human? The Catholic tradition has insisted on mediation: The divine is mediated in and through the human. This mediational aspect sometimes is called the sacramental principle,[1] the analogical imagination,[2] or the incarnational principle. The incarnation stands as the basic illustration of mediation. The divine becomes human—the word was made flesh in Jesus, but no one has ever seen the divinity of Jesus. The divine is mediated in and through the humanity of Jesus. This incarnational understanding is paradigmatic of the divine-human relationship, based on mediation. The Catholic understanding of the church illustrates mediation well. God comes to us through Jesus and in the Spirit through the visible human community of the disciples of Jesus, which also has human officeholders. The church is not just an invisible reality involving the relationship of the individual soul immediately with God; it is the visible human community through which God comes to individuals and individuals go to God. The church is the body of Christ.

The Catholic emphasis on the sacraments illustrates another aspect of the principle of mediation. God is present in and through the community primarily at the Eucharist. The Eucharist as a celebratory meal reminds us of all the celebratory meals that we share with family and friends. At these meals we celebrate our relationships, remember our joys and sorrows, comfort one another in the present, and encourage one another in hope for the future. The Catholic tradition has taken over this fundamental way for human beings to celebrate their love for one another within a community and uses it as the way in which God is present to the ongoing community in time and space. Notice how in all the sacraments the divine is mediated in and through the human—water, wine, bread, oil. The very word *sacrament* itself means *sign*. The human is the sign of the divine presence and activity in our midst.

The Catholic approach—as illustrated in Thomistic and later neoscholastic philosophy—insisted that reason can prove the existence of God by moving from the natural and created world to the divine. Analogy or mediation formed the basis for this claim. The shadow of God is present in all creation; we can learn something about God from what we see in creation. God tells us something about creation and the human, and creation and the human tell us something about God. This is the famous Catholic insistence on the analogy of being. All created existence in this world shows the glory of God and tells us something about God.[3] Catholicism—especially in the neoscholastic period beginning with Pope Leo XIII—gave great importance to natural theology or theodicy as an understanding of God and God's existence that is based totally on human reason. Today some people question this emphasis on strictly proving God's existence from reason, but natural theology's existence and role in the Catholic tradition exemplifies the Catholic insistence on mediation.[4]

This chapter illustrates how the Catholic insistence on universality, the goodness of creation, and mediation ground important aspects of theological methodology in modern papal social teaching. Even more fundamentally, they ground the existence of and need for Catholic social teaching. In the beginning of *Quadragesimo anno* (1931), Pius XI points out that Leo XIII and many other Catholics dedicated themselves to overcoming the undeserved misery of the working classes because they did not believe that the vast inequality "in the distribution of temporal goods was really in harmony with the designs of an all-wise Creator" (n. 5, O-S, p. 43). In justifying the involvement of the church in social and economic issues, Pope John Paul II insists, "At stake is the *dignity* of the human person whose *defense* and *promotion* have been entrusted to us by the Creator. . . (*Sollicitudo rei socialis*, n. 47, O-S, p. 429). The very existence of Catholic social teaching and involvement in working for justice and peace in the world recognizes that God has a purpose for creation and human beings must work in accord with that purpose. As time went on, however, the grounding for the social teaching and mission of the church included more than creation and its goodness.

REASON AND NATURAL LAW AS SOURCES OF MORAL WISDOM

A fundamental methodological question for theological ethics concerns the sources of moral wisdom and knowledge. Do the Christian, Christian social teaching, and Christian ethics find moral wisdom and knowledge only in revelation, in Jesus Christ, and in Scripture? The Catholic tradition—in keeping with its universality, its "both-and" approaches, and its insistence on the goodness of creation—

has recognized a considerable role for human reason as a source of moral wisdom and knowledge. The Catholic moral tradition understands reason in moral matters in light of natural law. Natural law has two significant dimensions: the theological and the philosophical. The theological aspect responds to the question of the sources of moral wisdom and knowledge for the Christian and explains how human reason is related to God. The philosophical aspect of the natural law question refers to the precise meaning of human reason and human nature (which I consider in chapter 2).

Although many theories of natural law were in existence even before the time of Christ, in the thirteenth century Thomas Aquinas developed a natural law theory that became generally acceptable within Roman Catholicism.[5] Aquinas does not reduce all morality to natural law; in fact, his discussion of natural law comes only at the end of his treatment of ethics—after he first considers the virtues and human acts.[6]

To properly understand the Thomistic concept of natural law, one must recognize the intrinsic nature of Thomistic morality and its insistence on mediation. Morality is what contributes to human goodness, fulfillment, and happiness. Morality is not a law imposed on human beings from the outside by someone who wants to force the human being to do the will of the legislator; morality is based on what contributes to human flourishing.[7]

Aquinas was a rationalist, not a voluntarist, with regard to his understanding of law. Law is not primarily an act of will by the legislator but an ordering of reason. For Aquinas, something is commanded because it is good—never the other way around. For Aquinas, law in all its different understandings (e.g., eternal law, natural law, human law) refers to an ordering of reason. Notice how this understanding accentuates the importance of wisdom as the primary virtue of the legislator.[8]

The very term *natural law* seems to indicate a legal or deontological ethical model with law as the primary way of understanding the moral life, but such is not the case. Thomistic natural law really exemplifies a teleological model rather than a deontological model. A teleological model understands morality primarily in terms of ends. For Aquinas, the end plays the primary role in morality. The first question Aquinas asks with regard to ethics is the question of the ultimate end of human beings, which is happiness or the full flourishing of the individual.[9] The human being must strive to attain the true end or purpose of all of the God-given inclinations and powers (e.g., passions, intellect, will) that make up human nature.[10] Perhaps the most accurate understanding of the way in which Aquinas develops natural law—although he does not use this expression himself—is as follows:

Natural law is human reason directing human beings to their ultimate end in ac-]
cord with their nature.

Thomistic natural law theory well illustrates the Catholic insistence on mediation. Aquinas understands natural law in relationship to eternal law. Eternal law is
God's rational plan or ordering for the world. Natural law is the participation of
eternal law in the rational creature. How does this participation or mediation
work? How can human beings know the plan or rational ordering that God has for
the world? Do we go immediately to God and ask? No. God created the world in
accord with God's plan but also gave human beings reason so that, reflecting on
human nature and all that God created, we can discover what God wants us to do.
Thus, natural law is the participation of eternal law in the rational creature. Human reason reflecting on the creation made by God can determine how God wants
us to act or what constitutes our own flourishing and happiness.[11] The plan of God
and our flourishing and happiness are the same.

Without doubt, natural law theory fit very well with the nineteenth-century papal opposition to liberalism. Philosophical liberalism so exalted human reason that
it denied the divine and cut off human reality from any relationship to God and
God's law. Aquinas insisted on the role of human reason but regarded human reason as related to the divine reason through mediation.

Leo XIII officially imposed the neoscholastic approach to Thomism that came to
the fore in the nineteenth century and is associated with figures such as German Jesuit Josef Kleutgen and Italian Jesuits Matteo Liberatore and Luigi Taparelli. Today
some Thomists point out the shortcomings and even distortions of this version of
Thomism. Above all, the strong neoscholastic distinction (at times almost a separation) between the supernatural order and the natural order strongly influenced the
development of papal social teaching. The natural order involved life in this world
under the rule of reason and natural law, whereas the supernatural order involved
the life of faith and grace mediated by Jesus and the church. Thus, grace, faith, and
Jesus Christ have very little to say about life in this world.[12] H. Richard Niebuhr, the
American Protestant ethicist, referred to this supernatural-natural distinction and its
approach as a "Christ above culture" model in which Christ does not directly influence culture in the world but is limited to the supernatural sphere.[13]

Early Encyclicals

Even a cursory glance at *Rerum novarum* shows that the encyclical heavily depends on neoscholasticism and its natural law approach. Nine of the thirty-nine

footnotes refer to Thomas Aquinas; all but two of the others refer to Scripture (the exceptions are two references to Gregory the Great and Tertullian from the era of the early church). Notice that there is no dialogue with contemporary thinkers.

Rerum novarum recognizes the important role of reason as a source for moral teaching and frequently invokes natural law and its principles. The first part of the encyclical proves the human right to private property, in opposition to the socialist position. The right to have property as one's own is based on human nature and is one of the chief points of distinction between human beings and all other animals. In keeping with the thought of Aquinas, Leo XIII describes human beings as having reason and the power of self-determination in carrying out their instincts for self-preservation and the propagation of the species. Precisely because human beings alone of all the animals have reason and the power of self-determination, they need stable and permanent possession of private property to achieve their end (n. 5, O-S, p. 16). Through reason, human beings need to plan for the future, and the inexhaustible fertility of the earth provides a storehouse for human needs and wants (n. 6, O-S, p. 16). Leo XIII goes on to point out

> another proof that private ownership is according to nature's law.... [W]hen the human being thus spends the industry of one's mind and the strength of one's body in procuring the fruits of nature by that act one makes one's own that portion of nature's field which one cultivates—that portion on which one leaves, as it were, the impress of one's own personality, and it cannot but be just that one should possess that portion as one's own, and should have a right to keep it without molestation (n. 7, O-S, p. 17).

Despite some contrary positions, the common opinion "has found in the study of nature, and in the law of nature herself . . . the principle of private ownership as being preeminently in conformity with human nature, and as conducing in the most unmistakable manner to the peace and tranquility of human life" (n. 8, O-S, p. 17).

Leo XIII clearly understands natural law in terms of mediating the law of God. Human beings govern themselves by their own reason "under the eternal law and the power of God whose Providence governs all things" (n. 6, O-S, p. 16). In describing Leo XIII's approach, Pius XI in *Quadragesimo anno* (1931) points out that the right to own property has been given to human beings by nature, or the Creator (n. 45, O-S, p. 52).

The opening section on private property in *Rerum novarum* illustrates the natural law methodology at work. The role of Scripture is entirely subordinate to the basic natural law structure. Only after developing the natural law arguments does this section end with the simple recognition that, "The authority of the divine law adds its sanction, forbidding us in the gravest terms even to covet that which is an-other's. . . ." and then cites the commandment from Deuteronomy 5:21 (n. 8, O-S, pp. 17–18).

The methodology of Leo XIII's social teaching is based on natural law. In keep-ing with the nature and custom of encyclical letters, *Rerum novarum* is formally ad-dressed to all the bishops of the world. In his commentary forty years later, howev-er, Pius XI correctly points out that Leo XIII addressed himself "to the entire Church of Christ and indeed to the whole human race" (n. 8, O-S, p. 43). The natu-ral law methodology logically allows one to address all human beings because the arguments proposed are not primarily based on uniquely Christian sources. Leo XIII cites particular Scriptural texts to support conclusions already reached by nat-ural law. The primary positions he defends—including the rights of workers to a just wage, fair working conditions, and organizing—are all based on reason and natural law.

Subsequent documents continue the natural law approach. Pius XI's *Quadra-gesimo anno* and John XXIII's *Mater et magistra* (1961) commemorate anniver-saries of *Rerum novarum*, review the teaching of the earlier document, clarify some of its aspects, and apply its principles to new circumstances and conditions. These two documents continue to use the same methodology as *Rerum novarum*, with its emphasis on human reason, human nature, and natural law. After reviewing *Re-rum novarum*, *Quadragesimo anno* sets out its own method.

> But reason itself clearly deduces from the nature of things and from the individual and social character of human beings what is the end and object of the whole eco-nomic order assigned by God the Creator. For it is the moral law alone which com-mands us to seek in all our conduct our supreme and final end, and to strive directly in our specific actions for those ends which nature, or rather the Author of nature, has established for them . . . (nn. 42–43, O-S, p. 51).

John XXIII continues to use the same methodology by proclaiming "a social mes-sage based on the requirements of human nature itself and conforming to the pre-cepts of the Gospel and reason" (n. 15, O-S, p. 86).

Pacem in terris

John XXIII's encyclical *Pacem in terris* (1963) does not commemorate an anniver-sary of *Rerum novarum* and thus does not begin by reviewing the earlier docu-ments. More explicitly than any other encyclical, however, *Pacem in terris* clearly spells out a natural law methodology.

How would one expect a Christian leader to address the question of peace in the world? One obvious approach would begin with the words of Jesus to the disciples after the resurrection: "My peace I leave you; my peace I give you." Peace will be established only if the reconciling love of Jesus becomes present in our hearts and in our world. Through conversion and change of heart, we too can share in the peace of Jesus and make it more present in our world. Hatred, jealousy, and division set up barriers among persons and nations that lead to war. The Gospel call to forgiveness and reconciliation and the life of grace lived in accord with that message alone can overcome the evils, divisions, and barriers that bring about war.

Such is not the approach in *Pacem in terris*, however. The opening paragraph sets out the method that will be used. The pope begins by noting, "Peace on earth, which all people of every era have most eagerly yearned for, can be firmly established only if the order laid down by God be dutifully observed" (n. 1, O-S, p. 131). Note again the emphasis on the ordering of reason. Human greatness allows us to understand that order and create suitable instruments to harness the forces of nature and use them properly. The gracious God created the universe and human beings themselves, pouring into them the abundance of goodness and wisdom. God created human beings in God's own image and likeness, especially endowing them with intelligence and freedom to carry out the divine plan for the world (nn. 2–3, O-S, p. 131).

Some people think that human relationships can be controlled only by force.

> But the Creator of the world has imprinted in the human heart an order which conscience reveals to us and enjoins us to obey. . . . But fickleness of opinion often produces this error, that many think that the relationships between people and States can be governed by the same laws as the forces and irrational elements of the universe, whereas the laws governing them are of quite a different kind and are to be sought elsewhere, namely where the Father of all things wrote them, that is, in the nature of human beings (nn. 5–6, O-S, p. 132).

Thus, *Pacem in terris* in its very beginnings explicitly and clearly sets out its natural law methodology. Jesus Christ and grace do not enter into the picture. The short introduction summarized above contains six citations from Scripture, but they are all used to buttress the natural law theory. The only citation from the New Testament is Romans 2:15, the classic text for proving the existence of natural law. In concluding the letter, John XXIII summarizes what the encyclical has pointed out:

> [P]eace will be but an empty-sounding word unless it is founded on the order which this present document has outlined in confident hope: an order founded on truth,

built according to justice, vivified, and integrated by charity, and put into practice by freedom (n. 167, O-S, p. 159).

The final paragraph of the introduction outlines the entire encyclical by pointing out that by these laws human beings are taught how to conduct their mutual dealing among themselves (part 1); how the relationships between citizens and public authorities of each state should be regulated (part 2); how states should deal with one another (part 3); and finally the relationship of individuals and states within the world community (part 4).

Criticism of This Approach

John XXIII explicitly recognizes one of the strengths of the natural law methodology—its openness to dialogue with all human beings—when he formally addresses his letter to all people of good will. Natural law, however, fails to highlight the central role of Jesus Christ in Christian morality. The Gospel, Jesus Christ, and grace should play a significant role in the moral life of Christians. The natural law theory in general and the early papal social encyclicals in particular downplay this role.

Pacem in terris does not entirely neglect the role of grace and the Gospel, however. After describing the order on which peace can be established, the conclusion points out that human resources alone are not enough to bring about such a noble and exalted task, but help from on high is necessary. By his passion and death (no mention is made of the resurrection) Jesus overcame sin, the root of all discord, and reconciled human beings to the gracious God. Citing Ephesians 2:14–17, John XXIII points out that Jesus is our peace and announces the good news of peace to all people, near and far. The conclusion then goes on to refer to Jesus' gift of peace to his disciples after the resurrection (nn. 169–171, O-S, p. 159). With such an approach, *Pacem in terris* remains in continuity with the earlier documents, which in their concluding sections also appeal to the need for grace and change of heart. *Quadragesimo anno*, for example, calls for the need for diffusion throughout the world of the Gospel spirit that can bring about the desired renewal of human society (n. 138, O-S, p. 74).

These references to grace, Christ, and the Gospel appear at the very ends of the documents, after the ethical principles and norms have been proposed in the light of natural law. Grace and God's redeeming love are necessary to live out fully the demands of natural law. Such an approach is in keeping with the neoscholastic theological thesis that fallen human beings without grace cannot observe the whole natural law for long.[14] The scholastic thesis is highly nuanced. Inability to observe natural law—understood collectively, embracing all the precepts belonging to it—is a moral inability, not a physical impossibility. This moral inability with regard to all the precepts of natural law does not deny the possibility of such observance in the short run. The bodies of these documents give the impression, however, that all human beings can observe what natural law entails for justice and peace. Without doubt, these documents severely restrict the role of grace, Gospel, and Jesus Christ in the Christian life, reducing them to means for observing the demands of natural law.

A second theological criticism of the natural law approach as illustrated in *Pacem in terris* involves the failure to recognize the reality of sin and its effects. By basing the whole teaching on reason and the order that the author of nature has put into the world, *Pacem in terris* and similar documents neglect the aspect of sin. As a result these documents suffer from a natural law optimism that often fails to explicitly acknowledge the harsher realities of human existence.

Sin here primarily refers not to individual sinful acts but to the presence and power of evil in the world. One could very well have written an encyclical entitled *Bellum in terris*—War on Earth. Every human generation has known the existence of war. Disorder, greed, and selfishness exist in the hearts of human beings and in the structures of our world. Sin makes it difficult for all the members of different nations to work together for the common good. In the four different parts of *Pacem in terris,* one could speak of disorder as well as order existing and affecting such relationships. Human experience and history continue to testify to the many wars, violence, and injustices that exist in our world.

Papal documents have not negatively criticized other papal documents, even after Vatican II. The emphasis in this canon of hierarchical documents is on continuity, not discontinuity. In a 1973 commentary on the tenth anniversary of *Pacem in terris,* however, Cardinal Maurice Roy, president of the Pontifical Commission on Justice and Peace, points out the many forms of violence in our world today and suggests that a new chapter (with the title *Bellum in terris*) would have to be added to *Pacem in terris.* Cardinal Roy takes the sting out of his criticism, however, by grounding the violence he cites in the radical social changes that had occurred in the ten years since *Pacem in terris.* [15] My criticism, which is more theological and radical, is directed at the encyclical's failure to fully recognize the reality of sin.

Failure to appreciate the reality of sin and its effects also influences substantive issues such as conflict and power. Sin does not totally destroy the goodness of creation, but it certainly affects all creation and human endeavors in this world.

A third criticism of the theological methodology of *Pacem in terris* concerns the ③ distinction between the natural and supernatural orders. As the encyclical indicates, the distinction in the Catholic approach at the time tends to put real distance between the natural order and the supernatural order, although there is a practical overarching unity. Papal social encyclicals dealt with the natural order and thus did not appeal to grace and the Gospel, which belong to the supernatural order.

Related to this supernatural/natural distinction were similar distinctions: spiritual/temporal; hierarchy and religious/lay; gospel/daily life and natural law; divinization/humanization. The level of the supernatural corresponds to the spiritual sphere, whereas the natural corresponds to the temporal sphere. This distinction is the basis for the distinction between hierarchy, clergy, and religious—who operate on the supernatural spiritual level—and laity, who operate on the lower level of the temporal and the natural. Clergy and religious have left the world or the temporal and have chosen to follow evangelical counsels. Note that the Gospel is a counsel for the few who leave the world, not an imperative for all. Those who stay in the world—the realm of the natural and the temporal—are lay people, who are called to follow natural law, which also is codified in the Ten Commandments. Natural law orders and directs the temporal and natural spheres, and lay people who live in these realms are called to act in accord with that law. The proper role of the laity is to transform the temporal and natural orders. Thus, the laity have a very clear and distinct role—which is subordinate, however, to that of the hierarchy.[16]

A twofold mission of the church corresponds to these other distinctions. Divinization and sanctification take place on the spiritual or supernatural level and are the work of the hierarchy and ministerial priesthood. Humanization takes place on the temporal or natural level and is the work of the laity. Divinization is the primary and more important role; humanization is the secondary but distinctive role of the church that is carried on by the laity. The hierarchical role mediates the grace and teaching of the church to the laity, who then mediate this grace and teaching to the world by their own actions. Fortified by the grace of the sacraments and the teaching of the hierarchical church (at the time the word *church* often referred only to the hierarchy), the laity carries out the humanizing mission of the church in the temporal realm under the direction of the hierarchy and of natural law. Thus, there is a clear distinction between the supernatural and the natural, and the laity have the role of mediating the supernatural to the natural.[17]

Pius XI did much to encourage this role of the laity in the church through what he called Catholic Action and the lay apostolate.[18] The original impetus for this approach came from the work of Joseph Cardijn (1882–1967), who founded the Young Christian Workers in Belgium. Cardijn's "Jocist" movement quickly spread throughout the Catholic world. A characteristic tenet of this movement involved the apostolate of like to like: Workers should try to transform other workers.[19]

It is no surprise, then, to find that Pius XI in *Quadragesimo anno* appeals to the role of the laity in transforming the temporal and natural realms. The laity who participate in this apostolate are "auxiliary soldiers of the church" (n. 141, O-S, p. 75). Note the important but secondary role of the laity as *auxiliary* soldiers. *Quadragesimo anno* points out that the best lay apostles for working people will be workers themselves (n. 142, O-S, p. 75). *Pacem in terris* ends with pastoral exhortations calling for the apostolate of a trained laity in the temporal sphere (n. 149, O-S, p. 155).

Like its predecessors, *Pacem in terris* emphasizes the theoretical distinction and an almost practical separation between the natural and supernatural orders. The problem remains that in this conception the natural constitutes a distinct and somewhat separate sphere that is not directly transformed by grace or negatively affected by sin.

CHANGE AT VATICAN II AND AFTERWARD

A dramatic change in theological ethical methodology occurred after *Pacem in terris*. The Second Vatican Council (1962–1965) introduced a new theological methodology in social issues that modified the older natural law approach. Four significant shifts in Vatican II influenced these changes.

First, *Gaudium et spes,* the Pastoral Constitution on the Church in the Modern World—the document from the council that forms a part of the canon of hierarchical social teaching—maintains that the division between the faith that many Catholics profess and their daily life should be counted among the more serious errors of our age. The prophets of the Old Testament vehemently criticized this scandal, and in the New Testament Jesus himself threatens it with grave punishment. There can be no false opposition between professional and social activities, on one hand, and religious life on the other (n. 43, O-S, p. 192). Grace, Jesus Christ, and the Gospel are related to our daily life in the world and should have some impact on it. The Constitution on the Liturgy of Vatican II insists on a close relationship between liturgy and life. The liturgy, especially the Eucharist, constitutes the summit toward which all of the activity of the church is directed and the font from which all of its power and life flows.[20] (Subsequent documents of Catholic social teaching have not explicitly developed the relationship between the liturgy and social justice, however.) Thus, the world and the temporal order in the approach of *Gaudium et spes* involve more than merely the natural and are related not only to the Creator but also to the Redeemer and the Sanctifier. "[T]he same God is Savior and Creator, Lord of human history as well as of salvation history..." (n. 41, O-S, p. 191). The earthly and the heavenly city penetrate one another (n. 40, O-S, p. 189). The reign of God includes what occurs in our world and in daily life.

Second, *Gaudium et spes* insists on the universal call of all Christians to holi-ness. Not just bishops, religious, and priests but "all Christians in any state or walk of life are called to the fullness of Christian life and to the perfection of love." The Gospel call to perfection is addressed to each and every one of the disciples without distinction. Laity, living in the world, are called to holiness and perfection and thereby "a more human manner of life is fostered also in earthly society." Life in the world, then, is intimately connected with the Gospel and Jesus' call to discipleship.[21]

Third, Vatican II restored the essential role of Scripture in the life of the church and the disciples of Jesus. Christians are encouraged to meditate on the Scriptures and understand their lives in light of Scripture.[22] The Constitution on the Liturgy (n. 24) recognized the importance of the Word of God that goes together with sacraments.[23] Vatican II itself pointed out the need for moral theology to be more grounded in Scripture. Moral theology before Vatican II, like the documents of hierarchical social teaching, had relied primarily on a natural law methodology. *Optatam totius*, the Decree on the Training of Priests of Vatican II (n. 16), called for special care in perfecting moral theology: "Its scientific presentation should draw more fully on the teaching of holy Scripture and should throw light on the exalted vocation of the faithful in Christ and their obligation to bring forth fruit and charity for the life of the world."[24]

Fourth, theologians came to recognize that the natural order was only a theological construct. The realm of the natural was a remainder concept, a metaphysical abstraction. The natural order was postulated to show that God could have made human beings without calling them to the supernatural order of divine love and friendship. This understanding guaranteed the free gift of God's saving love. In fact, the natural order as such never existed. All that we have ever known are people who have been called by God to share in God's loving friendship.[25]

Gaudium et spes

The significant shift in theological ethical methodology at Vatican II involved the realization that grace, faith, redemption, the Gospel, Jesus, and the Spirit affect and influence life in the world. The world and social issues do not involve the realm of the natural only. *Gaudium et spes,* the Pastoral Constitution on the Church in the Modern World, illustrates this dramatic contrast to the approach of *Pacem in terris* and earlier encyclicals.

Part I of *Gaudium et spes* considers the church and the human vocation. The first chapter discusses the dignity of the human person, beginning with the creation. God created human beings in God's own likeness. Human beings are not isolated monads; they are social beings who are called to live in relationships with all others. The chapter then discusses sin and its effects on human living. Experience testifies to the existence of these evil inclinations in human beings. The subsequent discussion makes clear that sin does not destroy the image of God in the human creature. Bodily, corporeal, and material things are basically good; they are not so infected by sin that they lose their goodness entirely. In conscience, the human being can discover the law of God and through freedom direct himself or herself toward goodness. The chapter ends with a long section on Christ as the new human being and then discusses the need to see the human person and life in the world in light of the redemptive love of Jesus. The Christian person, conformed to the likeness of Jesus—who is the first-born of many brothers and sisters—receives the first fruits of the Spirit and becomes capable of living the new law of love. Through Christ, the human riddles of sorrow and death receive a meaningful answer (nn. 12–22, O-S, pp. 172–79).

Chapter 2 follows the same approach in its discussion of the community of humankind. The Creator has written into human nature the law of social life, showing the interdependence of persons in society and the importance of the common good within society. Consequences of sin bring about disturbances in this order, but they do not entirely destroy the basic reality that arises from creation. A final section on the Incarnate Word stresses the communitarian character of existence and describes the new community of the church that is the body of Christ (nn. 23–32, O-S, pp. 179–185).

Chapter 3 focuses on human activity in the world and very clearly and distinctly shows the newer theological methodology at work. The first part deals with the plan of the Creator; the chapter then points out that human activity is infected by sin, finds its perfection in the paschal mystery, but will realize its fulfillment only in the new earth and the new heaven (nn. 33–39, O-S, pp. 185–89). Thus, working for justice and living in this world do not involve only the natural order of creation; they also must be seen in light of sin, as well as the redeeming love of God through Jesus and the Spirit—which comes to its fulfillment only in the heavenly Jerusalem.

Subsequent Documents

As might be expected, the significant change in *Gaudium et spes* did not immediately replace the older approach. In fact, Vatican II's Declaration on Religious
Freedom still employs the older approach, which is based on the distinction between the natural and supernatural orders. The declaration itself has two chapters.
The first chapter develops the argument for religious liberty "based on the dignity
of the person, the demands of which have become more fully known to human reason through centuries of experience."[26] The second chapter discusses religious liberty from the perspective of revelation. Although revelation does not affirm in so
many words the right to immunity from external coercion in religious matters, this
teaching is rooted in divine revelation; for that reason, Christians are bound to regard it all the more conscientiously.[27] Thus, the two chapters of the Declaration on
Religious Liberty follow the older distinction between the natural order and the supernatural order. (I discuss the Declaration on Religious Freedom in great detail in
chapter 7.)

Paul VI's encyclical *Populorum progressio* (1967) also does not follow the new
theological ethical methodology of *Gaudium et spes* in its discussion of development. Like all creatures, human beings, as spiritual beings, are ordered to the Creator—the first truth and the supreme good. Thus, although human development
and fulfillment summarize our duties, harmonious enrichment of nature by personal and responsible effort is ordered to a further perfection. By reason of union
with Christ the source of life, human beings attain a new fulfillment of themselves,
a transcendent humanism that leads to the greatest possible perfection. Because
we are social beings, human development also involves social, political, and cultural aspects. The encyclical understands development on the basis of a true and
authentic humanism whereby human beings move from less human conditions
(the basic material necessities of life, freedom from oppression by unjust social
structures, exploitation) to the higher level, which involves the growth of knowledge and the acquisition of culture; to a further level of esteem for human dignity
and cooperation for the common good; to the deeper humanization of the ac-
knowledgment of supreme values with God as their source and end; and finally to
faith, whereby we share in the life of God as God's own children (nn. 14–21, O-S,
pp. 243–45). Such an understanding of human development and fulfillment in the
context of an integral and transcendent humanism depends heavily on the thought
of French neo-Thomist Jacques Maritain.[28] Maritain is the only contemporary author cited twice in the footnotes of *Populorum progressio*.[29]

Subsequent documents in Catholic social teaching have tried to incorporate the theological ethical methodology of *Gaudium et spes* that has now become the standard approach. A few illustrations suffice to indicate this development. *Justitia in mundo*, from the international Synod of Bishops in 1971, reflects this shift in what may be the most-quoted sentence from any of these documents: "Action on behalf of justice and participation in the transformation of the world fully appear to us as a constitutive dimension of the preaching of the Gospel, or, in other words, of the church's mission for the redemption of the human race and its liberation from every oppressive situation."[30] Thus, the distinction between the natural and the supernatural is no longer accepted; action on behalf of justice is a constitutive dimension of the preaching of the Gospel and the redemptive mission of the church.[31]

In his 1975 apostolic exhortation *Evangelii nuntiandi*, Paul VI sums up the objectives of Vatican II, on the tenth anniversary of its closing, in the single theme of making the church of the twentieth century better fitted for proclaiming the Gospel (n. 2, O-S, p. 304). Paul VI echoes *Gaudium et spes* (without explicit citation) by pointing out that the split between the Gospel and culture is without doubt the drama of our time. Cultures have to be regenerated by an encounter with the Gospel (n. 20, O-S, p. 310). *Evangelii nuntiandi* insists on avoiding any reductionistic interpretation of evangelization, which by definition is many-faceted. One of the essential elements of evangelization involves transforming humanity, including the personal and collective consciences of people, the activities in which they engage, and the lives and concrete milieu that are theirs (n. 18, O-S, p. 309).

John Paul II devotes section five of *Sollicitudo rei socialis* (1987), which commemorated the twentieth anniversary of *Populorum progressio*, to "a theological reading of modern problems." John Paul II discusses obstacles to development as structures of sin, negative features working against the common good. "Sin" and "structures of sin" are categories that seldom are applied to the contemporary world, but they emphasize the roots of the evils that afflict us. Structures of sin include the all-consuming desire for profit and the thirst for power. For Christians, the diametrically opposed reality of the Christian virtue of solidarity can overcome the structures of sin with the help of divine grace. Solidarity helps us see the "other"—whether that other is a person, people, or nation—not just as an object to be exploited but as our neighbor and helper, called with us to share in the banquet of life to which all are invited equally by God. The church has an evangelical duty to take her stand beside poor people, helping them satisfy their basic rights without losing sight of other groups and the common good. Awareness of the common fatherhood of God, of the brotherhood and sisterhood of all in Christ, and of the presence and life-giving action of the Holy Spirit will bring to our vision of the world a new criterion for interpreting it. Beyond human and natural bonds, the light of faith provides a new model of the solidarity and unity that should be in our world—the model of the unity and solidarity of three persons in one God (nn. 35–40, O-S, pp. 419–24).

The development of liberation theology, especially in the South American context, also shows the influence of the approach of *Gaudium et spes*. The world and the struggle for justice are not just the realm of the natural. The Gospel call to liberation includes freedom from sin as well as from all oppressive historical, political, and economic situations.[32] I have more to say in chapters 2 and 6 about liberation theology and its relationship to Catholic social teaching; for the present it is sufficient to point out that the theory of liberation theology could not have been developed within the framework of a pre-Vatican II natural law methodology.

There can be no doubt that *Gaudium et spes* called for a more theological approach to the social teaching of the church. In the last section of this chapter, however, I point out and try to explain the lack of an integrated theological approach, especially in the papal documents that constitute Catholic social teaching.

OTHER THEOLOGICAL METHODOLOGICAL ISSUES

The theological methodological shift in *Gaudium et spes* had significant consequences for the method and approach of Catholic social teaching. These consequences involved issues of eschatology, the role of grace and faith in dealing with issues of social teaching and their relationship to other sources of moral wisdom and knowledge, the use of Scripture, and the relationship between change of heart and change of structures.

Eschatology

Contemporary eschatology deals with the relationship between the reign of God and the present realities of the world in which we live. Protestant Christian ethics—as exemplified in *Christ and Culture,* the classical work of H. Richard Niebuhr—has dealt with issues of eschatology for quite some time.[33] As long as life in the world and the pursuit of justice in the worldly moral order were considered in terms of natural law, however, there was no need for Catholic social teaching to deal explicitly with the issue of eschatology.

Gaudium et spes rightly tried to overcome the split between faith and daily life—the split between the supernatural order and the natural order. The danger in overcoming such a split is to regard grace and Jesus Christ as being too present in our world here and now. One can readily forget that the fullness of grace and redemption will come only at the end of time and history. *Gaudium et spes* did not entirely avoid this danger. The first chapter of *Gaudium et spes* ends with a section on "Christ as the New Human Being" (n. 22, O-S, pp. 178–79), and chapter 2 ends with a section on "The Incarnate Word and Human Solidarity" (n. 32, O-S, pp. 184–85). The danger is forgetting that the fullness of the reign of God will never be present in this world. Chapter 3 corrects this problem by bringing in the question of eschatology, ending with a section on "A New Earth and a New Heaven." The eschatological expectation should not weaken but stimulate our concern for cultivating this world. Earthly progress must be carefully distinguished, however, from the growth of Christ's reign. The reign of God is present in mystery in this world, but it will be brought into full flower only in the new heaven and the new earth (n. 39, O-S, pp. 188–89).

The theology of Vatican II in *Gaudium et spes* and its understanding of life in the world tended to be too optimistic precisely because it failed to recognize significant discontinuity between the present and the future. The Catholic tradition is never going to see total discontinuity or opposition between the present and the future. Insistence on the goodness of creation and the fact that grace affects our present world indicate strong continuity between the present and the future reign of God. The danger of forgetting sin and the fullness of the eschaton as future always lurks in the Catholic tradition, however.

Subsequent documents in Catholic social teaching often have been overly optimistic precisely because they do not recognize a greater tension between the presence of the reign of God and its fullness at the end of time. Perhaps this optimistic view comes from the intention of galvanizing Catholics and others to work for social change now. The conclusion of *Sollicitudo rei socialis* (1987), for example, explicitly recognizes the reality of sin and the future aspect of the kingdom, but

> the Church must strongly affirm the *possibility* of overcoming the obstacles which . . . stand in the way of development. And she must affirm her confidence in a *true liberation* . . . based on the *Church's awareness* of the divine promise guaranteeing that our present history does not remain closed in upon itself but is open to the kingdom of God (n. 47, O-S, p. 429; emphasis in original).

The most extended discussion of eschatology appears in the 1983 document of the U.S. bishops, "The Challenge of Peace: God's Promise and Our Response."

Eschatology greatly influences the teaching on peace and the possible justification of war in some circumstances. The fullness of eschatological peace remains before us in hope, yet the gift of peace is already here in Jesus Christ through the Holy Spirit. A special section on the kingdom and history points out the tension between the vision of the reign of God and its concrete realization in history. This tension often is described in terms of "already but not yet." We are a pilgrim people in a world marked by conflict and injustice. This eschatology grounds the Catholic approach. Justice is the fullness of peace. In history, unlike in the fullness of the reign of God, peace and justice are somewhat in tension (nn. 55–65, O-S, pp. 504–506). Peace is possible but never assured in this world, and its possibility must be continually protected. Thus, eschatology grounds the general ethical approach of the goal of peace, the presumption in favor of peace, and the reluctant acceptance of justified war in some limited circumstances. The ethical criteria spell out this position in greater detail. The bishops' document still seems too optimistic, however, in asserting "that peace is possible but never assured and that its possibility must be continually protected and preserved" (n. 60, O-S, p. 505).

I have incorporated eschatology into what I call the stance, basic posture, or perspective of Christian ethics that forms the horizon from which the individual Christian person and Christian ethics look at the world in which we live. Christian ethics surveys our world from the perspective of the fivefold Christian mysteries of creation, sin, incarnation, redemption, and resurrection destiny. Creation, incarnation, and redemption ground what is good and positive in human existence; sin and resurrection destiny as future ground what is limited and imperfect in the present world. The perennial temptation in Catholic ethics has been to be too optimistic and to forget about the presence of sin now and the future aspect of the reign of God.[34]

Grace and the Human

A second issue concerns the relationship of the aspects of grace, redemption, and the Gospel to the human aspects of the social, cultural, and political realties of our world. Recall that in pre–Vatican II approach, these "supernatural" elements did not enter the understanding of our life in the world.

At minimum, the nonfaith aspects continue to exist and have a significant role to play. Faith and Gospel realities do not do away with the realities and elements of our human existence in the cultural, social, economic, and political spheres. In the political realm, for example, Catholic social teaching does not call for a theocracy. The Declaration on Religious Liberty of Vatican II called for religious freedom and a government that does not impose religious positions on its citizens. *Gaudium et spes* explicitly raised the objection from many contemporaries that a closer bond between human activity and religion will work against the independence of human beings, societies, and the sciences. *Gaudium et spes* responds by accepting and defending "the autonomy of earthly affairs"—meaning "that created things and societies themselves enjoy their own laws and values which must be gradually deciphered, put to use, and regulated" by human beings (n. 36, O-S, p 186). Independence or autonomy of temporal affairs cannot mean, however, that such things and their use are not also related to God. The document goes on to claim that "by no human law can the personal dignity and liberty of human beings be so aptly safeguarded as by the Gospel of Christ which has been entrusted to the church. . . . By virtue of the Gospel committed to her, the church proclaims the rights of human beings" (n. 41, O-S, pp. 190–91).

Perhaps the most pointed way to raise the question about the relationship between faith, grace, and the Gospel, on one hand, and the human realities of political, social, economic, and cultural life, on the other hand, is as follows: Is there a unique Christian content regarding social justice in the world and the transformation of human society that is not shared by non-Christians and all people of good will? This question refers to moral obligations that are incumbent on all human beings insofar as they are human and are not the role or vocation of a particular individual. The documents of Catholic social teaching answer this question by indicating that Christians should work with all others for the same basic human rights and common good and imply that there is no unique content that calls for Christians to act in different ways from non-Christians. Many arguments support this position.

First, from a negative perspective, there is no explicit indication in the documents of something that Christians are called to do in working for transforming the world that is different from what all others are called to do. The documents could imply some differences, but in light of the following arguments that possibility also can be ruled out.

Second, ever since *Pacem in terris* the major encyclicals in this tradition have been addressed to all people of good will. The popes are speaking to all humankind, not just to Christians. It was obvious that even though earlier encyclicals were not directly addressed to all humankind, they were intended for them and open to their acceptance precisely because they were based on natural law and did claim any uniquely Christian aspects.

Sollicitudo rei socialis, the 1987 encyclical of John Paul II, does contain an explicit section on a theological reading of modern problems directed to Christians.

In this section, however, the pope is careful to express the hope that those who are not inspired by religious faith will accept the same basic approach with the urgent need to change spiritual attitudes in light of the higher values of the common good (n. 38, O-S, p. 421).

Third, the documents not only often address all people of good will; they propose principles and values such as human dignity, human rights, freedom, justice, and peace that apply to all human beings. The Catholic emphasis on the common good as a fundamental criterion of the good society by its very definition claims to be something that is shared by all members of the pluralistic human community. If Catholic social teaching proposed a unique material content for social justice, there could be no common good.

Fourth, the documents themselves propose what is good for humanity and all people and urge Christians to work together with all other human beings to achieve social justice. Paul VI highlights the universal aspect of the church's concern in the first paragraph of *Populorum progressio:*

> Following on the Second Vatican Ecumenical Council a renewed consciousness of the demands of the Gospel makes it her duty to put herself at the service of all, to help them grasp their serious problem in all its dimensions, and to convince them that solidarity in action at this turning point in human history is a matter of urgency (n. 1, O-S, p. 240).

Paul VI knew that the church alone cannot bring about true human development; all people must work together for the same goal. *Populorum progressio* ends with a final appeal to renew the temporal order that is directed first to Catholics, then to non-Christian believers, and finally to all people of goodwill:

> All of you who have heard the appeal of suffering peoples, all of you who are working to answer their cries, you are the apostles of a development which is good and genuine, which is not wealth that is self-centered and sought for its own sake, but rather an economy which is put at the service of human beings . . . (n. 86, O-S, p. 260).

With regard to John Paul II, it suffices to cite the concluding part of *Sollicitudo rei socialis:*

> At stake is the *dignity of the human person* whose *defense* and *promotion* have been entrusted to us by the Creator and to whom the men and women at every moment of history are strictly and responsibly *in debt. . . . Every individual* is called upon to play his or her part. . . . The Church too feels profoundly involved in this enterprise, and she hopes for its ultimate success (n. 47, O-S, p. 429; emphasis in original).

The pastoral letters of the U.S. bishops on peace and the economy continue this approach. They too insist on the need to strengthen the common moral vision and sustain a common culture and a common commitment to moral values in our society. The economic pastoral insists that the common bond of humanity that links all persons is the source of the bishops' belief that the country can attain a renewed public moral vision (nn. 22–27, O-S, pp. 583–84). The peace pastoral addresses two overlapping but different audiences: members of the church and the broader human society. In addressing members of the church, the bishops appeal to faith and its ramifications; in appealing to the broader public, however, they use more inclusive approaches (n. 17, O-S, p. 496). The economic pastoral does the same (n. 27, p. 584). In reality, however, the documents do not separate the two distinct audiences and the two different ways of proposing their teaching. The same basic demands are made of both audiences.

What ultimately explains the common appeal to Catholics, Christians, and all people of goodwill—whether they are believers or not—to work together for the same common good? Although one should not expect documents of Catholic social teaching to directly address more complex theoretical reasons for the common principles and values shared by all, the documents allude to three explanations that help to explain the basis for such communality.

First, Catholic teaching by definition is universal. A Catholic ethic must include a concern for the whole world, all people in the world, and what is happening in it. The earlier natural law approach illustrated a universal ethic shared by all. A greater role for faith and the Gospel in daily life does not eliminate the Catholic concern for working for the good of the entire human society and all people. A strong pragmatic concern for being effective in working for a better society also calls for working together. No single religious group can be effective. Effectiveness requires all people of different religions, races, cultures, and languages to work together for the common good.

Second, grace in the Catholic understanding—as *Populorum progressio* points out repeatedly—brings humanity to its fullness. Grace and the human are not opposed; grace brings the human to its true fulfillment. This is the basis for the transcendent and true humanism proposed in *Populorum progressio* and implied in all of the other documents. *Sollicitudo rei socialis* insists that the church is an expert in humanity (n. 41, O-S, p. 424).

Third, Catholic universality also affects grace and anthropology. The difference between Christians and others based on grace and salvation might not be as great as it appears. In *Sollicitudo rei socialis* John Paul II maintains that despite human evil and sinfulness, the church has confidence in humanity. This confidence is based on the fact of creation by a good and gracious God; it also obtains because of the "redemptive influence of Christ who 'united himself in some fashion with every human being,' and because the efficacious action of the Holy Spirit 'fills the earth' (Wis 1:7)" (n. 47, O-S, p. 429). In *Centesimus annus* John Paul II makes the central point very clearly. The last section of the document, "The Human Being is the Way of the Church," grounds all Catholic social teaching on the care and responsibility for human beings that have been entrusted to the church by Christ himself. "We are not dealing here with humanity in the 'abstract' but with the real 'concrete,' 'historical' human being. We are dealing with each individual, since each one is included in the mystery of Redemption, and through this mystery Christ has united himself with each one forever" (n. 53, O-S, p. 479). Here John Paul II repeats what pre-Vatican II theology called the universal salvific will of God who wants to save and offer salvation to all human beings. Christians do not have a monopoly on salvation and God's grace.[35]

Use of Scripture

The theological shift at Vatican II naturally raises a methodological question about how the Scripture should be used in Catholic social ethics. As should be expected, the documents under consideration in this volume do not explicitly raise the deeper methodological issue; one can learn something about the underlying methodology by studying the documents themselves, however.

The Scriptures are not the only source of moral wisdom and knowledge for Catholic social teaching. The "and" that is so characteristic of Roman Catholicism has insisted on faith or Scripture *and* reason, as exemplified in the natural law tradition. The post–Vatican II documents (e.g., *Centesimus annus*) insist that reason and the human sciences contribute to our understanding of the human (n. 54, O-S, p. 479). Despite the emphasis on the importance of Scripture in *Gaudium et spes,* this Vatican II document accentuates the autonomy of earthy affairs—meaning that human realities and societies have their own laws and values, which human beings of all and no religious beliefs must decipher and use (n. 36, O-S, p. 186).

The Catholic use of Scripture also is not fundamentalistic. One cannot claim that the words of Scripture are to be understood as literally true for all times and places. The traditional Catholic "and"—in this case the emphasis on Scripture *and* tradition—argues against any fundamentalistic use of Scripture in general or in ethics in particular. The Scriptures show the influence of the particular human authors who wrote them and the historical, cultural, and social conditions of the times in which they were written. Tradition essentially maintains that the Christian must understand, live, and appropriate the word of God in light of the ongoing historical and cultural situations of time and place. One cannot simply repeat the words of the Scripture. Recall here even the Trinitarian dogma of the three persons in one God and how it developed in the early church: There is no explicit description in Scripture of three persons in one God. In accord with the Catholic tradition, the U.S. bishops' peace pastoral recognizes that Scripture does not provide us with detailed answers to the questions we face today (n. 55, O-S, p. 504).

How, then, should the documents use the Scripture? In light of the realization of the historical limitations of the Scripture, one must differentiate more general aspects from more specific aspects of moral teaching and ethics. The general aspects of biblical moral teaching are more likely to be true and helpful for all people, whereas the more specific and historically conditioned aspects might not be applicable in other circumstances. With regard to specific aspects that are no longer applicable, consider the New Testament teaching on slavery or the role of women in society. On the other hand, the twofold commandment to love God and neighbor is valid for all Christians in all times. The problem often comes down to what the love of neighbor requires in this particular situation. Does love of neighbor call for affirmative action, universal health care, and absolute condemnation of violence? The documents should rely heavily but not exclusively on Scripture to make fundamental points about human dignity, care for poor people, and proper distribution of the goods of this world. The Scripture has much to contribute in the area of broad theory, basic vision, and fundamental values. In the discussion of more specific principles and norms such as the right to religious freedom, however, Scripture alone can never adequately address the issue. The historical conditioning of the Scripture means that its use will be more significant on the general level and less significant on the more specific level.

The economic pastoral illustrates such an approach. Chapter 2 begins with a discussion of biblical perspectives, including human creation in God's image, a covenant people, the reign of God and justice, a community of discipleship, poverty and riches, and hope. The second section goes on to propose "ethical norms for economic life." This section is more specific than the biblical perspectives that deal more with the basic Christian vision. The ethical norms develop the rights and duties of all people, such as the duties of justice and the basic civil and political rights as well as social and economic rights. This section differs methodologically from the first section, which appeals only to the biblical perspective; the Scriptures play a lesser role in the area of norms. Thus, the pastoral letter recognizes a greater role for Scripture on the more general level but a lesser role with regard to specific considerations that require heavy emphasis on human and scientific reasoning and a reading of signs of the times (nn. 28–95, O-S, pp. 584–601).

A significant problem in using and interpreting the Scriptures in Christian social ethics concerns the eschatological coloring of much of the Gospel ethic. Jesus and the early church expected the end time to come quickly. This expectation colored their moral teaching and advice. Perhaps because of the very nature of Catholic social teaching that dealt with contemporary issues of the day, there is little or no discussion about the eschatological coloring of some of the Gospel ethic. In particular, the Sermon on the Mount has always raised significant issues for Christian ethicists. Before Vatican II, Catholic approaches—unlike Protestant considerations—did not have to deal with the issue. John Courtney Murray, in his defense of natural law, brushes aside questions about the Sermon on the Mount with another question: What makes you think that morality is identical with the Sermon on the Mount? For Murray the Sermon on the Mount has nothing to do with social and political morality.[36] Bernard Häring illustrates a common contemporary Catholic approach; he regards the Sermon on the Mount as containing goal commandments or ideals and values toward which we must strive.[37] The U.S. bishops' letter on peace seems to follow this approach. The eschatological peace of the full realization of God's reign provides us with a direction in which we must urgently go (n. 55, O-S, p. 504).

Even the post–Vatican II documents tend to use the Scriptures in proof-text fashion. The documents never even allude to a critical approach to the Scriptures in the form of historical, form, source, redaction, or literary criticism. The documents do not consider the Scriptures in and for their own sake; they use the Scriptures to give support to moral teachings. The instrumental way in which the documents employ the Scriptures contributes to their failure to recognize explicitly the contemporary critical understandings of the Bible.

Change of Heart and Change of Structures

Catholic social teaching focuses primarily on changing institutions and structures. In the process, the documents also emphasize the values and principles that should be incorporated in practice—human dignity; truth, justice, charity, and freedom; civil and political as well as social and economic human rights. The tradition of Catholic social teaching also recognizes, though in a comparatively minor key, the need for a change of heart. To bring about a more just society, all people should recognize the need not only to change structures but also to change hearts. From a theological perspective, the basic change of heart is very important. The primary message of Jesus calls for repentance or change of heart. Without a change of heart, there will never be a change of structure. Yet the documents of Catholic social teaching do not give central importance to the change of heart. What explains this fact?

The pre–Vatican II documents generally emphasize the need for the change of heart only at the end. The concluding paragraph of *Rerum novarum* (n. 45 O-S, p. 38) points out that religion alone can destroy at its root the evil that is present in our world. An outpouring of Christian love can bring about the happy results longed for on the social scene. Near its end, *Pacem in terris* maintains that peace based on truth, justice, charity, and freedom is such a noble and elevated task that even the highest human resources cannot bring it to realization. For human society to reflect as faithfully as possible the reign of God, help from on high is absolutely necessary (n. 168–69, O-S, p. 159). One sees here the understanding of grace as necessary if one is to observe the demands of the natural law fully. Grace becomes primarily a means to live out in full the demands of natural law developed in the main part of the encyclical.

The post–Vatican II documents, in accord with the changes of that time, tend to give more importance to the interior change of the person, do not reduce grace only to a means to observe the law, and use more biblical language to describe the change that is required. These documents do not make change of heart the central part of their teaching, however.

By virtue of its very subject matter (i.e., evangelization), *Evangelii nuntiandi* gives greater centrality and significance to this interior change than any of the other documents.

> The purpose of evangelization is therefore precisely this interior change, and if it had to be expressed in one sentence, the best way of stating it would be to say that the Church evangelizes when she seeks to convert, solely through the divine power of the Message she proclaims, both the personal and collective consciences of people, the activities in which they engage, and the lives and concrete milieux which are theirs (n. 18, O-S, p. 309).

The biblical concept of conversion summarizes the basic change that is required. *Evangelii nuntiandi* goes on to maintain that the church is "conscious that the best structures and the most idealized systems soon become inhuman if the in-human inclinations of the human heart are not made wholesome, if those who live in those structures or who rule them do not undergo a conversion of heart and of outlook" (n. 36, O-S, p. 316).

John Paul II's *Sollicitudo rei socialis* devotes only one chapter (the fifth of seven) to a theological reading of modern problems. Structural sin constitutes the obstacle to development. "For *Christians,* as for all who recognize the precise theological meaning of the word *sin,* a change of behavior or mentality or mode of existence is called 'conversion' to use the language of the Bible" (n. 38, O-S, p. 421; emphasis in original). In keeping with the universality of the message, this same paragraph also points out that even people without explicit religious faith can and should change their basic attitudes (n. 38, O-S, p. 421).

Centesimus annus brings in explicit theological considerations only in the sixth and last chapter on "The Human Being as the Way of the Church." Although this document does not develop the need for conversion or change of heart as such, it recognizes that the "theological dimension is needed both for interpreting and solving present-day problems in human society" (n. 55, O-S, p. 480).

Why do the documents not highlight or at least give equal time to conversion or change of heart? The foregoing considerations point toward an answer. First, social teaching or social ethics primarily deals with social structures and institutions. Second, this teaching addresses all people of good will, not just members of the church. Third, to be truly effective in overcoming the grave social problems of our times, all people must cooperate and work together. Recall that *Evangelii nuntiandi*—the one document addressed explicitly to a church audience—concentrates more on evangelization and conversion. *Centesimus annus,* on the other hand, succinctly alludes to the three foregoing reasons to explain the lack of emphasis on conversion or change of heart. According to *Centesimus annus,* John XXIII was convinced (with Leo XIII) "that the grave problems caused by industrial society could be solved only by cooperation between all forces. This . . . explains why Pope John XXIII addressed his encyclical on peace to 'all people of good will'" (n. 60, O-S, p. 483).

Thus, documents of social teaching that are addressed to all people of goodwill downplay the basic Christian call to conversion and tend not to emphasize the need for a change of heart. The following section explores the tension that derives from the twofold audience of Catholic social teaching: the Catholic faithful and all people of goodwill.

An Unresolvable Tension

Gaudium et spes called for a newer methodological approach by insisting on the need to overcome the division between faith and daily life. In the two preceding sections of this chapter I have discussed some aspects of this theological methodology and how it should function. There is a deeper problem, however. The papal documents of Catholic social teaching generally do not propose a well-integrated theological methodology that permeates the documents and is used to address the particular issues under discussion. In part this approach might reflect the fact that Catholic social teaching by definition deals with teaching, not with a systematic ethical approach. Nevertheless, the documents propose church teaching that is based on the various sources of Christian moral wisdom and knowledge and is attempting to relate faith to daily life.

Ironically, an integrated approach—especially between the general explanation of the theory and the practical application to specific areas and issues—does not exist even in *Gaudium et spes* itself. Recall that the first part of that document deals with the church and the human vocation by developing the dignity of the human person, human community, human action, and the church in the modern world. This more general and theoretical part develops the more integrated theological methodology, as contrasted with the older natural law approach. The second part of *Gaudium et spes* deals with five areas or problems of special urgency: marriage and family, culture, socioeconomic life, political community, and peace. The discussion of these areas does not put into practice the more theoretical methodology discussed in the first part of the document, however. There is comparatively little mention of the role of faith, Gospel, grace, and Jesus Christ in this part. In a sense, the document suffers from methodological split personality! The theological methodology developed in part 1 is not followed to a great extent in part 2. Why not?

The lack of integration between the two parts of *Gaudium et spes* derives somewhat from the historical fact that they were developed on separate tracks and really were not integrated to form a coherent whole. The first part went through several drafts during the four years of the council. For a long time, the plan was to publish the second part merely as an appendix rather than as an official part of the document. As a result, there was no integrated relationship between the two parts.[38] In addition, the very nature of more specific discussions do not necessarily depend on broader theological understandings.

I have pointed out the absence of an integrated theological approach in the Declaration on Religious Freedom. The first chapter is based on reason; the second

THEOLOGICAL METHODOLOGY   49

chapter is based on revelation. This document deals with a specific and complex issue of constitutional law: the role and function of the state with regard to religion. As noted in the discussion on the use of Scripture, complex issues dealing with very specific topics are not much affected by the broader theological sources of faith, grace, and the Gospel; they are influenced more by the specific demands of the topic under discussion.

The document of Catholic social teaching with the most integrated theological method is *Evangelii nuntiandi*, the apostolic exhortation of Paul VI dealing with evangelization in the modern world. This document situates the social mission of the church as part of this mission of evangelization. Note, however, that in this case the document is addressed to a church audience only and does not consider many specific issues. Undoubtedly, the audience and focus of the document make a coherent and integrated theological approach much easier. *Justitia in mundo*, the document from the 1971 Synod of Bishops, likewise has a more consistent theological approach throughout. The audience for that document also is primarily the church and its members, and its focus is to develop "the mission of the People of God to further justice in the world" (O-S, p. 288).

The papal encyclicals that are the major documents of Catholic social teaching do not employ a coherent, consistent, and integrated theological approach. The best illustration is *Sollicitudo rei socialis*. This encyclical devotes one of its seven sections to "A Theological Reading of Modern Problems" (nn. 35–40, O-S, pp. 419–24). Thus, the document makes no attempt to develop a coherent and integrated theological approach to all of the matters it discusses. Theology does not permeate and unify the entire document. Again, why not? The modern papal documents of Catholic social teaching beginning with *Pacem in terris* are explicitly addressed to two different audiences: members of the church and all people of good will. This dual audience explains the lack of a coherent, cohesive, and integrated theological approach. By definition, a document with a dual audience cannot develop a unified theological approach because part of the audience does not accept such a theology. This tension is not unique to Catholic social teaching. Catholic social ethicists writing for two audiences face the same problem.[39] The twofold audience for Catholic social teaching is one of the tradition's strengths, but it is not without some problems and tensions. In fact, an irresolvable tension remains.[40]

In this chapter I analyze (with special emphasis on historical development) and criticize the theological methodology behind the documents that constitute Catholic social teaching. In chapter 2 I treat the more ethical aspects of methodology employed in these documents.

NOTES ▬▬▬▬

1. Richard P. McBrien, *Catholicism,* rev. ed. (San Francisco: Harper, 1994), 9–12.

2. David Tracy, *The Analogical Imagination: Christian Theology and the Culture of Pluralism* (New York: Crossroad, 1981); Andrew M. Greeley, *The Catholic Myth: The Behavior and Beliefs of American Catholics* (New York: Charles Scribner's Sons, 1990), especially 36–64

3. Aquinas, *Ia,* q.2, a.3.

4. McBrien, *Catholicism,* 209–23.

5. Philippe Delhaye, *Permanence du droit naturel* (Louvain: Nauwelaerts, 1960).

6. Aquinas, *IaIIae,* q. 94.

7. For a discussion of different contemporary understandings of Aquinas and natural law, see Charles E. Curran and Richard A. McCormick, eds., *Natural Law and Theology: Readings in Moral Theology No. 7* (New York: Paulist, 1991), 101–463.

8. Aquinas, *IaIIae,* q. 90–97.

9. Ibid., q. 1–5.

10. Ibid., q. 94, a.2.

11. Ibid., q. 91, a. 2.

12. Gerald A. McCool, *Catholic Theology in the Nineteenth Century: The Quest for a Unitary Method* (New York: Seabury, 1977), especially 7*ff.*, 197*ff.*, and 221*ff.*

13. H. Richard Niebuhr, *Christ and Culture* (New York: Harper, 1975), 116–48.

14. Severino Rivas, *De Gratia,* in *Patris Societatis Jesu Facultatum Theologicarum in Hispania Professores, Sacrae theologiae summa* (Madrid: BAC, 1956), 3, 521–29.

15. "Reflections by Cardinal Maurice Roy on the Occasion of the Tenth Anniversary of the Encyclical *Pacem in terris* of Pope John XXIII (April 11, 1973)," in *The Gospel of Peace and Justice: Catholic Social Teaching Since Pope John,* ed. Joseph Gremillion (Maryknoll, N.Y.: Orbis, 1976), 548.

16. Theodore M. Hesburgh, *The Theology of Catholic Action* (Notre Dame, Ind.: Holy Cross, 1946); Louis Joseph Putz, *The Modern Apostle* (Chicago: Fides, 1957).

17. John Courtney Murray, "Toward a Theology for the Layman: The Problem of Its Finality," *Theological Studies* 5 (1944): 43–75.

18. Raymond Francis Cour, "Catholic Action and Politics in the Writings of Pope Pius XI" (Ph.D. diss., University of Notre Dame, 1952); Liliana Ferrari, *Una storia dell' Azione cattolica: gli ordinamenti statuari da Pio XI à Pio XII* (Genoa: Marietti, 1989).

19. Michael De La Bedoyère, *The Cardijn Story* (New York: Longmans, Green, 1958).

20. Constitution on the Sacred Liturgy, n. 40, in *Vatican Council II: The Conciliar and Post-Conciliar Documents,* rev. ed., ed. Austin Flannery (Collegeville, Minn.: Liturgical, 1992), 6.

21. Constitution on the Church, n. 40, in Flannery, *Vatican Council II,* 397.

22. Constitution on Divine Revelation, nn. 21–26, in Flannery, *Vatican Council II,* 762–65.

23. Flannery, *Vatican Council II,* 10.

24. Ibid., 720.

25. Stephen Duffy, *The Graced Horizon: Nature and Grace in Modern Catholic Thought* (Collegeville, Minn.: Liturgical, 1992).

26. Flannery, *Vatican Council II,* 806.

27. Ibid.

28. Jacques Maritain, *True Humanism* (London: G. Bles, 1938). The original French work is *Humanisme intégral* (Paris: Fernand Aubier, 1936).

29. *Populorum progressio,* fn. 17 and 44, in O'Brien-Shannon, *Catholic Social Thought,* 261–62. Note that footnote 44 refers to Maritain, *Humanisme intégral.*

30. *Justitia in mundo* (Justice in the World), in O'Brien-Shannon, *Catholic Social Thought,*

289. There are no paragraph numbers in this document.

31. For the exact meaning of the very strong term "constitutive," see Charles M. Murphy, "Action for Justice as Constitutive of the Preaching of the Gospel: What Did the 1971 Synod Mean?" *Theological Studies* 44 (1983): 298–311.

32. The best one-volume compendium of liberation theology is Ignacio Ellacuría and Jon Sobrino, eds., *Mysterium Liberationis: Fundamental Concepts of Liberation Theology* (Maryknoll, N.Y.: Orbis, 1993).

33. Niebuhr, *Christ and Culture.*

34. Charles E. Curran, *The Catholic Moral Tradition Today: A Synthesis* (Washington, D.C.: Georgetown University Press, 1999), 30–59.

35. For a position that disagrees with mine, see Norbert J. Rigali, "The Uniqueness and Distinctiveness of Christian Morality and Ethics," in *Moral Theology: Challenges for the Future: Essays in Honor of Richard A. McCormick, S.J.,* ed. Charles E. Curran (New York: Paulist, 1990), 74–93, and Norbert J. Rigali, "Christian Morality and Universal Morality: The One and the Many," *Louvain Studies* 19, no. 1 (spring 1994): 18–33. For an analysis and criticism of this debate, see James J. Walter, "The Question of the Uniqueness of Christian Morality: An Historical and Critical Analysis of the Debate in Roman Catholic Ethics," and Todd A. Salzman, "Specificity, Christian Ethics, and Levels of Ethical Inquiry," in *Method and Catholic Moral Theology:*

The Ongoing Reconstruction, ed. Todd A. Salzman (Omaha, Neb.: Creighton University Press, 1999), 157–208; see also Vincent MacNamara, *Faith and Ethics: Recent Roman Catholicism* (Washington, D.C.: Georgetown University Press, 1985).

36. Murray, *We Hold These Truths,* 275ff.

37. Bernard Häring, *Free and Faithful in Christ: Moral Theology for Clergy and Laity,* vol. 1, *General Moral Theology* (New York: Seabury, 1978), 75–76. For discussion of the use of the Sermon on the Mount by contemporary theologians and ethicists, see Siker, *Scripture and Ethics,* 203–10.

38. Mark G. McGrath, "Note storiche sulla Costituzione," in *La Chiesa nel mondo di oggi,* ed. Guilherme Baraúna (Florence: Vallecchi, 1966), 150.

39. For the best example of an integrated theological approach to public issues, see Michael J. Himes and Kenneth R. Himes, *Fullness of Faith: The Public Significance of Theology* (New York: Paulist, 1993).

40. This chapter addresses the two audiences of Catholic social teaching from the perspective of the church and theology. For a discussion of the proper way for the church to be present in the public square from the perspectives of the U.S. Constitution and effectiveness, see Charles E. Curran and Leslie Griffin, eds., *The Catholic Church, Morality, and Politics: Readings in Moral Theology No. 12* (New York: Paulist, 2001).

CHAPTER 2

Ethical Methodology

The understanding of natural law in the pre–Vatican II documents of Catholic social teaching entails a clear distinction between theological aspects and philosophical aspects. The theological aspect of natural law justifies human reason as a source of moral wisdom for Christians and Christian ethics by recognizing natural law as the participation of eternal law in the rational creature. The philosophical aspect of natural law considers the precise meaning of human nature and human reason.

The post–Vatican II documents in theory overcome the strict separation between the supernatural and the natural, grace and nature, and the spiritual and the temporal. This understanding likewise challenges the total separation between theological and philosophical methodological aspects. The pre–Vatican II approach would title this chapter "Philosophical Methodology." The title I use here, "Ethical Methodology," refers to what is common to theological and philosophical ethics. Philosophical considerations play a significant role here, but theological aspects also have a contribution to make.

The ethical methodology of Catholic social teaching has changed significantly over the years. In analyzing and criticizing the ethical methodology of these documents in their historical development, I discuss three significant changes and their contemporary implications: the shifts to historical consciousness, greater emphasis on the person as subject, and use of a relationality-responsibility model. In a fourth section I discuss the need for Catholic social teaching to develop the theory and practice with regard to conflict and power, and in a final section I explore the meaning of moral truth.

Shift from Classicism to Historical Consciousness

Classicism tends to see reality in terms of the eternal, the immutable, and the unchanging.[1] Natural law in neoscholasticism illustrates a classicist approach.[2] The word "nature" has many meanings and much ambiguity.[3] As developed in Catholic neoscholasticism, natural law refers to the eternal plan of God, discovered by reason and true for all times, places, and circumstances. As a participation in the eternal law of God, it shares the characteristics of universality and unchangeableness. In addition, nature in a more philosophical sense refers to the principle of operation in every living thing. Everything has its own nature and should act in accord with that nature. Thus, the acorn has a nature that directs it to develop into an oak tree, provided its development is not thwarted. It will not become a pine, a maple, or an elm. Cats have their own nature and act according to it. Cats meow; dogs do not. Human beings have a rational nature by which human reason is to direct us to our end in accord with our nature. All human beings have the same nature and therefore should act in the same way, despite historical and cultural differences.

Neoscholastic natural law tradition—in keeping with its classicist approach—uses a deductive methodology, as illustrated by the syllogism as its form of reasoning. The syllogism contains a major premise that is true always and everywhere (e.g., all human beings are rational). The minor premise of the syllogism is a statement of fact (e.g., Mary is a human being). The conclusion, which is as certain as the premises if the logic is correct, maintains that Mary is rational. Note that deduction tries to arrive at certain answers—that is, answers that are as certain as the premises from which the conclusion is drawn. These conclusions therefore are true in all times, places, and circumstances.

Historical consciousness gives more importance to the particular, the contingent, the historical, and the changing. Historical consciousness maintains continuity and discontinuity, however, so it differs from existentialism. Existentialism regards the present reality in a particular time and space, with no connection to what has gone before or what will come afterward, and as an isolated monad with no connection or relationship to other beings. Historical consciousness retains some relationship to past and future and some relationship to other present realities.

A historically conscious methodology employs a more inductive approach. Such a method by definition induces its conclusions by examining different contingent historical situations. An inductive methodology by its very nature can never claim the absolute certitude of deduction; it is satisfied with moral or practical certitude.

Historical consciousness strives to be a middle position between classicism and existentialism. Classicism has the virtue of being universal and applicable to all; its weakness is failure to give sufficient attention to history, individuality, diversity, and particularity. On the other hand, existentialism emphasizes the particular and the individual to such an extent that it has no place for continuity or any universality.

By definition, the Catholic tradition tends to be universal. In its social teaching, the Catholic tradition has a concern for the whole world and everyone in it. The needs of our times also call for some universality. We are living on one planet and ultimately are connected with all other people living in our world. Economic power, for example, now exists on a global scale. Many corporations have larger budgets than some nations. To work for justice and peace in our world, we need a global ethic that is universal enough to include everyone in a basic and general way (e.g., the human dignity of all, basic human rights for all), yet is open to diversity, particularity, and individuality.[4] The challenge for social ethics and Catholic social teaching calls for precisely such an approach.

A word of caution is in order. The concepts of classicism, historical consciousness, and existentialism are broad so that many varieties of these approaches exist. A more precise understanding of historical consciousness proposed here will emerge in the discussion that follows. Despite these general and expansive categories, Catholic social teaching clearly has undergone a shift from classicism to historical consciousness—although Pope John Paul II pulled back from the historical consciousness of Paul VI.

Pre–Vatican II Documents

As with theological methodology, Vatican II marks a change in ethical methodology. As expected, Leo XIII and his immediate successors appealed primarily to natural law, especially in its neoscholastic understanding, as the basis of their social teaching. Because these popes were dealing with Catholic social teaching rather than Catholic social ethics as such, they did not develop the theory or methodology behind this approach. They merely appealed to natural law for their positions. In *Rerum novarum* (1891), Leo XIII begins by insisting that private property is based on "human nature" and "natural law" (nn. 6–7, O-S, pp. 16–17). The "most sacred law of nature" demands that a father provide food and necessities for his children (n. 9, O-S, p. 18). Socialism is "against natural justice" and "contrary to the natural rights of workers" (nn. 11–12, O-S, p. 19). Thus, natural law grounds the basic teachings of *Rerum novarum*.

Pacem in terris (1963) explicitly calls attention to its methodology in its introduction. The laws governing the relationships between human beings are to be sought "where the Father of all things wrote them, that is, in human nature" (n. 6, O-S, p. 132). These laws teach us how we should conduct our mutual dealings among ourselves, how citizens should relate to states, how states should relate to one another, and how the community of all peoples should act toward each other (n. 7, O-S, p. 132).

Quadragesimo anno (1931) insists on the existence of "unchanging principles" (n. 11, O-S, p. 44). Natural law manifests God's will (n. 53, O-S, p. 54). In this document Pius XI refers to "a fundamental principle of social philosophy fixed and unchangeable" (n. 79, O-S, p. 60). Although these eternal and unchangeable laws and principles do not determine all of the specifics, they constitute the framework within which more specific determinations occur. In talking about the counsels of Leo XIII with regard to workers' unions (note that *Quadragesimo anno* uses the word counsel, which by definition is not a strict law), Pius XI points out that they have been reduced to practice in different ways in different places (n. 34, O-S, p. 49). *Quadragesimo anno* also points out that the government should specify laws governing property when natural law does not do so. In light of the more general direction given by natural law, the state makes specific what natural law leaves indeterminate (n. 44, O-S, p. 53). Thus, laws and principles derived from natural law are universal and unchanging; they are somewhat general, however, and leave room for further specification by individuals or public authority.

Quadragesimo anno clearly recognizes the deductive nature of natural law. "But reason itself clearly deduces from the nature of things and from the individual and social character of human beings what is the end and object of the whole economic order assigned by God the Creator" (n. 42, O-S, p. 51). *Rerum novarum* had followed an essentially deductive approach in developing its natural law arguments for private property. This encyclical proposes three arguments in defense of private property. First, human nature is distinguished from animal nature precisely because human beings alone are rational animals. Other animals are directed by instinct to achieve their ends of self-preservation and propagation of the species; the human being alone has reason and can provide for self-preservation and propagation of the race only by having stable and permanent possession of things. Rational human beings can achieve their God-given ends only by having private

property. Developing the same basic argument deduced from rational human nature, the encyclical maintains that the human need to provide for the future requires stable possession of private property (n.5, O-S, p. 16). A second argument is
deduced from the work that human beings do to cultivate the earth. The earth produces what is required for the preservation of life—but only through the work and
cultivation of human beings. The human being has a right to the fruits of nature,
which become one's own by reason of the work one does on them (n. 7, O-S, p.
17). A third argument is deduced from the social nature of human beings. Fathers
have the obligation to provide for their children, but this obligation can be fulfilled
only if fathers have private property to provide for them (n. 9, O-S, p. 18).

Quadragesimo anno itself exemplifies a deductive methodology at work in the
most important part of the encyclical that calls for a reconstruction of the social order. Recall that Pius XI wrote this encyclical in light of the worldwide depression
and the problems it created. On the basis of his understanding of human nature,
Pius XI proposed a system of moderate corporatism or solidarism. The opposition
between capital and labor must be eliminated and replaced by functional groups
that bind human beings together not according to the position they occupy in industry but according to the diverse functions they exercise in society. Groups are
proposed on the basis of their function in society or the work they do with capital,
labor, and what we would call consumers working together for the good of the particular industry. There also is an overall group ordering the various particular industries (nn. 81–87, O-S, pp. 60–62). Pius proposed this plan for the whole world,
although obviously the world for him was primarily Eurocentric. In reality this particular plan never had a chance to succeed precisely because it came not from the
bottom up but from the top down. Interestingly, subsequent popes tended to move
further away from the plan, until it was not mentioned again. This plan illustrates,
however, the deductive methodology at work that moves from the understanding of
human nature to how society should be structured. Thus, the documents before
Vatican II clearly insist on a natural law basis for their teaching and see reason op-
erating in a deductive manner on the basis of the unchangeable nature that is common to all human beings.

The pre–Vatican II documents employ a classicist approach—which does not
mean they do not recognize some significant historical changes and developments.
Rerum novarum itself responds to new circumstances that had arisen concerning
the social question and the role of workers (n. 1, O-S, p. 14). The encyclicals on the
fortieth and seventieth anniversaries of *Rerum novarum* praise what *Rerum novarum* did but recognize that new developments had occurred that required a

response. Natural law and its unchangeable principles had to be applied to these new situations.[5]

Some changes toward historical consciousness appear in the documents of John XXIII. For example, *Mater et magistra* (1961) points out "that the greater amount of responsibility desired today by workers in productive enterprises, not merely accords with human nature, but also is in conformity with historical developments in the economic, social, and political fields" (n. 93, O-S, p. 99). The obvious implication is that this understanding of responsibility was not present earlier but had come about in light of these historical developments and modifies our understanding of the human person.

Vatican II Documents

The influential Canadian Jesuit Bernard Lonergan, who taught for many years in Rome, first proposed that the change that occurred at Vatican II can be explained best in terms of the shift from classicism to historical consciousness.[6] The best illustration of historical consciousness at work in Vatican II comes from the Declaration on Religious Liberty (*Dignitatis humanae*, 1965). Vatican II acknowledges for the first time the right to religious liberty, even though previous Catholic teaching, including the writings of Leo XIII, condemned religious liberty. At best, religious liberty could be tolerated in some countries but could never be accepted as a basic good.[7] At Vatican II, the more fundamental issue before the council in its discussion of religious liberty involved the question of the development of doctrine. How could the church teach in the twentieth century what it denied in the nineteenth?[8]

American Jesuit John Courtney Murray exercised a predominant influence in this matter at Vatican II. Murray had been working on the issue of religious liberty since the 1940s. In his examination of Leo XIII's many teachings on the subject, Murray distinguished three transtemporal principles that are always true but are applied in different historical and political circumstances. In the conditions Leo XIII addressed in 1891, his answer was correct. In our conditions, the same three transtemporal principles call for a different answer.[9] Note that Murray himself was still somewhat close to a classicist approach with his insistence on the unchangeable transtemporal principles. In the late 1960s, after Vatican II, Murray began to employ Lonergan's notion of historical consciousness to explain the development. Murray recognized that historical consciousness cannot accept the notion of truth as something that objectively exists "out there," apart from history and the subject and expressed in unchangeable propositions.[10] Even then, however, Murray did not fully appreciate how historical consciousness differed from the merely historical hermeneutic he had applied to understand how the teaching changed. Lonergan regards historical consciousness not only as recognizing historical change but also as involving differentiation of subjective human consciousness. Murray did not always appreciate this meaning of historical consciousness. Lonergan saw the teaching on religious liberty as well as the new developments in Vatican II in general precisely in terms of historical consciousness.[11]

Gaudium et spes (1965), with its emphasis on the signs of the times, illustrates a more historically conscious methodology at work. Classicism starts with human nature and deduces principles from it. Such an approach still guided the methodology of John XXIII's encyclical *Pacem in terris* (1963), which finds the laws governing human and social relations in "human nature" (n. 6, O-S, p. 132). These laws govern human relations in the four areas that became the four major parts of the encyclical. After considering what these basic laws call for, however, each of these four parts concludes with a discussion of the characteristics of the present day or the signs of the times. Thus, the first part—on order and relationships between human beings—ends with the distinctive characteristics of our age: workers have gained ground in economic and public affairs; women are now taking part in public life; and almost all nations have achieved independence and self-government (nn. 39–45, O-S, pp. 137–38). Part 3, "Relations between States," ends with "signs of the times" that recognize the growing conviction that disputes among people should be settled by negotiation rather than by arms (nn. 126–129, O-S, p. 151).

Gaudium et spes begins each of its discussions of five particular areas in part 2 with a consideration of signs of the times. Disputes arose about the signs of the times at Vatican II. Earlier drafts of *Gaudium et spes* used the term much more often, but some council fathers objected because *the signs of the times* is a biblical term that refers to the eschatological signs of the last day.[12] Consequently, the final draft used the term more sparingly. Each of the five problems of special urgency treated in part 2 of *Gaudium et spes* begins, however, with signs of the times or characteristics present in the modern world. Thus, the first chapter of part 2 (on the family) begins with marriage and the family in the modern world (n. 47, O-S, pp. 195–96). Chapter 2 (on culture) discusses contemporary circumstances—pointing out that the living conditions of modern human beings have been so profoundly changed that we can speak of a new age in human history (n. 54, O-S, p. 202). Chapter 3 (on socioeconomic life) points out that human beings' increasing domination over nature, greater mutual dependence among all, and more frequent government intervention characterize our modern age; there also are negative signs of the times, however, such as materialism and growing economic inequalities (n. 63, O-S, pp. 208–209). The same approach appears in chapters 4 and 5, which deal with political life (n. 73, pp. O-S, pp. 215–16) and fostering peace (n. 77, O-S, p. 219).

Post–Vatican II Documents

Without doubt, *Octogesima adveniens* (1971)—Paul VI's letter to Cardinal Maurice Roy, president of the Council of the Laity and of the Justice and Peace Commission—best incorporates a historically conscious methodology. This document points out the wide diversity among the situations in which Christians find themselves today—diversity of regions, sociopolitical systems, and culture.

> In the face of such widely varying situations it is difficult for us to utter a unified message and to put forward a solution which has universal validity. Such is not our ambition, nor is it our mission. It is up to the Christian communities to analyze with objectivity the situation which is proper to their own country, to shed on it the light of the Gospel's unalterable words, and to draw principles of reflection, norms of judgment, and directives for action from the social teaching of the Church (n. 4, O-S, p. 266).

How different this methodology appears from the approach of Pius XI, who proposed a general plan that was meant for the whole world. The inductive nature of *Octogesima adveniens* is evident:

> It is up to these Christian communities, with the help of the Holy Spirit, in communion with the bishops who hold responsibility and in dialogue with other Christian brethren and all people of good will, to discern the options and commitments which are called for in order to bring about the social, political, and economic changes seen in many cases to be urgently needed (n. 4, O-S, p. 266).

Note both the word "discern" to discuss the process involved—which is quite different from deduction—and the emphasis on beginning with the local and the particular.

Octogesima adveniens does not embrace existentialism, however. Despite the emphasis on change, the document recognizes some continuity.

> In the present changes, which are so profound and so rapid, each day the individual human being discovers oneself anew, and questions self about the meaning of one's own being and collective survival. Reluctant to gather the lessons of a past that they consider over and done with and too different from the present, human beings nevertheless need to have light shed upon their future which is perceived to be as uncertain as it is changing—by permanent eternal truths. These are truths which are

certainly greater than human beings but, if we so will, we can find their traces (n. 7, O-S, p. 267).

Yes, there are eternal truths—but one does not deduce moral principles from them. Instead, human beings can find the traces of these truths and thus shed some light on their situation.

In light of new developments, two aspirations persistently make themselves felt in these new contexts, and they grow stronger as human beings become better informed and better educated: the aspiration to equality and the aspiration to participation (n. 22, O-S, p. 273). These important moral values have not been deduced from human nature; they have been inductively realized in the course of historical development.

Direct appeals to natural law in *Octogesima adveniens* are muted. For the first time, however (and for the last time), Paul VI calls attention to the role of utopias, which are future-oriented perceptions that can critique present realities:

> But it must clearly be recognized that this kind of criticism of existing society often provokes the forward-looking imagination both to perceive in the present the disregarded possibility hidden within it, and to direct itself toward a fresh future; it thus sustains social dynamism by the confidence that it gives to the inventive powers of the human mind and heart; and, if it refuses no overture, it can also meet the Christian appeal. The Spirit of the Lord, who animates human beings renewed in Christ, continually breaks down the horizons within which our understanding likes to find security and the limits to which our activity would willingly restrict itself; there dwells within us a power which urges us to go beyond every system and every ideology. At the heart of the world there dwells the mystery of human beings discovering themselves to be God's children in the course of a historical and psychological process in which constraint and freedom as well as the weight of sin and the breath of the Spirit alternate and struggle for the upper hand (n. 37, O-S, p. 278).

Utopias and imaginative future constructs that serve as critiques of present structures and offer some guidance for direction into the future differ considerably from natural law as a discovery of the eternal law or order that God has put into the world. There is no order or blueprint put into the world that human beings can decipher, but imaginative visions of the future can criticize the present and provide some direction toward the future.

John Paul II

Paul VI's successor did not continue the emphasis on historical consciousness in *Octogesima adveniens*.[13] From a methodological perspective, John Paul II's first social encyclical, *Laborem exercens* (1981), stands in contrast with *Octogesima adveniens*. *Laborem exercens* involves a theological and philosophical reflection on work. The document discusses work in light of the human person. Here John Paul II quotes his first encyclical, *Redemptor hominis* (1979): "that the human being is the primary and fundamental way for the church." Work is a fundamental and perennial aspect of humanity that is always relevant and constantly demands attention, with fresh problems always arising (n. 1, O-S, pp. 352–53). John Paul II is proposing an understanding of work that is applicable to all situations in the modern world. The method does not begin with signs of the times or recognize any important role for local communities. This methodological approach does not necessarily mean, however, that the encyclical simply endorses the status quo. Far from it. Gregory Baum concludes his commentary on the encyclical by describing it as radical; socialist but not Marxist, although it integrates certain Marxist paradigms; and liberationist.[14] Although others would not necessarily agree,[15] *Laborem exercens* certainly does not constitute an apologia for the status quo. *Sollicitudo rei socialis* (1987) likewise does not embrace a historically conscious methodology in its discussion of development. Although John Paul II maintains that the division of the world into East and West blocs presents a major obstacle to the transformation of less-developed countries (n. 22, O-S, pp. 407–8), the method of the encyclical is from the top down, rather than from the bottom up. *Centesimus annus* (1991) follows the same basic approach in its method as it speaks to the whole world.

Why did John Paul II step back from the more historically conscious approach of *Octogesima adveniens*? Three reasons help to explain this move. First, Karol Wojtyla himself is a philosopher and an ethicist. The phenomenology of Max Scheler influences him to some extent, but he also remains in the neoscholastic tradition— the school in which he was trained.[16] As a phenomenologist and a neoscholastic, John Paul II reflects on the important concept of human existence, drawing out the implications of the meaning of work for human beings in our world today. All of us obviously are influenced by our past, and Wojtyla is no exception. He writes as a philosopher-theologian contemplating the meaning of important realities and values for life in the world.

Second, John Paul II as pope was worried and fearful about what was happening in local churches throughout the world. Everyone recognizes the tension in most parts of the Catholic world between the local church and the papacy. John Paul II emphasizes papal authority and greater centralization in response to what he regards as unacceptable ideas from local churches.[17] How, then, could John

Paul II say that it is not his responsibility, in the face of such widely varying situations, to utter a unified message and put forward a solution that has universal validity as *Octogesima adveniens* maintained? The pope disagreed with what some local churches were doing and consequently did not want to encourage them to come up with their own solutions for their own circumstances. John Paul II's ethics and ecclesiology, which I discuss in chapter 3, definitely are in harmony.

A third reason for John Paul II's opposition to historical consciousness is even more fascinating. In the late 1970s the French Dominican Marie-Dominique Chenu—a well-respected medieval scholar and Thomist, but no supporter of neoscholasticism—published a short book in Italian and then in French titled *The "Social Doctrine" of the Church as Ideology*.[18] The title itself is provocative. Chenu understands the social doctrine of the church as an ideology in the pejorative sense. In this small book he paints the development in papal documents as I have proposed, with a definite move toward a more inductive methodology—as exemplified especially in *Octogesima adveniens*. In fact, the chapter on *Octogesima adveniens* bears the title "An Inductive Method."

Chenu understands "the social doctrine of the church" as the teaching proposed by Leo XIII in 1891 and developed for sixty years until John XXIII. John XXIII introduced some changes that came to full fruition in Paul VI's *Octogesima adveniens*—which marked the end of Catholic social doctrine. The social doctrine constituted an ideology because—on the basis of abstract and prefabricated understandings that claimed to be the eternal demands of natural law—the popes authoritatively proposed plans and models for all people to follow. This authoritative, deductive, top-down approach corresponded with the hierarchical church's older claim to have indirect power over the temporal sphere. Vatican II proposed a very different ecclesiology of the church as the people of God living in the world and, through their concrete experience under the inspiration of the Holy Spirit, striving to be faithful to the Gospel call for liberation. How Christians are to act in the social sphere is not deduced from an eternal abstract plan; it results from the creative urgings of the Holy Spirit on Christian people striving to overcome injustice in dialogue with human sciences and all people of good will. Social change results not from moralizing principles and models authoritatively imposed from above on a passive people but from active involvement by the people themselves, especially those who are poor and oppressed. Thus, Chenu sees a change in papal teaching on social issues that emphasizes discontinuity, not continuity. The newer approach is inductive, from the ground up, beginning with the concrete experience of Christian people trying to live out the liberating Gospel of Jesus Christ in their social situations. This teaching does not come from preconceived ideas called natural law that are authoritatively proposed by the hierarchy on a passive laity.

Chenu refers to the older approach as "the social doctrine of the church"—a term that often was employed in the first seventy years of this tradition. This expression still appears frequently in *Mater et magistra* (1961) but is absent from *Pacem in terris* (1963) and purposely excluded from *Gaudium et spes* (1965), which explicitly uses other terms. *Octogesima adveniens* illustrates the new approach.[19]

Without mentioning Chenu by name, John Paul II responded to his book by claiming a great continuity within the documents themselves, by not personally embracing so historically conscious a methodology, and even by reviving the term "social doctrine." In this context, *Sollicitudo rei socialis*—written on the twentieth anniversary of *Populorum progressio* (1967)—is fascinating:

> In this way I wish principally to achieve *two objectives* of no little importance: on the one hand to pay homage to this historical document of Paul VI and to its teaching; on the other hand, following in the footsteps of my esteemed predecessors in the See of St. Peter, to reaffirm the *continuity* of the social doctrine as well as its constant *renewal*. In effect, continuity and renewal are a proof of the *perennial value* of the teaching of the Church.
>
> This twofold dimension is typical of her teaching in the social sphere. On the one hand it is *constant,* for it remains identical in its fundamental inspiration, in its "principles of reflection," in its "criteria of judgment," in its basic "directives for action," and above all in its vital link with the Gospel of the Lord. On the other hand it is ever *new,* because it is subject to the necessary and opportune adaptations suggested by the changes in historical conditions and by the unceasing flow of the events which are the setting of the life of people and society (n. 3, O-S, p. 396).

The introduction to the encyclical explicitly refers to the social doctrine of the church, with emphasis on its continuity, perennial value, and renewal. In the paragraphs immediately before and after, John Paul II writes of social teaching and refers to the teachings of other popes. Thus, he strives to rehabilitate the term *social doctrine*—but regarding it as embracing continuity and perennial values as well as the need for renewal. The way in which he does this, however, is even more fascinating.[20]

Chenu regarded *Octogesima adveniens* as the death knell for the "social doctrine of the church." John Paul II claims what is constant and identical in this doctrine: its fundamental inspiration, "its principles of reflection," "its criteria of judgment," its basic "directives for action," and its vital link with the Gospel of the

Lord. The words within quotation marks come from the famous paragraph 4 of *Octogesima adveniens,* in which Paul VI calls for local churches to come up with their own solutions. A few paragraphs later in *Sollicitudo rei socialis,* John Paul II again makes his point that the social doctrine of the church offers "principles of reflection," "criteria of judgment," and "directives for action" in applying the word of God to people in their daily life and the life of society (n. 8, O-S, p. 398). Later in the same document, John Paul II again discusses the social doctrine of the church, cites the same three aspects of continuity from the words of *Octogesima adveniens,* and explicitly claims that the social doctrine is moral theology rather than ideology (n. 41, O-S, p. 425). This statement directly attempts to refute Chenu's thesis.

Very early in his pontificate, John Paul II had dealt in the same manner with the Chenu thesis. In his opening address to the Latin American Bishops' Conference at Puebla in 1979, he used the term "social doctrine" four times in one comparatively short section and appealed to the aforementioned citation from *Octogesima adveniens.*[21] There can be no doubt that John Paul II consciously intended to refute the Chenu thesis by resurrecting the term "social doctrine," emphasizing the constant and perennial nature of the principles involved, and downplaying a more historically conscious methodology in his writings. John Paul II has not merely turned the clock back to Leo XIII. As I point out in chapter 1, John Paul II has accepted and employed many of the newer theological developments associated with Vatican II, especially overcoming the supernatural-natural dualism and thereby giving a greater role to Scripture, Jesus Christ, and grace in his social teaching. John Paul II clearly has moved back, however, from the more historically conscious approach of Paul VI.

A serious tension exists between historical consciousness and the neoscholastic approach to natural law. John Paul II seldom refers explicitly to natural law in his social encyclicals, but his 1993 encyclical *Veritatis splendor* defends and employs the theory of natural law. The encyclical strongly supports the absolute moral norms taught by the hierarchical magisterium.[22] In defending such absolute norms John Paul II maintains, "The church has often made reference to the Thomistic doctrine of natural law, including it in her teaching on morality" (n. 44). John Paul II explicitly cites Aquinas in defining natural law as the participation of eternal law in the rational creature (n. 43). The positive precepts of natural law are "universally binding" and "unchanging"; they are "universal and permanent laws." "The negative precepts of the natural law are universally valid . . . without exception" (n. 52). This neoscholastic understanding regards natural law as based on the eternal plan of God for the world, employs a deductive methodology, and insists on the absolute certitude and unchanging character of particular laws belonging to natural law.

Developments Outside Catholic Social Teaching

The shift to historical consciousness appears explicitly in the broader world of Catholic social ethics, especially in liberationist and feminist ethics. Liberation theology first appeared in the Latin American context not as a new area of theology but as a new method.[23] This new approach took root in the soil first plowed by Vatican II. Liberation theology maintains that the Gospel message of liberation affects not only the religious level but also the social, cultural, political, and economic levels of human existence. The Gospel calls for liberation from all forms of oppression. Liberation theology begins with the perspective and experience of poor and oppressed people. It is a theology and ethics from the underside and the bottom up. It does not insist on universal principles, and it strongly rejects the so-called universal, objective, and neutral perspective of Catholic social teaching and Western ethics in general. The emphasis on praxis indicates that one comes to understand the truth by being involved in the struggle for liberation, not studying in the library. Tension developed between the papal teaching office, especially under John Paul II, and liberation theology.[24] Precisely because liberation theologians are Catholic, however, they have continued in their own way to insist on a universal aspect of this approach. The teaching on liberation ultimately is for the good of all human beings. The starting point and method differ considerably, however, from the traditional starting point of Catholic social teaching.

Catholic feminist thought in ethics has come to the fore, especially in the United States, as a form of liberation theology.[25] Feminism begins with a particular experience of oppressed women, not from an objective, neutral, or pretended universalist perspective. Women historically have suffered because of a patriarchal mentality that often claimed to be an objective, neutral, value-free starting point. Catholic feminists, however—in keeping with their Catholic self-understanding—do not want to abandon some universality in ethics; they promote the welfare and well-being of all human beings and the planet, not just the welfare of women.

There can be no doubt that Catholic social ethics in general and Catholic social teaching in particular until recently have stressed the universal and have not given enough importance to the contingent, the historical, the particular, and the diverse. Likewise, these approaches have failed to be self-critical and to recognize that what they claim to be an objective, neutral, value-free perspective was susceptible to limitation, blindness, and prejudice of many kinds. Liberationist and feminist methodologies correctly remind us that there is no truly neutral, objective, universal starting point. As finite and sinful human beings, we have our own limitations and prejudiced perspectives. The solution is to develop a historically conscious methodology that can appreciate particularity and diversity but also recognizes the need for some universality that is increasingly necessary today in light of our global relationships.

In the last section of this chapter and in the next chapter I suggest methodological approaches for Catholic social teaching in keeping with these two goals. Such an approach will have to give much more attention to what occurs on the local level throughout the world; it cannot impose things from the top down.

GREATER EMPHASIS ON THE PERSON AS SUBJECT

In addition to the shift from nature to greater appreciation of history, there also is a shift from human nature to greater appreciation of the person as subject, with the different attributes that belong to the personal subject. *Octogesima adveniens* calls attention to this significant methodological shift. In light of significant developments, "two aspirations persistently make themselves felt in these new contexts, and they grow stronger to the extent that human beings become better informed and better educated: the aspiration to equality and the aspiration to participation, two forms of human dignity and freedom" (n. 22, O-S, p. 273). Thus, Paul VI points out new developments that embrace human freedom, equality, and participation.

As in any development, significant continuities exist. Catholic social thought in general always gave great importance to the individual human being. *Rerum novarum* points out that human beings alone of all animals possess reason and the power of self-determination (n.5, O-S, p. 16). Note here the Thomistic influence. According to Leo XIII, the fact that human beings are masters of their own destiny grounds the right to private property. The human being is prior to the state and holds the right of providing for physical well-being prior to the formation of any state (n. 6, O-S, p. 16). The Catholic tradition in general and Catholic social teaching in particular traditionally have emphasized the basic dignity of the human being, who is an image of God through reason and the power of self-determination. As *Octogesima adveniens* points out, however, there was a shift to greater consideration of human freedom, equality, and participation in Catholic social teaching.

Leo XIII

Leo XIII did not advocate freedom, equality, and participation; in fact, he opposed all three. He strongly condemned modern liberties in his encyclicals, especially in the 1888 letter *Libertas praestantissimum*. Liberty of worship goes against the "chiefest and holiest duty" that calls for worship of the one true God and the one true religion, which can be recognized easily by its external signs. Freedom of speech and the press mean that nothing will remain sacred. Truth will be obscured by darkness, and error will prevail. One has the right to fully propagate the truth but not lying, opinions, and vices that corrupt the heart and the moral life. It is absurd to suppose that nature is indifferent to truth or falsehood, to justice or injustice.

With regard to freedom of speech and the press, Leo XIII points out that the excesses of an unbridled intellect, which unfailingly end in oppression of the untutored multitude, should be controlled by the authority of law, just as law restricts violence and harm to people who are physically weak. Freedom of teaching means freedom to teach the truth; there is no right to teach what is false in the supernatural or natural order. At best, public authority can tolerate what is opposed to truth and justice for the sake of avoiding greater evils or preserving some good. The deadly vice of liberalism denies God's authority and truth.[26] Note here the position on religious freedom that endured in Catholic thought until Vatican II. At best, religious freedom could be tolerated in certain circumstances. Thus, Leo XIII was no friend of the modern freedoms.

Leo XIII did not promote equality as a value for the individual or society; he stressed the importance of inequality. Inequality is a fact of nature. Differences exist with regard to health, beauty, intelligence, thought, and courage. These natural inequalities necessarily involve social inequalities that are essential for the good functioning of society.[27] Elsewhere Leo XIII recognizes a basic equality of human beings with regard to origin, value, and end, with corresponding rights and duties but differences in abilities, powers of mind and body, and manners and character that call for inequalities in the institutions of civil life.[28] In *Rerum novarum*—while attacking socialism but still seeking to protect the basic rights of workers—Leo XIII maintains that it is impossible to reduce all human beings to the same level because individual differences of the most important kind exist among human beings. Such inequalities are good for individuals and for society (n. 14, O-S, p. 20). On several occasions in *Rerum novarum*, Leo XIII refers to "masters" and workers (nn. 33, 43, 45, O-S, pp. 30, 36, 38).

In keeping with his views of freedom and inequality, Leo XIII proposes a very hierarchical view of society, with no participation by ordinary citizens in running society and government. His favorite word for rulers is "princes." The citizen primarily obeys the laws of the ruler, which must be in conformity with eternal law and natural law. Leo XIII even quotes the maxim *qualis rex talis grex* ("as the king, so the flock").[29] He refers to citizens as the untutored or ignorant multitude that must be led and protected by the ruler.[30] At best, Leo XIII's approach to the state and authority is paternalistic, with subjects compared to children who need the guidance and direction of their father.[31]

Leo XIII proposes an important moral role for the state in *Rerum novarum*. "Since it is the end of society to make human beings better, the chief good that society can be possessed of is virtue" (n. 27, p. 27). He spells out in more detail what the ruler and the state should do:

> This is the proper office of wise statesmanship and the work of the heads of the State. Now a State chiefly prospers and flourishes by morality, well-regulated family life, by respect for religion and justice, by the moderation and equal distribution of public burdens, by the progress of the arts and of trade, by the abundant yield of the land— by everything which makes the citizens better and happier. Here, then, it is in the power of a ruler to benefit every order of the State, and amongst the rest to promote in the highest degree the interests of the poor . . . (n. 26, O-S, p. 26).

Leo XIII's authoritarian and paternalistic view of the state makes no distinction between society and the state—a distinction that later provided some basis for accepting religious liberty. He proposes an ethical society-state in which the total common good of the society, including the religious and moral good of all individuals, is entrusted to the rulers. Society is constructed from the top down, with rulers protecting and guarding the untutored multitude from all moral and physical dangers as a father protects his children.[32] Leo XIII strongly attacks the concept of the sovereignty of the people that maintains that the will of the people is supreme and the princes are simply delegates to carry out the will of the people, without any reference to God and God's law. For Leo XIII, all power comes from God; princes share and participate in this power, ruling not for their own good but for the good of all.

In the eighteenth and nineteenth centuries, Roman Catholicism and Leo XIII opposed liberalism in its religious, philosophical, and political dimensions, as well as the movements associated with these aspects—the Protestant Reformation, the philosophical Enlightenment, and democracy as seen especially in the French

Revolution. All of these developments were fatally flawed by their exaltation of the freedom and reason of the individual or the people as a whole, with no recognition of God and God's law. God and God's law—represented and mediated by the church in the spiritual realm and by the prince in the temporal realm—are necessary to the true flourishing of human existence as individuals and as a society. A passage from *Immortale Dei*, Leo XIII's 1885 encyclical, clearly indicates his perspective:

> But that harmful and deplorable passion for innovation which was aroused in the sixteenth century threw first of all into confusion the Christian religion, and next, by natural sequence invaded the precincts of philosophy whence it spread amongst all classes of society. From this source, as from a fountain-head burst forth all those later tenets of unbridled license which, in the midst of the terrible upheavals of the last century, were wildly conceived and boldly proclaimed as the principles and foundation of that new conception of law which was not merely previously unknown, but was at a variance on many points with not only the Christian, but even the natural law.
>
> Amongst these principles the main one lays down that as all human beings are alike by race and nature, so in like manner all are equal in the control of their life; that each one is so far one's own master as to be in no sense under the rule of any other individual; that each is free to think on every subject just as one may chose, and to do whatever one may like to do; that no human being has any right to rule over other human beings. In a society grounded upon such maxims all government is nothing more nor less than the will of the people, and the people, being under the power of itself alone, is alone its own ruler.[33]

In one sense, the problems arising from the Industrial Revolution manifested this same origin—excessive liberalism with its emphasis on the freedom and rights of the individual. The capitalist or owner is free to make as much profit as possible. Leo XIII, as a representative of the Catholic approach at the time, logically opposed economic liberalism just as Roman Catholicism had opposed religious liberalism, philosophical liberalism, and political liberalism. God and God's law put limits on what owners and capitalists can and should do.

Rerum novarum, however, recognizes another false philosophy that had appeared on the scene: socialism. For this reason, *Rerum novarum* has a different tone from most of Leo's encyclicals that deal primarily with the political order. This encyclical begins with socialist proposals to deal with the problems of the Industrial Revolution. Socialists maintain that property and possessions should become the common property of all, to be administered by the state or municipal bodies.

Thus, they take away from individuals the possessions to which they have a right, and they give too great a role to the state (nn. 1–3, O-S, pp. 14–15). *Rerum novarum* defends the basic rights of the individual and the family and their priority with regard to the state (nn. 28–29, O-S, pp. 27–28). It spells out various rights of the worker: the right to just wages, decent working conditions, limited hours of work, some rest, and above all to form associations to work for their good (nn. 29–41, O-S, pp. 29–35).

Note what is happening here: In his disagreement with the socialists, Leo XIII defends the basic dignity and rights of the individual—a position that has some similarities with liberalism. Thus, *Rerum novarum* sets the parameters in which Catholic social teaching develops over the succeeding century. Catholic social teaching opposes liberalism—with its deification of the reason, freedom, and conscience of the individual—but it also opposes socialism, which gives too great a role to the state and fails to recognize the true dignity and rights of the individual. As the twentieth century developed, socialism or communism came to be regarded as the leading threat, so Catholic social teaching began to stress even more the dignity, freedom, equality, and rights of the individual.

Pius XI

In reviewing *Rerum novarum* and in discussing the contemporary reality, *Quadragesimo anno* follows the parameters set by Leo XIII in regarding Catholic social teaching as opposed to both liberalism and socialism. Liberalism stands at the root of the problems of the modern world. The power of law and respect for authority have been considerably weakened ever since liberalism denied God, the Creator and Ruler of the world, as the source of all law and authority. Liberalism overstressed the freedom and rights of the individual.[34] In *Quadragesimo anno*, Pius XI points out how Leo XIII "attacked and overthrew the idols of liberalism" (n. 14, O-S, p. 44) and "completely overthrew those tottering tenets of liberalism which had long hampered intervention by the government" (n. 27, O-S, p. 47). Economic affairs cannot be left to rugged competition, as the individualistic school advocates (n. 88, O-S, p. 62). The liberalistic tenets of the so-called Manchester School helped capital appropriate excessive advantages (n. 54, O-S, p. 54). Notice the triumphalistic tone—as if Leo XIII had single-handedly taken care of the problems caused by liberalism.

In *Quadragesimo anno*, however, socialism constitutes more of a problem than liberalism. Pius XI devotes a special section to changes that had occurred in

socialism (nn. 111–126, O-S, pp. 66–70). In light of socialism's emphasis on material aspects, Pius XI defends the higher human goods (especially freedom), maintains
that human dignity can never be reduced to the possession of material goods, and
excoriates excessive compulsion involved in socialism (n. 119, O-S, pp. 68–69).

Later encyclicals of Pius XI show that the primary problem in his mind was not
individualistic liberalism but totalitarianism of the right and the left. Shortly after
publication of *Quadragesimo anno*, Pius XI wrote an encyclical condemning fas-
cism, especially its failure to recognize the rights of the church, individuals, and
families. In this context, Pius XI is "happy and proud to wage the good fight for the
liberty of consciences"—which he is quick to point out does not mean absolute independence of conscience from God's law.[35] Against the incursions of the state,
Pius XI defends the liberty of consciences, but in the context of natural law.

The encyclical *Mit brennender Sorge* (1937) condemned Nazism. Again, Pius XI
appeals to natural law to oppose the practice of the Nazis in violating the rights of
the church, the rights of believers, and the rights of parents with regard to their children.[36] A few days later in 1937, Pius XI published *Divini Redemptoris*, which condemns the false messianism and dialectical materialism of atheistic communism.

> Communism moreover strips the human being of liberty, which is the principle of
> one's life as a rational being, robs the human person of all its dignity.... There is no
> recognition of any right of the individual in one's relations to the collectivity; no nat-
> ural right is accorded to the human person, which is a mere cogwheel in the Commu-
> nist system.[37]

Often the word "person" and not "human being" is now used.

Under Pius XI, papal teaching in opposition to totalitarianism staunchly defended the dignity, freedom, and rights of the person. It is fair to say that Pius XI
was always more fearful of totalitarianism from the left than from the right.[38] Again,
a pope set the stage for subsequent development. The Vatican became the most
vocal opponent of communism from that time forward and continued so for a long
time during the cold war. In opposition to communism, Roman Catholicism now
championed the dignity and freedom of the person.

Pius XII

Although Pius XII (whose pontificate covered the years 1939–1958) did not write
an encyclical specifically on the social question, he wrote and delivered many addresses on all aspects of human existence, concentrating especially on medical
ethics.[39] History remembers Pius XII most for his public silence on the Nazi persecution of Jewish people.[40] His 1944 Christmas address, written in the midst of

World War II, insists on the dignity and freedom of the human person and calls for greater participation by individuals in the governing of society. The human being is not the object of social life or an inert element in it but the subject, foundation, and end of social life. Pius XII strongly appealed to natural law as the basis for his teaching and maintained that a democratic form of government appears to many people as a postulate of reason itself.[41] Here was the first cautious acceptance of democracy as the best form of government. The influential French Catholic philosopher Jacques Maritain, who spent the war and postwar years in the United States, had been advocating the cause of democracy on the basis of Thomism since the late 1930s.[42] After the war, Europe saw the rise of Christian democratic parties, which played significant roles in Germany, France, and Italy in postwar politics—especially in strongly opposing communism.[43]

John Courtney Murray pointed out a significant development in Pius XII's understanding of the state. Pius XII abandoned Leo XIII's ethical or moral concept of the society-state and accepted a juridical and limited constitutional state. For Leo XIII, there was no distinction between society and the state. Rulers have the task of protecting and promoting the virtue of all the subjects. By emphasizing the dignity, freedom, and responsibility of individuals, Pius XII accepts a much more limited view of the state that does not paternalistically look after the life of its subjects. The state has the limited juridical role of defending basic human rights and promoting the freedom of the people; it is no longer the parent directing the entire lives of the children. Rulers are not princes who guide and direct the untutored or ignorant multitude but representatives of the people, who are themselves responsible citizens.[44]

Although Pius XII helped Catholic teaching move in the direction of emphasizing the freedom of the person and limited constitutional government, he remained a transitional figure. Pius XII advanced beyond the position of Leo XIII, who simply accepted the many inequalities in human existence, but Pius still upheld such inequalities in education, earthly goods, and social positions that do not constitute obstacles to brotherhood and community if they are not arbitrary and are in accord with justice and charity.[45] Note that there are some limits on the inequalities that must be in accord with justice and charity. An Italian commentator still detects in Pius XII an aristocratic approach.[46]

John XXIII

Under Pius XII the church regarded communism as its primary foe. This attitude logically led to an emphasis on the dignity and freedom of people, as well as a more limited role for government. Significant nuances developed in the pontificate of John XXIII; for our purposes, however, one fascinating development, which was never explicitly acknowledged by the pope himself, occurred between *Mater et magistra* (1961) and *Pacem in terris* (1963).

Part 4 of *Mater et magistra* is titled "Reconstruction of Social Relationships in Truth, Justice, and Love" (nn. 212–265, O-S, pp. 118–27). It indicates what basic goods constitute the values in a just society. This is not simply an isolated citation; it constitutes the entire fourth part of the encyclical. In *Pacem in terris*, John XXIII maintains that truth, justice, charity, and freedom make civil society well ordered, beneficial for all, and in keeping with human dignity (n. 25, O-S, p. 136). Chapter 3 · deals with relationships between states, and here the encyclical cites four values that guide and direct those relationships: truth, justice, solidarity, and freedom. Here John XXIII substitutes solidarity for love, but this substitution makes sense because the topic involves the global relations of all states. Again, note how central this comment is to the encyclical as a whole (nn. 86–129, O-S, pp. 145–51). Thus, a fascinating change occurred in the two years between *Mater et magistra* and *Pacem in terris*. Whereas the former does not mention freedom, in the latter it becomes one of the four basic values that must be found in a well-ordered political society and in the whole world. This development testifies to the growing importance of freedom in Catholic social teaching.

Pacem in terris also illustrates, in an ambiguous way, the transition from an older authoritarian and moralistic view of society to a more democratic one. *Pacem in terris* insists, "The chief concern of civil authorities must therefore be to insure that these rights are acknowledged, respected, coordinated with other rights, defended and promoted, so that in this way each one may more easily carry out one's duties" (n. 60, O-S, p. 141). The chief concern of public authorities is not to direct the subject to truth, justice, virtue, and religion but to protect and defend these human rights. The older understanding of the legislator and law as participating in eternal and natural law also is developed in this encyclical, however, so the concept of law directing other individuals to the common good and one's own good continues to be present here. Society needs authority "directing all to strive earnestly for the common good . . . and this authority . . . has its source in nature, and has consequently God for its author." Because authority "is the power to command according to right reason, authority must derive its obligatory force from the moral order which in turn has God for its first source and final end." Recalling that law is an ordering of reason that should move reasonable human beings by moral force rather than coercion, John XXIII insists that "civil authority must appeal primarily to the conscience of individual citizens, that is to each one's duty to collaborate readily for the common good of all" (nn. 46–48, O-S, pp. 138–39). The Catholic tradition will always recognize some directing force of law for the common good; the problem is how to reconcile that authority with the freedom and rights of the individual.

Vatican II

Gaudium et spes and *Dignitatis humanae* continue the fascinating development toward greater emphasis on the person as subject. *Gaudium et spes* regards the dignity of the human person as the grounding of the whole teaching by making this phrase the title of its very first chapter. The Pastoral Constitution on the Church in the Modern World within that chapter extols the excellence of freedom, hinting that the church has become aware of this issue from our contemporaries who rightly extol freedom. Freedom is not the same as license, however. Freedom must direct human beings toward goodness. Human dignity demands that the human being act according to a knowing and free choice for the good (n. 17, O-S, p. 175). Catholic social ethics will never regard the person as an isolated individualistic monad who is free to do whatever he or she pleases.

Gaudium et spes recognizes the complex reality of freedom and refuses to absolutize it. The document emphasizes the subjective aspect of the person in its discussion of conscience. An older approach regarded law as the objective norm of morality and conscience as the subjective norm that had to conform itself to the objective. *Gaudium et spes* stresses the primacy of the subjective without, however, denying the objective. In discussing the dignity of conscience, the pastoral constitution points out that in conscience the human being recognizes the law written by God. Conscience is the most secret core and sanctuary of a human being—where the human is alone with God, whose voice echoes in its depths. The document calls Christians and all others to join in the search for truth and genuine solutions to the numerous problems that arise in the life of individuals and social relationships. The search for truth in the depth of conscience is much more than simply recognition of a particular law. Conscience is much more complex. The antidote to the danger of license in an older approach was the objective law; now, however, it is fidelity to conscience. Yes, conscience strives to be correct—that is, in accord with the demands of truth—but conscience frequently errs from invincible ignorance without losing its dignity (n. 16, O-S, p. 174). Thus, in the complex matter of conscience *Gaudium et spes* emphasizes the primacy of the subjective without denying the objective and sees the search for moral truth as taking place in the depth of the person's conscience.

Religious liberty was a significant topic at Vatican II. The existing Catholic teaching following Pius IX and Leo XIII still condemned religious freedom; at best this teaching only tolerated religious liberty as a lesser evil. The older teaching collided head on, however, with the developing emphasis in Catholic social teaching on the dignity and freedom of the person as subject. Ultimately, the newer emphasis on the freedom and dignity of the person changed the older teaching, but the whole issue of religious freedom is much more complex than most people realize. Four aspects of the Declaration on Religious Freedom (*Dignitatis humanae*) show how religious liberty is to be properly understood and the growing emphasis on the freedom and dignity of the person.

First, the very first paragraph of the declaration clearly states the basis for the new teaching: the dignity of the human person that has been expressing itself more and more deeply on the consciences of contemporary people.[47] Note how the document recognizes development and historical consciousness.

Second, the precise meaning of religious liberty in the document again indicates that in accepting the importance of freedom, Catholic social teaching still opposes individualistic license. The declaration makes this point in a clumsy way by insisting that all individuals and societies have a moral duty to the true religion and the one church. Religious freedom does not mean that a human being is morally free to recognize God or not. Religious freedom in its true understanding involves an immunity of the person from external coercion by the state or other individuals in matters of religion. The object of this immunity is twofold: No person is to be forced to act against that person's conscience in religious matters, and no person is to be restrained from acting in accord with her or his conscience in religious matters. Religious liberty is primarily a political or civil right, not a personal moral choice. To fulfill the obligation to seek religious truth, the person must be free from all external coercion.[48]

Third, the document further develops the nature of religious liberty as a political freedom by considering religious liberty in light of limited constitutional government. The private and public acts of religion by which people order their lives to God transcend limited constitutional government.[49] Religious liberty involves a constitutional and jurisprudential issue regarding the proper role of the state or government. The declaration accepts the fundamental principle of limited constitutional government: as much freedom as possible and as little restraint as necessary. The state has no competence in matters of religion; it should leave this area to the freedom of the citizen. The state can intervene only for the sake of public order, which involves public peace, public morality, and justice.[50]

Dignitatis humanae proposes a very different understanding of the state from that of Leo XIII. The latter proposed an authoritarian or paternalistic state that had the moral role of guiding and directing all of the activities of the untutored or igno- rant multitude toward virtue. This approach fit with the understanding of sacred and secular authority as applying God's law to all the actions of people. In a limit- ed constitutional democracy, however, government no longer has the moral task of guiding people to moral and religious truth. Government must respect the dignity and conscience of its individual citizens in religious and moral matters to choose for themselves. Government can interfere and act only when public order is at stake.

Fourth, the move to the person as subject that changed the understanding of the state grounded another important factor in the changed teaching on religious liberty. The older denial of religious liberty was based on the primacy of truth: The Catholic Church is the one true church of Jesus Christ, and all people have an obli- gation to embrace it. In response to the objection in the name of conscience, the older approach responded that error has no rights. Notice how this approach em- phasized the objective aspect of truth or law and simply regarded conscience as having the obligation to follow it.[51] Now, however, the dignity of the human person constitutes the grounds for overturning the older emphasis on the objective while still recognizing a significant role for the free search for moral truth. (I discuss reli- gious freedom in greater detail in chapter 7.)

Gaudium et spes also illustrates a move to a greater emphasis on equality and participation. The pastoral constitution still defends some inequalities, but the recognition of inequalities appears in subordinate clauses; the principal clauses af- firm equality. For example,

> True, all human beings are not alike from the point of view of varying physical power and the diversity of intellectual and moral resources. Nevertheless, with respect to the fundamental rights of the person, every type of discrimination, whether social or cul- tural, whether based on sex, race, color, social condition, language, or religion, is to be overcome and eradicated as contrary to God's intent. . . . Moreover although right- ful differences exist between human beings, the equal dignity of persons demands that a more humane and just condition of life be brought about. For excessive eco- nomic and social differences between the members of the one human family or popu- lation groups cause scandal, and militate against social justice, equity, the dignity of the human person, as well as social and international peace (n. 29, O-S, p. 183).

Gaudium et spes also emphasizes the importance of participation in all aspects of social life. The will to play one's own role in common endeavors should be encouraged. The largest possible number of citizens should participate in public affairs with genuine freedom (n. 31, O-S, p. 184). For all people to exercise responsibility and participation, they need a greater share in education and culture. Economic enterprises should promote active participation by all (n. 41, O-S, p. 68). The juridical and political structure should "afford all their citizens the chance to participate freely and actively in establishing the constitutional bases of a political community, governing the state, determining the scope and purpose of different institutions, and choosing leaders" (n. 75, O-S, p. 217).

In light of this development, Paul VI's insistence in *Octogesima adveniens* (1971) on the importance of equality and participation as forms of human dignity and freedom comes as no surprise. The papal understanding of human nature had changed dramatically since Leo XIII. Changing historical circumstances—especially the growth of totalitarianism and, above all, communism—influenced this development. Greater continuity exists in the area of participation precisely because in dealing with workers Leo XIII emphasized the right of workers to form their own associations and thereby work for their own betterment. In the same context, Pius XI in *Quadragesimo anno* urged a modification in the wage contract to a contract of partnership so that workers become sharers in ownership or management or participate in the profits (n. 65, O-S, p. 57). As with the shift to historical consciousness, *Octogesima adveniens* clearly demonstrates the dramatic shift in the understanding of human nature that now gives greater emphasis to human freedom, equality, and participation. Catholic social teaching clearly had come to appreciate some aspects of liberalism, although it still criticizes liberalism's one-sided individualism and failure to give importance to our relationships to God, one another, all people on the globe, and the earth itself.

John Paul II

John Paul II has steadfastly continued the emphasis on the person as subject. His philosophical work before he became pope stressed the person—as illustrated in the English titles of his best known works: *The Acting Person* and *Love and Responsibility*.[52] John Paul II's emphasis on the person as subject stands out very clearly in his first encyclical on social issues—*Laborem exercens* (1981), issued on the ninetieth anniversary of *Rerum novarum*. The two most important points in the encyclical illustrate this emphasis on the person as subject.

First, *Laborem exercens* extols the priority of labor over capital (n. 12, O-S, pp. 367–68). Throughout this encyclical, John Paul II frequently cites the Genesis command to Adam to subdue and have dominion over the earth. The human be-ing, as the subject of work and independent of the work done, is a person with do-minion over all other created realities. This truth has important and decisive conse-quences—one of which is the priority of labor over capital. Capital is only a means or instrument. The person is the master of all other creatures put into this world for her or his disposal. The consistent teaching of the primacy of the person over things also governs the relationship between capital and labor. Extolling capital over labor involves the fundamental error of economism or materialism (n. 13, O-S, pp. 369–70).

Second, *Laborem exercens* emphasizes the priority of the subjective aspect of work over the objective aspect precisely because the person is a subject (nn. 5–6, O-S, pp. 357–60). In light of the Genesis command to subdue the earth and have dominion over it, work involves a "transitive" activity (i.e., an activity beginning in the human subject and directed toward an external object). Thus, work involves two aspects: the object or the thing done and the subject who does it. The objective aspect of work or what is done has an infinite variety, ranging from the physical to the intellectual areas in which human beings carry out the divine command of sub-duing the earth. The human being as a person, however, is the subject of work. The person is the one who "dominates." Thus, dominion refers to the subjective aspect more than the objective aspect. Work has its ethical value precisely because the one who carries it out is a person, a conscious and free subject, who in the process of working shapes herself or himself. Work is for the person, not vice versa. Such an understanding tends to lead to a radical evaluation of a basic equality of all who work regardless of the object of their work. According to John Paul II, "Such a concept practically does away with the very basis of the ancient differentiation of people into classes according to the kind of work done" (n. 6, O-S, p. 359). Notice here that John Paul II uses this notion to overcome the class conflict and even war-fare that communism so often extols.

John Paul II draws out some ramifications of this basic criterion of the priority of labor in his discussion of both wages and the worker's role. The demand for a living family wage is based on the notion of worker as subject (n. 19, O-S, pp. 378–80). Not only does the priority of the subjective aspect of work call for greater equality among all workers; it also calls for effective participation by the worker in the whole productive process (n. 13, O-S, p. 369). The subjective aspect of work also grounds the very important role of, and need for, worker solidarity. Today there is a need for new movements of solidarity of workers with other workers (n. 8, O-S, pp. 361–63). Thus, *Laborem exercens* uses the concept of the person as subject to ground the priority of labor over capital and the priority of the subjective aspect of work over the objective, with greater emphasis on the equality, participation, and solidarity of all workers.

Sollicitudo rei socialis (1987) continues this emphasis on the person as subject in its central theological development. At stake is the dignity of the human person (n. 47, O-S, p. 429). The human person is the protagonist of development (n. 30, O-S, p. 415). Sollicitudo rei socialis emphasizes "the creative subjectivity of the citizen" (n. 15, O-S, p. 403). John Paul II continues along the same lines in Centesimus annus (1991), insisting that the grounding principle of all of the church's social directives comes from a correct view of the human person made in the image and likeness of God, with an incomparable dignity and rights that flow from that dignity (n. 11, O-S, p. 447).

The foregoing discussion of the move to the person as subject, with emphasis on freedom, equality, and participation, is much longer than any of the other methodological sections in this chapter. Elaboration of this perspective requires greater length because it also includes the developing understanding of the state in Catholic social teaching that now can be summarized succinctly in the substantive consideration of the state in part 2.

The contemporary emphasis in Catholic social teaching on the human person—with a recognition of the importance of freedom, equality, and participation—must continue in the future. The dignity and rights of human persons are central to any social ethics in this new century. A full Catholic anthropology must incorporate freedom with justice, truth, and love. Roman Catholicism has learned much from liberalism, but it should continue to disagree with the one-sided individualism of classical liberalism.[53] John Paul II, who is no fan of liberalism, sometimes so emphasizes the divine command to human beings to dominate and subdue nature that he does not give enough importance to the ecological aspects of existence in our world. The human person occupies a very importance place in Catholic social thought; as the following section shows, however, the person always must be considered in terms of multiple relationships with God, neighbor, the earth, and self.

A SHIFT IN ETHICAL MODELS

The shift to historical consciousness and a greater emphasis on the person as subject goes hand-in-hand with the shift in the ethical model in Catholic social teaching. Three generic models exist for moral theology. The deontological model understands morality primarily in terms of duty or law and conformity to duty or law. The teleological model considers morality in terms of ends or goals: One decides the normative ends or goals and judges means in relationship to obtaining these ends. The third model, relationality-responsibility, sees the human person in multiple relationships with God, neighbor, world, and self and acting responsibly within these relationships.

These models are generic and broad, and many different varieties of deontology and teleology exist. One important difference for our purposes in teleological approaches concerns intrinsic or extrinsic teleology. Extrinsic teleology, which is identified with consequentialism and utilitarianism, regards the end as extrinsic to the human person and her or his act. These ends are consequences that follow from the act. Intrinsic teleology regards the ends as constitutive inclinations of the human person, who obtains fulfillment by achieving the ends to which the person is inclined.

Another word of caution about models is necessary. The ethical model constitutes an important consideration in ethics, but ethics involves many other aspects and considerations. In addition, the primacy of one model does not and should not exclude aspects of the other models within the primary model.

Early Approaches

As we would expect from the foregoing considerations, the earlier documents tend to employ a deontological model, based on their use of natural law. *Rerum novarum* appeals often to natural law and the law of nature to justify its positions on private property, rejection of socialism, the role of government, and the rights of workers.

Quadragesimo anno likewise bases its teaching on natural law. In a short explanation of its methodological approach, however, this document briefly summarizes its understanding of natural law and shows the different strands in the Thomistic model of natural law:

> But reason itself clearly deduces from the nature of things and from the individual and social character of the human being what is the end and object of the whole economic order assigned by God, the Creator.
>
> For it is the moral law alone which commands us to seek in all our conduct our supreme and final end, and to strive directly in our specific actions for those ends which nature, or rather, the Author of nature has established for them, duly subordinating the particular to the general. If this law be faithfully obeyed, the result will be that particular economic aims, whether of society as a body or of individuals, will be

intimately linked with the universal teleological order, and as a consequence we shall be led by progressive stages to the final end of all, God himself, our highest and lasting good (nn. 42–43, O-S, p. 51).

The foregoing passage is remarkable because it brings together teleological and deontological approaches. This passage reminds us that Thomas Aquinas's ethics generally was teleological, not deontological.[54] Aquinas begins his treatment of ethics with the ultimate end of human beings, which for him is happiness. When are we happy? We are happy as human beings when we achieve our ultimate end and good. Because we are rational creatures composed of intellect and will, these two powers have as their ends the knowledge of truth and love of goodness. When these two intrinsic powers have achieved their end, we achieve happiness—when we know the full truth and love the perfect good, who is God. Experience itself also testifies that any lesser good—wealth, honor, health, power, or popularity—will never satisfy the basic human yearning for the true and the good whose possession alone means the final end and happiness have been achieved.

In this passage Pius XI also points out that the individual precepts of natural law are derived teleologically. Reason discovers the end and object of the whole economic order and directs us to this end through appropriate means. This passage recognizes that natural law should be understood as human reason directing us to our end in accord with our nature. In dealing with more specific issues, however (as these encyclicals generally do), the encyclicals emphasize precepts of natural law rather than the teleological manner in which they are derived. Hence, in early Catholic social teaching natural law comes across as a deontological approach even though its grounding is teleological.

Earlier in this chapter I use *Pacem in terris,* the 1963 encyclical of John XXIII, to show a more classicist methodology at work precisely because of its natural law basis. The laws governing human relationships are to be found where the Author of all things wrote them—that is, in human nature (n. 6, O-S, p. 137). These laws are then developed and applied in the remainder of the encyclical. Thus, *Pacem in terris* explicitly calls attention to the deontological model that the encyclical follows.

A Change

The shifts to historical consciousness and to the emphasis on the person as subject, together with recognition of the global aspect of social problems, tend to favor a relationality-responsibility model rather than a deontological model. In light of these changes, it is harder to speak of an unchanging eternal law with specific precepts guiding human actions as the primary ethical model. Needless to say, there will always be some place for principles and norms.

Gaudium et spes shows traces of the primacy of a relationality-responsibility model. For example, in discussing culture the pastoral constitution claims that we are witnesses of a new humanism in which the human being is defined first by one's responsibilities to one's brothers and sisters and to history itself (n. 55, O-S, p. 202). *Dignitatis humanae* insists that the moral principle of personal and social responsibility should guide the citizen in using her or his political freedoms.[55] In some ways, Paul VI's *Populorum progressio* employs a more teleological approach by insisting on complete development as the end of human existence in this world.

As should be expected, once again Paul VI's *Octogesima adveniens* best illustrates the shift to a relationality-responsibility model. The description of Catholic social teaching in this document clearly indicates such a model at work:

> It is with all its dynamism that the social teaching of the Church accompanies human beings in their search. If it does not intervene to authenticate a given structure or to propose a ready-made model, it does not thereby limit itself to recalling general principles. It develops through reflection applied to the changing situations of this world, under the driving force of the Gospel as the source of renewal when its message is accepted in its totality and with all its demands. It also develops with the sensitivity proper to the Church which is characterized by a disinterested will to serve and by attention to the poorest. Finally, it draws upon its rich experience of many centuries which enables it, while continuing its permanent preoccupations, to undertake the daring and creative innovations which the present state of the world requires (n. 42, O-S, pp. 280–81).

Recall *Octogesima adveniens*'s emphasis on utopias that provoke the forward-looking imagination that perceives in the present the discarded possibilities hidden within it and at the same time drives toward a new future. At the heart of the world dwells the human person discovering himself or herself to be a child of God in the midst of personal and historical struggle (n. 37, O-S, p. 278). The apostolic letter ends with a recognition of shared responsibility, a call to action, and a realization of the pluralism of possible options (nn. 47–52, O-S, pp. 283–85).

In *Sollicitudo rei socialis* John Paul II at times highlights the primacy of the relationality-responsibility model. In overcoming sin and the structures of sin, Christians are called to conversion—which involves a relationship to God, to the sin committed, to the consequences of sin, and hence to the neighbor whether an individual or a community. Through conversion we become more aware of the interdependence among all individuals and all nations. Solidarity constitutes the virtue that deals with this interdependence that guides our relationships in the contemporary world in its economic, cultural, political, and religious aspects. John Paul II has made solidarity a primary theme in his development of Catholic social teaching. Solidarity, with its emphasis on the unity of the human race, finds its grounding in the unity and diversity of the Trinity itself (nn. 38–40, O-S, pp. 421–24).

The very title of the U.S. Catholic bishops' pastoral letter on peace—"The Challenge of Peace: God's Promise and Our Response" (1983)—indicates a relationality-responsibility model at work. The introduction states that the letter is an invitation and a challenge to Catholics in the United States to join with others in light of our grave human, moral, and political responsibilities to see that a conscious choice is made to save humanity (n. 4, O-S, pp. 492–93). Thus, from the time of Leo XIII Catholic social teaching has moved from the primacy of a deontological model to accepting, to some degree, a relationality-responsibility model.

In any shift or change within a tradition, the newer approach exists in uneasy tension with older approaches. The problem is even more complex in considering the ethical model because there is a place for the concerns of the three different models; the question is which one is primary.

Consider John Paul II's three social encyclicals as examples of the ambiguity regarding models in Catholic social teaching. At times he seems to highlight the primacy of a relationality-responsibility model. Unlike earlier popes, he seldom if ever even mentions the term "natural law" in these three social encyclicals. As I discuss in chapter 7, however, he stoutly defends neoscholastic concepts of natural law—with all of its characteristics—in other documents, especially *Veritatis splendor* (1993). This amazing difference in his approaches to social and personal morality raise many questions.

Although John Paul II's social encyclicals avoid the term "natural law," there are strong indications of a more deontological model at work in these documents. Recall that he frequently describes Catholic social teaching in the words taken from *Octogesima adveniens*—principles of reflection, criteria of judgment, and directives for action. These concepts clearly point in a deontological direction.

John Paul II, in keeping with his generic understanding of the contents of Catholic social teaching, frequently uses the term "principles" in his encyclicals. The words "principle" or "principles" appear more than twenty times in *Centesimus annus*. This encyclical uses the term to refer not only to good and positive principles but also to bad and negative principles such as "the unilateral principle of the exploitation of the natural resources" (n. 33, O-S, p. 464). At times the insistence on principles clearly indicates an older natural law approach at work with some deontological aspects. "If there is no transcendent truth, in obedience to which the human person achieves one's full identity, then there is no sure principle for guaranteeing just relations between people" (n. 44, O-S, p. 473). In chapter 7 I discuss John Paul II's heavy insistence on moral truths. Such an emphasis on principles and moral truths indicates a deontological model at work.

John Paul II's approach appears to be ambiguous. In the social encyclicals he clearly abandons the term "natural law" and gives some indications of using a relationality-responsibility model, but he strongly insists on principles and their application. Other encyclicals, especially *Veritatis splendor*, are much more insistent on a neoscholastic, natural law approach.

The increasing complexities of social problems in our global society will continue to call for more emphasis on a relationality-responsibility model. Theological ethicists and Catholic hierarchical teaching alike must spell out more the specific criteria of such a model, however, and how it relates to the other models.

CONFLICT AND POWER

In its earliest stages, Catholic social teaching gave little explicit attention to the role of conflict and power in social justice. Even today, conflict and power remain undeveloped.

Factual Situation

An excellent illustration of this failure to recognize fully the role of conflict and power in Catholic social teaching appears in *The New Dictionary of Catholic Social Thought,* published in 1994. Although specialists have recognized this dictionary as a significant and helpful volume, it has no entries listed under conflict or power.[56] Thus, the dictionary truly manifests what has been the tradition of Catholic social teaching.

Conflict and power are related but obviously are not the same. We are all aware of conflicts in our personal lives, our relationships with others, and relationships among various groups in our society. How do I balance my responsibilities to family and to work? Conflicts exist in our relationship with others at home, at work, or at play. Political campaigns remind us of the political conflict between and even within political parties, to say nothing of conflicts between classes, genders, and especially religious groups throughout our world. Human beings and human society do not exist without conflict.

Everyone recognizes the role of power in social morality. In its broadest sense, power involves the capacity to influence others. Thus, power constitutes a broader concept than coercion, which is the power to influence others against their will. The power of good example entails no coercion of any kind.[57]

Why did Catholic social teaching in the period before Vatican II downplay the roles of conflict and power? Catholic social teaching has emphasized harmony, not conflict. Many factors contributed to the emphasis on harmony and the downplaying of conflict and power. The natural law methodology strongly emphasized harmony. Natural law is the participation of eternal law in the rational creature. Eternal law is the providential plan of God ordering all things in this world.

Catholic natural law theory is rationalistic, not voluntaristic. Law is an ordering of reason, not an act of will. The emphasis on order and ordering forms the ground from which natural law looks at the universe. The opening of *Pacem in terris* recognizes that "peace on earth . . . can be firmly established only if the order laid down by God be dutifully observed. . . . How strongly does the turmoil of individual human beings and peoples contrast with the perfect order of the universe" (nn. 1, 4, O-S, p. 131). The Creator of the world has imprinted in the human heart an order. Whatever God has made shows God's infinite wisdom, which is manifested more clearly in the creatures that have greater perfection, such as human beings (n. 5, O-S, p. 132).

Classicism's emphasis on the universal and unchanging added to the emphasis on harmony. Such an approach did not highlight change and the disruptions that come with change.

The emphasis on order and ordering in Catholic social thought manifested itself in a hierarchical understanding of human society, parallel to the hierarchical understanding of the church. A hierarchical approach to society downplays and even opposes freedom, equality, and participation. In the beginning—and even to this day, to some extent—Catholic social teaching insisted on an organic view of society. Such an organic view compares the political order to a body, with different parts performing different functions for the good of the whole body under the authority of the head.[58] Again, note the parallel with an ecclesiology that regards the church as the mystical body of Christ. Each part of the body is different and has its own function. Total equality of parts would mean there could never be a whole. The arm is not free to act like a leg. An emphasis on freedom, equality, and participation threatens the order, unity, and cohesion of the hierarchically structured body or organism. The corporatism in *Quadragesimo anno* illustrates the organic understanding of society. The positive aspect of this approach recognizes the social

and communitarian aspect of human existence and opposes a one-sided individualism. The authoritarian or at best paternalistic understanding of an organic human society in the early documents fails, however, to give due importance to the
freedom, equality, and participation of all citizens. Recall the move that took place
within Catholic social teaching from the individual as part of the ignorant multitude to the person as citizen.

The hierarchical ordering of society and the classicist top-down approach also
contributed to downplaying the role of power. Power in society was tied to the authority of the rulers of society. There were no other sources of power. The authorities had responsibility for determining God's law for society, proposing it, and enforcing it. The fact that divine law and natural law sanctioned the just law of rulers
meant that the subjects simply had to obey God's law coming down from above.

A strictly theological dimension also influenced the downplaying of conflict in
Catholic social teaching. Recall that Catholic social teaching failed to give enough
importance to sin and its effects on human existence. The effects of sin definitely
contribute to conflict in the world, as well highlighted in the social ethics of Rein-
hold Niebuhr.[59] Conflict clearly does not result from sin only, but failure to recognize the effect of sin partially contributes to the failure to recognize the role of
conflict.

The theoretical downplaying of conflict and power existed in some tension
with a Catholic realism that acknowledged aspects of conflict in human existence.
Rerum novarum recognized the conflict between workers and owners and called for
state intervention to protect workers with the right to organize. Catholic social
ethics often has been identified with the "just war" theory that—while seeking to
limit violence and force—accepts limited use of force in certain situations. The
Catholic tradition has never been pacifist. The U.S. bishops began the Campaign
for Human Development in 1971. This organization supports and strengthens
community organizations that come together to form power groups to work for
powerless people. Much of the theory and practice behind the Campaign for Human Development came from Saul Alinsky, the agnostic Jewish founder of the Industrial Areas Foundation. Conflictual tactics formed an important part of Alinsky's approach, although he strongly recognized that conflict was only a means
and not an end.[60]

With recognition of social problems as global and worldwide, more recent documents of Catholic social teaching explicitly call attention to more conflictual areas—East and West, North and South, rich and poor, developed and underdeveloped, educated and noneducated. *Laborem exercens* recognizes that the present

situation "is deeply marked by many conflicts caused by human beings, and the technological means produced by human work play a primary role"—as illustrated by nuclear war (n. 12, O-S, p. 367). In *Centesimus annus* John Paul II briefly notes a positive role for conflict in struggling for social justice. In passing, he mentions that conflict must be restrained by ethical and juridical considerations, especially the common good (n. 14, O-S, p. 449).

Even the later documents of Catholic social teaching, however, do not develop in any detail their understanding of conflict and power and the role they play in working for justice. Why not? Six reasons help to explain why contemporary Catholic social teaching still fails to develop the role of conflict and power.

Why This Downplaying?

First, even contemporary Catholic social teaching appeals to all human beings on the basis of human reason. Reasonable people should see the truth in what is proposed and do it. Thus, the centrality of reason downplays any role for power. One can see here that Catholic social teaching fails to recognize fully the sinful aspects of human existence. The powerful will not always hear or heed reason or the truth. Reason is not the only factor that is important in bringing about greater justice in the world.

Second, the very word "teaching" accurately describes what is taking place here. Teaching means imparting knowledge to others. In some ways this concept describes what often takes place when there is a great difference between the teacher and the one who is taught. In light of the greater importance given to the creativity and participation of the student, teaching is much more than the mere imparting of knowledge. The teacher tries to stimulate and challenge the student to think for herself or himself. By its very nature, however, Catholic social teaching claims to be authoritative teaching and thus tends to emphasize the superior giving knowledge to the passive inferior or subject. (I discuss this aspect of authoritative teaching in more detail in chapter 3.)

The primacy of teaching, however it is understood, coheres with the Catholic emphasis on reason and truth as the primary forces in bringing about a more just society. Because the most important factor in bringing about social change is convincing people through reason of the truth of what is proposed, the Catholic Church thus sees its primary function for social change through its role as teacher. Conflict and power are not important factors in this understanding of how to bring about a better human society.

Third, the Catholic tradition's emphasis on harmony and wholeness, with all parts working together for a unified whole, goes much deeper than just the natural law tradition. Medieval theology, as well as medieval cathedrals, emphasized such an attempt to fit all the parts together into a unified whole. Catholic ecclesiology itself illustrates the emphasis on harmonious wholeness. All people have to admit that there can be no social justice or social ethic of any type without some overarching harmony and cooperation.

Fourth, Catholic social teaching even today still tends to move from the top down, from theory to practice. Once people know what truth and justice call for in these areas, they can reduce them to practice. Approaches that give more importance to moving from the bottom up and the centrality of praxis over theory will necessarily accentuate the conflictual nature of human existence. Liberation theology illustrates such an approach. Recent Catholic social teaching recognizes many of the conflicts in our global society, but the emphasis on moving from theory to practice gives much less importance to conflict and power as a means to obtain justice for people who are powerless and oppressed.

Fifth, in its opposition to Marxism, recent Catholic social teaching—as exemplified especially by John Paul II—opposes the concept of class struggle. All individuals and groups must cooperate and work together for the common good. By no means do I mean to imply that class struggle as an absolute is the correct approach, but Catholic social teaching tends to overreact and to stress harmony, cooperation, and the common good in contrast to Marxism. On the other hand, *Centesimus annus* explicitly recognizes some conflict while rejecting the class struggle that entails no ethical or juridical limits to conflict (n. 14, O-S, pp. 449–50).[61]

Sixth, Catholic social teaching tends to be general in approach rather than specific or particular. In chapter 3 I show the need for this type of generality in proposing authoritative church teaching. As a result, such teaching can avoid many of the conflicts in which various values collide. A more general approach stands above the nitty-gritty tensions and conflicts of concrete human existence.

In subsequent chapters I show the growing significance in Catholic social teaching of human rights as universal moral criteria applied to all. David Hollenbach has perceptively pointed out in his book on Catholic social teaching that human rights frequently involve claims in conflict.[62] The discussion of human rights in Catholic social teaching tends to be on a more general level, however, and seldom explicitly addresses the conflicts that so often arise on the concrete level of practice. Yes, contemporary Catholic social teaching recognizes some conflicts and insists, for example, on the priority of labor over capital; on the whole, however, such teaching remains more general and thus less conflictual.

Future Development

Conflict and power constitute important realities in working for social justice, and Catholic social teaching in the future must become more conscious of and reflective about these realities. Conflict and power differ greatly, but they share some significant characteristics. Two of these characteristics deserve further elaboration.

First, a tendency exists among some Christians to regard conflict and power as ultimately negative and thus related primarily to sin. Conflict brings about division and therefore should be avoided. The Tower of Babel story in Genesis, for example, portrays the conflict of languages as a result of human sinfulness. Power understood as *power over* and domination has very negative overtones; thus, theology regards such power as a result of sin. Without doubt, negative understandings of conflict and power exert real influence in the social world. Yet positive aspects also exist with regard to conflict and power. Phenomenologically, conflict has been and can be creative. In personal life, true human and moral growth occurs through conflict and tension. In human relationships, conflicts can be occasions for positive growth and development of those relationships. Power also has a positive aspect. Power includes not only domination but also empowerment. Social morality today recognizes the need to empower people who are poor and marginalized to enter more fully into participation in the life of society. On a personal level, people seek to develop all of their powers and abilities in striving to lead a better life.[63]

From a theological perspective, conflict and power do not relate to human sinfulness only. Human finitude—which from a theological perspective involves a positive but limited aspect of human existence—explains some of the positive aspects of both conflict and power. In addition, grace or God's redeeming love also can work through conflict and power. Catholic theology in other areas has recognized relationships between grace or redemption and power. Our liturgical prayer often addresses God as the all-powerful one. Grace empowers us to be people of God and to act as such.

Second, even the positive aspect of conflict and power cannot be absolutized. Conflict and power are limited by ethical and social considerations. For example, as *Centesimus annus* recognized with regard to conflict, the common good and respect for the dignity of persons constitute two important ethical considerations that give guidance and direction to conflict and power (n. 14, O-S, p. 449). Conflict and power in the service of selfish individualism or narrow tribalism or nationalism are morally evil. Future considerations must develop a better theory and practice of the role of conflict and power in trying to achieve social justice, but the common good and human dignity must always guide the theory and practice of conflict and power.

MORAL TRUTH

An important and even fundamental question in ethics concerns the existence of and the possibility of knowing moral truth. Ethics by its very nature pays attention to such deeper and methodological issues involving epistemology. Catholic social teaching rightly does not consider such epistemological issues, but presupposes that human beings can know moral truth. The very existence of Catholic social teaching proves that, in the mind of the authors, moral truths, values, and principles exist and all human beings can and should accept such truths.

The Approach of Catholic Social Teaching

Catholic social teaching came out of the neoscholastic tradition that strongly insisted on epistemological realism and the possibility of attaining certitude with regard to universal moral truth. With such a realistic epistemology, nineteenth-century neoscholasticism claimed to know universal moral truth, readily and with great certitude. God's law put an order into the world, and human reason can discover that order. A deductive methodology claimed to arrive at certain conclusions. The insistence on an essential human nature that is the same at all times, places, and circumstances grounded the existence of universal moral truths and downplayed pluralism, diversity, and difference.[64]

The three shifts I discuss earlier in this chapter—to historical consciousness, to the person as subject, and to a relationality-responsibility model—have affected epistemology or the ability to know universal moral truths and values. In general, Catholic theology in the post–Vatican II period has moved away somewhat from the epistemological approach of neoscholasticism but still holds on to a realistic epistemology and objective truth. Such realism and objectivity, however, are not the picture-book realism of the truth that is based on the analogy of sight (seeing the object "out there"). The turn to the subject in transcendental Thomism in the twentieth century, as in the approach of Bernard Lonergan, gives greater importance to the knowing subject and develops an epistemology on that basis. For Lonergan, intellectual conversion transforms the human knower from the myth that knowing is like looking at reality "out there" to recognizing the world mediated by meaning. Genuine objectivity and authentic subjectivity come together, but one cannot see objective truth in the way the eye sees external objects. Thus, objective truth is not as apparent and easy to grasp as an older neoscholasticism thought.[65]

Challenge to the Approach

Developments within the Catholic tradition itself, such as the three aforementioned shifts and recent liberationist and feminist ethics, together with challenges from dialogue with contemporary approaches such as postmodernism, have challenged three characteristics that are still present in the epistemological presuppositions of Catholic social teaching: universality, impartial and universal perspective, and certitude. Catholic social teaching should continue to maintain these three perspectives, but in a more nuanced and chastened way.

UNIVERSALITY

Today we are much more conscious of the great diversities of culture and traditions, with their different understandings of human realities such as marriage and the family as well as cultural, social, political, and economic institutions and structures. In light of this great diversity, some people have denied the possibility of a universal morality. Recall that Paul VI in *Octogesima adveniens* recognized the diverse situations in which Christians find themselves according to regions, sociopolitical systems, and cultures. In light of this diversity, Paul VI maintained that it was neither his mission nor his ambition "to put forward a solution that has universal validity" (n. 4, O-S, p. 256). Even in *Octogesima adveniens*, however, Paul VI intended to address the needs of all Catholics and the whole world. He insisted on the evils of discrimination on the basis of race, origin, color, culture, sex, or religion; the importance of the common good; the right to emigrate; the need to work for the establishment of universal brotherhood [sic]; the dangers of exploiting the environment; and the aspirations to equality and participation that are making themselves felt in these new contexts.

The approach in *Octogesima adveniens* indicates the approach that Catholic social teaching should take. In the midst of great diversity in our world there are no easy, ready-made solutions to the manifold problems facing the world. There are important moral values (e.g., equality, participation, justice) and principles (e.g., human rights, the common destination of the goods of creation to serve the needs of all), however, that have moral validity that can and should guide the building of more just social structures throughout our diversified world.

The Catholic tradition and the needs of the world today call for some universality, in the sense of general approaches and themes for all (such as human rights).[66] Such a chastened universality, as illustrated in *Octogesima adveniens*, is compatible with a historically conscious methodology. By definition, *catholic* means all-embracing and universal. This catholicity or universality finds its ground and support in basic Christian principles. Belief in a creator God who is mother and father of all means that all human beings are brothers and sisters of one another. Creation creates a bond among all human beings. In the Christian tradition, love has many different meanings; thousands of volumes have tried to put together the Christian understanding of love in a systematic way. Everyone agrees, however, that the object of Christian love of neighbor is universal and embraces all people—especially those in need and even enemies.

In addition, the realities of our world cry out for a universal or global morality. We live today in a global society. Scientific and technological progress has helped bring about this global society. The Internet provides instantaneous communication throughout the world. The economic reality today is global. What happens in one country has significant ramifications for what happens throughout the world. Pollution and environmental problems ignore national boundaries. Without some type of universal morality, the powerful will simply dominate. The poor will get poorer and the rich will get richer. In the midst of all of our diversity, a global morality will be somewhat general but absolutely necessary to overcome the individualism, tribalism, and power of the strong that so easily affect the world in which we live. Recent debates about human rights and growing recognition of human rights for all people indicate a significant aspect of a global morality that is so necessary for our world.

One significant contribution that the whole Judeo-Christian approach makes to a universal morality concerns speaking out for the rights and concerns of poor people at all times and in all places. At its best, Catholic social teaching has tried to be faithful to that tradition. This teaching has emphasized the preferential option for the poor. Very few people in the broader society speak up for poor people.[67] In the United States, powerful lobbies—corporations, labor unions, professional groups, and even churches and religious groups—who are involved to protect their own interests and concerns push the causes of special interests. The voice of poor people becomes even more muted. The church has an obligation to become an advocate for poor people throughout the world. The preferential option for the poor has universal validity in all cultures and societies, and Catholic social teaching must continue to be an advocate for poor people.

AN IMPARTIAL PERSPECTIVE

The question of an impartial and universal perspective is associated with but clearly distinguished from the issue of a universal morality. The impartial perspective relates to the social location of the knower. Does one begin as an objective, neutral observer discerning all aspects of the question in terms of what is required for everybody, or does one begin with concrete particular experience? Here we see perhaps the primary methodological difference between Catholic social teaching and liberation theology. Liberation theology begins with poor people's experience of oppression and their struggle to overcome it. Arriving at moral truth is not simply an intellectual matter done in the study or library; one comes to moral truth through involvement in liberating praxis. Postmodernism, liberation theology, and feminism have raised serious questions about the claim to work from an impartial epistemological perspective.[68]

Catholic social teaching has not avoided this problem of a particular perspective claiming to be universal. The early documents were almost entirely Eurocentric. The authors and their experience were heavily European, especially in their intellectual and cultural formation. To their credit, John XXIII in *Mater et magistra* (n. 6, O-S, p. 261) in 1961 and Paul VI in *Populorum progressio* in 1967 (n. 3, O-S, p. 261) recognized long before many others in the Western world that the social question had become a worldwide issue. The Eurocentric approach still comes through, however, as is evident in the extended treatment John Paul II in *Centesimus annus* gives to what happened in 1989 in Europe (n. 22–29, O-S, pp. 454–61). Furthermore, the male perspective comes through in almost every document of Catholic social teaching. Women tend to be invisible in the earlier documents, except in discussions of the family. Within the family, however, the earlier documents clearly portray and extol the subordinate position of women. Even today the role of women is primarily as mothers and educators of their children in the home.[69]

The very nature of Catholic social teaching speaking to the whole world implies a perspective that claims to be impartial and universal. I already have noted the problems with such a perspective. There also are problems with beginning from a particular social location. Such a perspective might be prejudiced in the negative sense and not open to recognizing all that must be considered. There are benefits and problems connected with both epistemological perspectives. Neither starting perspective is entirely correct or entirely erroneous. Consequently, those who begin with an impartial and universal perspective must be very self-critical and conscious of the potential problems associated with such an approach.

From a theological perspective, the problems for an impartial and universal perspective come from two distinct sources—our finitude and our sinfulness. Because of our finitude and limitations, we are unable to see the total picture. Every human being resonates with the experience of looking back on a particular decision in the past and bemoaning the fact that I did not know then what I know now. All human beings also are subject to human sinfulness, so we tend to bring into our perspective our own prejudices—mostly in the form of too much self-centeredness. Such negative prejudices affect our search for moral truth. The prudent human searcher for moral truth, claiming to have an impartial and universal perspective, must realize that such a perspective can never be fully achieved in this world. At the least, one must be self-critical. In chapter 3 I suggest some practical steps that Catholic social teaching should take in light of ecclesiology to overcome problems arising from an epistemological perspective that claims to be impartial and universal.

CERTITUDE

The neoscholastic approach to morality followed a deductive method and claimed great certitude for its conclusions. The shift to historical consciousness that has occurred within Catholic social teaching will not be able to claim such certitude. Within the broader discipline of Catholic moral theology, many revisionist moral theologians have challenged the absolute certitude with which the hierarchical magisterium has proposed absolute moral norms that are always obligatory with regard to contraception, homosexuality, and the prohibition of all direct killing.[70] No similar criticism has been made, however, about Catholic social teaching. What explains these differences?

Catholic social teaching has proposed general directives, values, and principles rather than specific concrete norms that are always obligatory. In chapter 3 I point out the ecclesial reasons for such an avoidance of more specific proposals. One can more easily claim some certitude on a more general level. Contemporary Catholic social teaching can and should follow the understanding developed by Aquinas in dependence on Aristotle, which unfortunately was not entirely accepted in the neoscholastic manuals of moral theology. Aquinas distinguishes between speculative truth and practical or moral truth. By its very nature, the certitude available in specific moral truth is less than that in speculative truth. Aquinas maintains that speculative truths are always and everywhere true. For example, every triangle has 180 degrees. More specific moral laws or truths admit of exceptions and therefore are not absolutely certain. The reason for this exception is that specific and complex moral issues involve many different circumstances that might affect the general principle. Thus, Aquinas asserts that deposits should always be returned. In this understanding, a deposit is something the owner gives to another person with the understanding that the other person will return the deposit whenever the owner asks for it. Aquinas points out, however, that there are some potential exceptions

to this norm. For example, if a person who has given you a sword as a deposit now demands the sword but is raving drunk and threatening to kill other people, you have an obligation not to return the sword. Specific moral norms by their very nature admit of exceptions because of the influence of individual circumstances.[71]

Contemporary Catholic social teaching should follow this general understanding. Moral certitude is easier to attain on the level of the more general (e.g., the dignity of the human person, basic human rights) but impossible to attain with regard to specific policy recommendations (e.g., affirmative action programs). There will always be room for discussion about how general is general, but that is unavoidable. With our contemporary recognition of greater diversity and pluralism, we should be even more conscious than Aquinas of the impossibility of claiming moral certitude on specific and complex issues.

In this chapter I have examined six significant aspects of ethical methodology that indicate significant changes in the historical development of Catholic social teaching and suggest how Catholic social teaching should develop its ethical methodology today. In chapter 3 I consider the historical development and contemporary needs of methodology from the perspective of the understanding of the church.

NOTES

1. See Bernard Lonergan, *Collection* (New York: Herder and Herder, 1967), 252–67, and "A Transition from a Classicist Worldview to Historical Mindedness," in *Law for Liberty: The Role of Law in the Church Today*, ed. James E. Biechler (Baltimore: Helicon, 1967), 126–33; see also Joann Wolski Conn, "From Certitude to Understanding: Historical Consciousness in the American Catholic Theological Community in the 1960s" (Ph.D. diss., Columbia University, 1974).

2. For the understanding of natural law in the manuals of moral theology, see Marcellinus

Zalba, *Theologiae moralis summa*, vol. 1 (Madrid: Biblioteca de autores cristianos, 1952), 345–66.

3. Philippe Delhaye, *Permanence du droit naturel* (Louvain, Belgium: Éditions Nauwelaerts, 1960).

4. Hans Küng, *Global Responsibility: In Search of a New World Ethic* (New York: Crossroad, 1991).

5. See, e.g., *Quadragesimo anno*, nn. 41–43, in *Catholic Social Thought*, ed. O'Brien and Shannon, 50–51.

6. See note 1.

7. Alfredo Ottaviani, *Institutiones iuris publici ecclesiastici*, vol. 2, *Ius publicum externum*, 3rd ed. (Rome: Typis Polyglottis Vaticanis, 1948).

8. Émile-Joseph de Smedt, "Religious Freedom," in *Council Speeches of Vatican II*, ed. Yves Congar, Hans Küng, and Daniel O'Hanlon (London: Sheed and Ward, 1964), 161–68.

9. John Courtney Murray developed his interpretation of Leo XIII in five articles: "The Church and Totalitarian Democracy," *Theological Studies* 13 (1952): 525–63; "Leo XIII on Church and State: The General Structure of the Controversy," *Theological Studies* 14 (1953): 1–30; "Leo XIII: Separation of Church and State," *Theological Studies* 14 (1953): 145–214; "Leo XIII: Two Concepts of Government," *Theological Studies* 14 (1953): 551–67; "Leo XIII: Two Concepts of Government, II: Government and the Order of Culture," *Theological Studies* 15 (1954): 1–33. A sixth article, "Leo XIII and Pius XII: Government and the Order of Religion," existed in galley proofs, but higher authority did not allow it to be published. This article appears in John Courtney Murray, *Religious Liberty: Catholic Struggles with Pluralism*, ed. J. Leon Hooper (Louisville, Ky.: Westminster/John Knox, 1993), 49–125.

10. John Courtney Murray, "The Declaration on Religious Freedom: Its Deeper Significance," *America* 114 (April 23, 1966): 592–93; John Courtney Murray, "The Declaration on Religious Freedom," *Concilium*, no. 15 (May 1966): 11–16.

11. J. Leon Hooper, *The Ethics of Discourse: The Social Philosophy of John Courtney Murray* (Washington, D.C.: Georgetown University Press, 1986), 140–43.

12. Charles Moeller, "Preface and Introductory Statement," in *Commentary on the Documents of Vatican II*, vol. 5: *Pastoral Constitution on the Church in the Modern World*, ed. Herbert Vorgrimler (New York: Herder and Herder, 1969), 94.

13. Mary Elsbernd, "What Ever Happened to *Octogesima adveniens?*" *Theological Studies* 56 (1995): 39–60.

14. Gregory Baum, *The Priority of Labor: A Commentary on* Laborem Exercens, *Encyclical Letter of Pope John Paul II* (New York: Paulist, 1982), 80–88.

15. See, e.g., Robert A. Destro, "Work: The Human Environment: *Laborem exercens* (1981)," in *Building the Free Society: Democracy, Capitalism, and Catholic Social Teaching*, ed. George Weigel and Robert Royal (Grand Rapids, Mich.: William B. Eerdmans, 1993), 163–86.

16. Ronald Modras, "The Moral Philosophy of John Paul II," *Theological Studies* 41 (1980): 683–97. For a more positive and appreciative evaluation, see Kenneth L. Schmitz, *At the Center of the Human Drama: The Philosophical Anthropology of Karol Wojtyla/Pope John Paul II* (Washington, D.C.: Catholic University of America Press, 1993).

17. Hans Küng and Leonard Swidler, eds., *The Church in Anguish: Has the Vatican Betrayed Vatican II?* (San Francisco: Harper and Row, 1986). For a criticism of centralization in the Roman Catholic Church from a retired American archbishop, see John R. Quinn, *The Reform of the Papacy: The Costly Call to Christian Unity* (New York: Crossroad, 1999).

18. Marie-Dominique Chenu, *La "doctrine sociale" de l'Église comme idéologie* (Paris: Cerf, 1979), 79–86. For an earlier discussion of this legacy, see Bartolomeo Sorge, "E superato il concetto tradizionale di dottrina sociale?" *La civiltà cattolica* 119 (1968), I, 423–36.

19. Chenu, *La doctrine sociale*, 87–96.

20. Some confusion arises from the English translation, which translates *doctrina socialis* sometimes as "social doctrine" and sometimes as "social teaching." There seems to be no discernable reason for distinguishing between the two translations. The term "social teaching" appears four times in the English translation of *Sollicitudo rei socialis*. Three times this phrase

translates *doctrina socialis.* In paragraph 9, however, *sociale . . . magisterium* also is translated as
"social teaching." The English translation of *Sollicitudo* uses the term "social doctrine" seven
times. Most often this phrase appears in the expression "social doctrine of the Church." Here
the Latin word is always *doctrina.* However, "social doctrine" also is used in paragraph 42 as
"Christian social doctrine." The five times *doctrina* appears in paragraphs 41 and 42, it is translated as "social doctrine." Obviously this translation is related to the attempt to refute Chenu.
Centesimus annus (n. 2, O-S, p. 440) uses three
terms in English as synonyms: "social doctrine,"
"social teaching," and even "social magisterium." The corresponding Latin phrases are *doctrina socialis, disciplina socialis,* and *Ecclesiae
Magisterium.* Thus, there is a tendency in the
original Latin and in the English translation
(which also sometimes translates the same Latin
word—*doctrina*—differently) to treat several different terms as synonymous. In this volume I
have used the term "Catholic social teaching."

21. Pope John Paul II, "Opening Address at the
Puebla Conference," in *Third General Conference of Latin American Bishops: Conclusions*
(Washington, D.C.: National Conference of
Catholic Bishops, 1979), 13. For different per-
spectives on the Chenu thesis, see Peter Heb-
blethwaite, "The Popes and Politics: Shifting
Patterns in 'Catholic Social Doctrine,'" in *Reli-
gion and America: Spiritual Life in a Secular Age,*
ed. Mary Douglas and Stephen Tipton (Boston:
Beacon, 1983), 190–204; Roger Heckel, *The So-
cial Teaching of John Paul II,* vol. 1, *General Aspects of the Social Catechesis of John Paul II: The
Use of the Expression "Social Doctrine" of the
Church* (Vatican City: Pontifical Commission
Justitia et Pax, 1980).

22. Pope John Paul II, *Veritatis splendor, Origins*
23 (1993): 297–334.

23. For the best one-volume overview of liberation theology from its own adherents, see Ignacio Ellacuría and Jon Sobrino, eds., *Mysterium*

*Liberationis: Fundamental Concepts of Libera-
tion Theology* (Maryknoll, N.Y.: Orbis, 1993).

24. Dorr, *Option for the Poor,* 320ff.

25. See Charles E. Curran, Margaret A. Farley,
and Richard A. McCormick, eds., *Feminist
Ethics and the Catholic Moral Tradition: Readings in Moral Theology No. 9* (New York:
Paulist, 1996).

26. Leo XIII, *Libertas praestantissimum,* nn.
19–37, in *The Church Speaks to the Modern
World: The Social Teachings of Leo XIII,* ed. Etienne Gilson (Garden City, N.Y.: Doubleday Image, 1954), 70–79.

27. Leo XIII, *Quod apostolici muneris,* nn. 5–6,
in Gilson, *The Church Speaks to the Modern
World,* 192–93.

28. Leo XIII, *Humanum genus,* n. 26, in Gilson,
The Church Speaks to the Modern World, 130–33.

29. John Courtney Murray, *The Problem of Religious Freedom* (Westminster, Md.: Newman,
1965), 55–56.

30. Leo XIII, *Libertas praestantissimum,* n. 23,
in Gilson, *The Church Speaks to the Modern
World,* 73.

31. Leo XIII, *Immortale Dei,* n. 5, in Gilson, *The
Church Speaks to the Modern World,* 163.

32. Murray, *The Problem of Religious Freedom,*
55–57.

33. Leo XIII, *Immortale Dei,* nn. 23–24, in
Gilson, *The Church Speaks to the Modern
World,* 172.

34. Terence P. McLaughlin, "Introduction," in
*The Church and the Reconstruction of the Mod-
ern World: The Social Encyclicals of Pius XI,* ed.
Terence P. McLaughlin (Garden City, N.Y.:
Doubleday Image, 1957), 6–9.

35. Pius XI, *Non abbiamo bisogno,* nn. 45–46,
in McLaughlin, *The Church and the Reconstruction of the Modern World,* 318–19.

36. Pius XI, *Mit brennender Sorge,* nn. 35–39, in
McLaughlin, *The Church and the Reconstruction
of the Modern World,* 351–53.

37. Pius XI, *Divini Redemptoris*, n. 10, in McLaughlin, *The Church and the Reconstruction of the Modern World*, 369–70.

38. Richard J. Wolff and Jörg K. Hoensch, eds., *Catholics, the State, and the European Radical Right* (Boulder, Colo.: Social Science Monographs, 1987).

39. John P. Kenny, *Principles of Medical Ethics*, 2d ed. (Westminster, Md.: Newman, 1962).

40. John Cornwell, *Hitler's Pope: The Secret History of Pius XII* (New York: Viking Penguin, 1999). For a defense of Pius XII, see Pierre Blet, *Pius XII and the Second World War: According to the Archives of the Vatican* (New York: Paulist, 1999).

41. Pope Pius XII, "1944 Christmas Message," in *The Pope Speaks: The Teachings of Pope Pius XII* (New York: Pantheon, 1956), 292–99.

42. Jacques Maritain, *Integral Humanism* (New York: Scribner, 1938); *Scholasticism and Politics* (New York: Macmillan, 1940); *The Rights of Man and Natural Law* (New York: Scribner, 1943); *Man and the State* (Chicago: University of Chicago Press, 1951).

43. Paul E. Sigmund, "Politics and Liberal Democracy," in *Catholicism and Liberalism: Contributions to American Public Philosophy*, ed. R. Bruce Douglass and David Hollenbach (Cambridge: Cambridge University Press, 1994), 225–27.

44. Murray, *The Problem of Religious Freedom*, 65–67.

45. Pope Pius XII, "Radio Message," December 24, 1944, *Acta apostolicae sedis* 37 (1945): 14.

46. G. B. Guzzetti, "L'impegno politico dei cattolici nel magistero pontificio dell' ultimo ventennio," *La scuola cattolica* 194 (1976): 202.

47. *Dignitatis humanae*, n. 1, in Flannery, *Vatican Council II*, 551.

48. Ibid., nn. 1–2, 552–53.

49. Ibid., n. 3, 553–55.

50. Ibid., n. 7, 558.

51. For Murray's formulation of the older position, see his *Problem of Religious Freedom*, 7–17.

52. John Paul II, *The Acting Person* (Dordrecht, Holland; Boston: D. Reidel, 1979); John Paul II, *Love and Responsibility* (New York: Farrar, Straus, Giroux, 1981).

53. Douglass and Hollenbach, *Catholicism and Liberalism*.

54. For a succinct overview of Thomistic ethics (in my judgment with an overly negative approach to contemporary developments in Catholic ethics), see Ralph McInerny, *Ethica Thomistica: The Moral Philosophy of Thomas Aquinas*, rev. ed. (Washington, D.C.: Catholic University of America Press, 1997).

55. Declaration on Religious Liberty, n. 7, in Flannery, *Vatican II*, 558.

56. Judith A. Dwyer, ed., *The New Dictionary of Catholic Social Thought* (Collegeville, Minn.: Liturgical, 1994). The dictionary includes an article of slightly more than one page on "Force" (pp. 398–400).

57. Joseph L. Allen, *Love and Conflict: A Covenantal Model of Christian Ethics* (Lanham, Md.: University Press of America, 1995), 183–84.

58. Johannes Messner, *Social Ethics: Natural Law in the Western Tradition*, rev. ed. (St. Louis: B. Herder, 1965), 118–21.

59. For an exposition and critique of Niebuhr on conflict and sin, see Allen, *Love and Conflict*, 88–99.

60. Lawrence J. Engel, "The Influence of Saul Alinsky on the Campaign for Human Development," *Theological Studies* 59 (1998): 636–61.

61. For somewhat different views on Catholic social teaching and the class struggle, see Gregory Baum, "Class Struggle and the Magisterium: A New Note," *Theological Studies* 45 (1984): 690–701, and Ivan Deschamps, "La doctrine sociale de l'Église catholique et le concept de 'lutte des classes,'" *Social Compass* 37 (1990): 367–90.

62. David Hollenbach, *Claims in Conflict: Retrieving and Renewing the Catholic Human Rights Tradition* (New York: Paulist, 1979).

63. Christine Firer Hinze, *Comprehending Power in Christian Social Ethics* (Atlanta: Scholars, 1995).

64. Zalba, *Theologiae moralis summa.*

65. Bernard J. F. Lonergan, *Method in Theology* (New York: Herder and Herder, 1972), 237ff.

66. For the 1993 "Declaration toward a Global Ethic" of the Parliament of the World's Religions and support for it, see Hans Küng, ed., *Yes to a Global Ethic* (London: SCM, 1996). For my reaction to the declaration, see Charles E. Curran, "The Global Ethic," *Ecumenist* 37 (spring 2000): 6–10.

67. Stephen J. Pope, "Proper and Improper Partiality and the Preferential Option for the Poor," *Theological Studies* 54 (1993): 242–71.

68. Lisa Sowle Cahill, "Feminist Ethics and the Challenge of Culture," *Proceedings of the Catholic Theological Society of America* 48 (1993): 65–83.

69. Christine E. Gudorf, "Encountering the Other: The Modern Papacy on Women," *Social Compass* 36 (1989): 295–310.

70. Charles E. Curran and Richard A. McCormick, eds., *Readings in Moral Theology No. 1: Moral Norms and Catholic Tradition* (New York: Paulist, 1979).

71. Aquinas, *IaIIae,* q. 94, a.4.

CHAPTER 3

Ecclesial Methodology

Ecclesial or church influences on the approach of Catholic social teaching are much more implicit than the theological and ethical aspects of methodology. The documents seldom if ever explicitly discuss ecclesiology, although the Catholic understanding of the church obviously colors the way the popes teach. In this chapter I discuss the most significant ecclesial factors affecting the method and approach of Catholic social teaching.

The most fundamental methodological direction from ecclesiology stems from the fact that Roman Catholicism is a church, not a sect, in the well-known typology of Ernst Troeltsch.[1] The sect type, as a small radical group, regards the world as evil and thus removes itself from the world so that the Christian community can live and follow the biblical demands of Jesus without being forced to compromise or to be contaminated by the evil world. The church type, on the other hand, comprises saints and sinners, lives in the world, and attempts to have a direct influence on what transpires in all aspects of worldly existence. Troeltsch correctly regards the Roman Catholic Church as the clearest example of the church type.

Such an understanding of church rests on its characteristic of catholicity and the theological assumptions I discuss in chapter 1. What God has made is good, although it is affected by sin. Grace affects not only persons but everything that has been created. The natural, the created, and the human are not basically evil.

Because the Roman Catholic Church is the best illustration of the church type, it will be concerned about what happens in the world. The history of the Catholic Church testifies to its involvement in working for a better human society, although at times the means were more than questionable. Consequently, there is nothing new in Catholic social teaching's involvement in working for a better human society. Even within the body of teaching going back to 1891, however, significant discontinuity exists with regard to the church's self-understanding and the way in which it teaches.

Changes in the Church's Self-Understanding

In the earlier documents, the church regards itself primarily as a juridical institution, often identified only with the hierarchy, triumphally claiming to be holy and without spot, with the pope or hierarchical teaching authority proclaiming the truth entrusted to it by God to the problems of the world. *Quadragesimo anno* (1931)—especially in its description of Leo XIII's encyclical *Rerum novarum* (1891)—illustrates this understanding of the church.

> The eyes of all, as often in the past turn toward the Chair of Peter, sacred repository
> of the fullness of truth whence words of salvation are dispensed to the whole world.
> To the feet of Christ's vicar on earth were seen to flock, in unprecedented numbers,
> specialists in social affairs, employers, the very working men themselves, begging
> with one voice that at last a safe road might be pointed out to them (n. 7, O-S, p. 43).

Later in the same encyclical, Pius XI describes his own role in similar terms. The church

> never can relinquish her God-given task; of interposing her authority not indeed in
> technical matters, for which she has neither the equipment nor the mission, but in all
> those that have a bearing on moral conduct. For the deposit of truth entrusted to us
> by God, and our weighty office of propagating, interpreting, and urging in season and
> out of season the entire moral law, demand that both social and economic questions
> be brought within our supreme jurisdiction, insofar as they refer to moral issues (n.
> 41, O-S, p. 51).

In keeping with the general understanding of the church at the time, Pius XI depicts the church primarily as a juridical institution that is practically identified with the hierarchy. Near its conclusion, *Quadragesimo anno* appeals to the role of Catholic Action (n. 138, O-S, p. 74). Pius XI clearly recognizes an important role for the laity and acknowledges the famous principle of the apostolate of like working with like by insisting that the immediate apostles of working people must themselves be working people (n. 141, O-S, p. 75). Pius XI defines Catholic Action as participation and collaboration of the laity in the apostolate of the hierarchy.[2] As such, the definition does not include the moral and social obligations that people have in their daily lives in the family or at work. Pius XII later expanded the definition of Catholic Action to include all organized groups of the lay apostolate recognized by the hierarchy. In such a view, even the social apostolate belongs primarily to the hierarchy, but they can and should involve laity in this by giving them a mandate or at least an official recognition of their role.[3]

Shift Away from Primacy of Juridical and Hierarchical

Lumen gentium (1964)—Vatican II's Constitution on the Church—reacted against a juridical and primarily hierarchical view of the church. Vatican II clearly affirms the role of the hierarchy, but it sees the hierarchy within its fundamental understanding of the church as mystery and as the people of God. The original drafts of *Lumen gentium* considered first the hierarchy and then the people of God or the laity, but even before the second session of the council the fathers rejected such an approach and insisted that the total church is the people of God, including laity and hierarchy.[4] Thus, in the final version of *Lumen gentium*, the first chapter treats the church as mystery, and the second chapter treats the church as the people of God. Only the third chapter discusses the hierarchical office in the church.[5]

Chapter 4 of part 1 of *Gaudium et spes* (1965)—The Pastoral Constitution on the Church in the Modern World—discusses the role of the church in the modern world and regards the church as the whole people or family of God, downplaying the heavy juridical emphasis on the church but still recognizing a special role for the hierarchy. "[I]t is the task of the entire People of God, especially pastors and theologians, to hear, distinguish, and interpret the many voices of our age, and to judge them in the light of the divine Word" (n. 44, O-S, p. 194). Secular duties and obligations belong properly, although not exclusively, to the laity. The well-formed conscience of lay people has the function of seeing that the divine law is inscribed in the life of the earthly city. Laity should not expect their pastors to be experts who can provide a solution to every problem that arises (n. 43, O-S, pp. 192-93). The subsequent documents continue to regard the church as the people of God.

Shift Away from Triumphalism

Lumen gentium devotes an entire chapter to the pilgrim church—an effort to move away from the older triumphalistic notion of the church as a perfect society. The church will receive its perfection only in the fullness of time.[6] *Gaudium et spes* explicitly recognizes and develops the pilgrim nature of the church (n. 40, O-S, p. 189). Some members of the church, clerical and lay, have been unfaithful to the spirit of God during the course of many centuries (n. 43, O-S, p. 193). Thus, the pilgrim church recognizes the sinfulness of its members and their actions.

By insisting on the practical aspects of being a pilgrim church, *Justitia in mundo* (1971) creatively introduces an important new aspect in Catholic social teaching.

> While the church is bound to give witness to justice, she recognizes that everyone who ventures to speak to people about justice must first be just in their eyes. Hence we must undertake an examination of the modes of acting and of the possessions and lifestyle found within the Church herself (O-S, p. 295).

The document then points out the need to safeguard rights in the church, including the rights of women, the rights of workers to a living wage, and rights to suitable freedom of expression and thought. In addition, the use of material goods in the church and the lifestyle of all of its members should bear witness to the Gospel (O-S, p. 295).

Paul VI explicitly apologized for actions of the Catholic Church that contributed to division among Christian churches.[7] John Paul II often has called on the church to examine its conscience and apologize for the wrongs that its members have committed. The contemporary church is somewhat conscious of its pilgrim nature, but further steps are necessary. Recognition of wrongs truly constitutes a new approach for the Roman Catholic Church, but it does not go far enough. Vatican II and, more recently, John Paul II make the distinction between the church and its members. They explicitly admit the sins and errors of some members but never seem to speak of the sins of the church itself.[8] By definition, however, the pilgrim church also is a sinful church. If the church is the pilgrim people of God on its journey to the fullness of perfection, not only limitation but also some sinfulness will mark the church itself.[9] The hierarchical magisterium must recognize explicitly the sinful nature of the church and its effects, while still recognizing the role of the Holy Spirit striving to make the church holy.

Changed Understanding of Papal Teaching Role

The shift away from a hierarchical, juridical, and triumphalistic understanding of the church in the documents of Catholic social teaching contributes to a change in understanding how the teaching role of the pope and the hierarchical church functions. The pre-Vatican II documents regard the pope as entrusted with the deposit of faith and knowledge of eternal and natural law to apply these realities to the social situation of the world. Thus, Catholic social teaching comes from the top down. Recognition of the pope as the authoritative interpreter of eternal and natural law stands in some tension with the realization that natural law is based on human reason and is open to all people of good will.

Vatican II again is a significant turning point in this understanding of how the hierarchical magisterium functions. Although *Lumen gentium* strongly upholds the authoritative teaching office of the hierarchical magisterium, it insists that all baptized people share in the prophetic and teaching function of Jesus.[10]

The Declaration on Religious Liberty of Vatican II puts flesh and blood on this theoretical recognition that the teaching role in the Catholic Church is broader than just the hierarchical teaching office.

> People nowadays are becoming increasingly conscious of the dignity of the human person; a growing number demand that people should exercise fully their own judgment and a responsible freedom in their actions and should not be subject to external pressure or coercion but inspired by a sense of duty.... This Vatican Council pays attention to these spiritual aspirations and, with a view to declaring to what extent they are in accord with truth and justice, searches the sacred tradition and teaching of the church, from which it draws forth new insights in harmony with the old.[11]

Here the Vatican Council clearly admits that it has learned from the experience of human beings. Recall that the Catholic Church came to its teaching on religious liberty very late in comparison with most secular governments, Christian churches, and other religious bodies. The Catholic Church clearly learned from people of good will.

In contrast to a divine law imposed authoritatively from above by divinely ordained teachers, *Gaudium et spes* describes the teaching function of the church with regard to the social conditions of our world in terms of dialogue. "Everything we have said about the dignity of the human person, and about the human community, and the profound meaning of human activity, lays the foundation for the relationship between the church and the world and provides the basis for dialogue between them" (n. 40, O-S, p. 189). The church strives to bring help to individuals, to society, and to human activity, but it also receives help from the modern world.

> [T]he church herself knows how richly she has profited by the history and development of humanity. Thanks to the experience of past ages, the progress of the sciences, and the treasures hidden in the various forms of human culture, the nature of

human beings is more clearly revealed and new roads to truth are opened (n. 44, O-S, p. 194).

The church has learned moral truth from the world. *Justitia in mundo* (1971) insists on the need for dialogue to bring about true peace and justice in the world (O-S, p. 292).

The post–Vatican II changed understanding of the hierarchical magisterium's mode of teaching on social justice corresponds with many of the other theological, philosophical, and ecclesiological developments in Catholic social teaching. Above all, a more inductive philosophical method calls for a more dialogical approach to hierarchical teaching that recognizes that all people of good will can and do contribute to our understanding of what it means to be truly human in our world.

In *Centesimus annus* John Paul II recognizes that Catholic social teaching must be in dialogue with the different disciplines that tell us about human beings. In addition to this interdisciplinary aspect, an experiential dimension of teaching and learning exists at the crossroads where Christian life and conscience come into contact with the world (n. 59, O-S, pp. 482–83). "Indeed, openness to dialogue and to cooperation is required of all people of good will, and in particular of individuals and groups with specific responsibilities in the areas of politics, economics, and social life, at both the national and international levels" (n. 60, O-S, p. 483). The hierarchical teaching office has changed from the authoritative source of eternal and natural law applied to human problems to a dialogue partner that has something to contribute to the world but also can learn from the world.

The shift in the church's understanding of its relationship to the state is intimately connected with the changes in Catholic social teaching regarding the nature of the church and its teaching function within the broader human society. Before Vatican II, the official Catholic position called for the union of church and state. In practice one could tolerate separation of church and state, but recognition of the church by the state remained the obligatory ideal.[12] Such a view highlighted the religious and moral supremacy of the church and supported the notion of the pope and hierarchical teachers authoritatively interpreting the demands of the eternal and natural law for the state and the ignorant multitude. The Catholic Church was not simply one among other institutions in society; it was *the* religious and moral leader. The Declaration on Religious Liberty proposed a very different relationship between church and state: The church speaks to the world not on the basis of privilege granted by the state but by the freedom the state gives it to pursue its own mission, which includes a social dimension. In freedom the church proposes its social teaching, and in freedom it asks all others to respond to it. The church regards itself as one of many voices in society working for the common good and neither expects nor receives any privileged recognition from the state.[13] Thus, the church's self-understanding and how it teaches in social matters has changed dramatically since 1891, although the teaching is still proposed as authoritative and in some ways does not always avoid the problems and triumphalistic overtones of the past (as I point out later in this chapter).

AUTHORITATIVE NATURE OF CATHOLIC SOCIAL TEACHING

The hierarchical teaching office in the Roman Catholic Church still authoritatively proposes Catholic social teaching for the guidance of all Catholics. In *Centesimus annus* John Paul II proposes "to show the fruitfulness of the principles enunciated by Leo XIII, which belong to the church's doctrinal patrimony and, as such, involve the exercise of her teaching authority" (n. 3, O-S, p. 441). All commentators agree that this social teaching falls into the category of authoritative, noninfallible teaching. This genre of official and authoritative church teaching clearly colors the content and approach of the documents.

Authoritative, Not Prophetic

The papal documents often have been compared and contrasted with the documents of the World Council of Churches, the worldwide association of Orthodox and Protestant churches. By its very nature, the World Council of Churches has no authoritative teaching role for the churches it comprises. The social documents issued by the World Council of Churches speak not *for* the churches but *to* the churches. They challenge the churches and their members.[14] The fact that Catholic social teaching represents authoritative church teaching for the whole body of Roman Catholics means that it carries much more weight and is much better known than similar documents of the World Council of Churches. One distinguished Protestant colleague in social ethics once remarked to me that probably 99 percent of American Protestants could not name the head of the World Council of Churches—but they all know the name of the pope!

Because the World Council of Churches speaks to the churches and not for the churches, however, its documents are free to be more radical and challenging. These documents have a more prophetic tone because they raise questions for the churches and challenge existing approaches. On the other hand, the documents of

Catholic social teaching propose guidelines that are to be followed by all the members of the church. Such documents must be careful not to propose things that are not binding on all its members. The authoritative nature of these documents definitely influences the approach they take.

Catholic social ethics, however, traditionally has recognized ways of holding on to what is obligatory for all as well as the particular vocation of individuals. The distinction between a precept that is binding on all and a counsel for an individual or a few individuals illustrates this approach.[15] For the most part, Catholic social teaching has not developed the prophetic role of individuals. The U.S. bishops' letter on peace, however, clearly supports the vocation of some people to bear witness to pacifism and the contribution they make to society, while recognizing that nations cannot embrace pacifism (nn. 111–121, O-S, pp. 517–18). The Catholic tradition has always recognized the vocation of religious who take vows of poverty, chastity, and obedience. Religious life bears witness to the significance of these values. Social ethics acknowledges many different values that at times can conflict. Think, for example, of justice and nonviolence. God calls some people to bear witness to a particular value and thereby remind the church and society of the importance of this particular value, even though not all people are called to embrace this particular value at all times because of possible conflicts.

Many significant Catholic individuals and movements have embraced voluntary poverty as a way of trying to live out their Christian lives. Although not all Christians are called to embrace voluntary poverty, the life of the Catholic Church and human society has been enriched by the witness of individuals and groups who try to live out voluntary poverty in the midst of our world. The limited focus of Catholic social teaching means that these "prophetic shock-minorities" usually are not mentioned.[16] Such individuals and groups challenge all of us by their witness to be more conscious of how we are to try to live out our Christianity in the midst of the world. Catholic social teaching in the future must call attention to these individual vocations and raise significant prophetic challenges for its own members and all people of good will.

General, Not Specific

From the perspective of Catholic ecclesiology, how does the fact that these documents constitute authoritative teaching for all members of the church affect their content? Catholic social teaching has justified and limited its teaching role in social questions on the basis of its responsibility to teach morality; the phrase that often is used is "the moral law." In *Sollicitudo rei socialis* John Paul II justifies the church's involvement in social questions because of the "dignity of the human person whose defense and promotion have been entrusted to us by the Creator" (n. 47, O-S, p. 429). *Centesimus annus* maintains that the human person is "the way of the church. . . . Her sole purpose has been care and responsibility for human beings" (n. 53, O-S, p. 479). The church claims (too triumphalisticly) to be an "expert in humanity."[17] Throughout the corpus of Catholic social teaching, popes have insisted that the church does not have teaching competence in political, economic, and social issues as such. Even the earlier, more authoritarian notion of the papal teaching role recognized its limits. *Quadragesimo anno* maintains that the church "never can relinquish her God-given task; of interposing her authority not indeed in technical matters, for which she has neither the equipment nor the mission, but in all those that have a bearing on moral conduct" (n. 41, O-S, p. 51). *Sollicitudo rei socialis* insists that "the church does not have technical solutions to offer . . . for the church does not propose economic and political systems or programs . . ." (n. 41, O-S, p. 424).

The church regards its mission as authoritatively teaching moral law or moral obligations that flow from the dignity and rights of human beings. How specific are the moral laws or requirements of human dignity taught by the hierarchical magisterium? In the very beginning, *Rerum novarum* refers to "the principles which truth and justice dictate" (n. 1, O-S, p. 14). John Paul II frequently refers to what is contained in Catholic social teaching by citing *Octogesima adveniens*—principles of reflection, norms of judgment, and directives for action. The content of the documents of Catholic social teaching bears out this emphasis on principles as opposed to more specific conclusions and concrete models. *Centesimus annus* points out that the pope's analysis of historical events does not involve binding magisterial teaching (n. 3, O-S, p. 441). Precisely because Catholic social teaching is authoritative and binding on Catholics to some degree, it remains somewhat general and avoids specifics.

This question of the specificity of the authoritative teaching of church documents on social matters came to the fore in the early 1980s when the U.S. bishops were drafting their pastoral letter on peace and war (*The Challenge of Peace*, 1983). The bishops already had made the point that their teaching was going to be more specific than the teaching in the documents coming from Rome. At the same time, other bishops' conferences, especially in Europe, also were in the process of drafting pastoral letters on the nuclear question. Even then it was clear that all of the different bishops' conferences would not agree on some of the specifics they were addressing. For example, the U.S. bishops opposed the NATO policy advocating first use of counterforce nuclear weapons, but not all the Europeans were in agreement with that position.

The Vatican Congregation for the Doctrine of the Faith under Cardinal Joseph Ratzinger called for a meeting in Rome of Vatican officials, with representatives of the U.S. bishops' conference and European bishops' conferences. The question was, What is the nature and binding force of the teaching in these pastoral letters? What if the various conferences come to different specific conclusions? At this meeting Cardinal Ratzinger insisted on the legitimate freedom of the Catholic believer, which could not be taken away. At first it might seem ironic that Cardinal Ratzinger, in his position as Prefect of the Congregation for the Doctrine of the Faith, was defending the legitimate freedom of the believer. Such a position is very much a part of the Catholic self-understanding, however. In matters of social and political concerns, the individual Catholic is free to make her or his own decisions on matters for which there is no authoritative church teaching.[18]

After the Rome meeting, subsequent drafts and the final version of the peace pastoral clearly distinguished three different levels of moral teaching: statements of universal moral principles, formal church teaching, and application of these principles and teachings to specific cases. Application of universal principles and formal church teaching to specific cases involves prudential judgments that are based on specific circumstances that can change or be interpreted differently by people of good will. The bishops refer specifically to their teaching that no first use of even counterforce nuclear weapons could ever be justified. These prudential judgments in specific cases and applications of principle do not bind Catholics in conscience, although Catholics should give them serious attention and consideration as they determine whether their moral judgments are consistent with the Gospel (n. 9, O-S, p. 494).

The Catholic notion of mediation explains such an approach. On one hand, specific issues of public policy involving economic and political realities are not simply legal, economic, or political questions. Public policy matters truly are moral issues; for the believer, they also are Christian issues. Many people in our society do not understand how these issues can be religious or Christian issues. Issues such as the unemployment rate or the first use of even small nuclear weapons seem to have no relationship to religion but are issues for experts in the respective sciences and disciplines. However, whatever affects human persons, human communities, and their environment is a human issue, a moral issue, and a Christian issue for the believer. Faith touches all aspects of our lives. *Economic Justice for All*

(1986), the pastoral letter of the U.S. bishops, in its opening paragraph justifies the bishops' discussion of particular issues facing the economy because of the human, moral, and Christian questions involved. "What does the economy do *for* people? What does it do *to* people? And how do people *participate* in it?" (n. 1, O-S, p. 578). On the other hand, the bishops acknowledge that on complex and specific issues there is no such thing as *the* obligatory or Catholic answer.

How does the principle of mediation explain these two aspects—that such specific issues are truly human and Christian issues but that many believers from the same church often will disagree on specifics? Mediation maintains that the divine is mediated in and through the human. Faith, Gospel, and grace are mediated through all aspects of the human down to the specific issue or question. The unemployment rate obviously is a human and moral issue because it affects persons, communities, and the environment. Unemployment involves considerable economic data and analysis, but it is more than just an economic issue. Yes, solutions to questions of unemployment and other questions in the political, economic, and urban policy areas require great expertise in specific fields, but they remain truly human and Christian issues. Christian and human values are mediated through knowledge of the particular sciences and analysis of the realities down to the bottom line of what should be done.

Because our Christian and human values are mediated in and through all of the relevant empirical and scientific data and analysis, people who share the same general values and faith commitments often find themselves in disagreement about the approach to a particular issue. In the second half of the twentieth century, one of the most controversial and divisive debates—for the country and for church communities—concerned the morality of the Vietnam War. People who opposed the war objected to our country's support for an apparently corrupt government that did not have much public support. Others regarded the war as a necessary opposition to the worldwide domination of communism and appealed to the "domino theory," which maintained that if one nation in Asia fell to communism it would bring about the fall of other countries to communism. People who shared the same faith came to different practical conclusions about a very important issue precisely because they interpreted the facts differently and because of their acceptance or rejection of certain political science theories such as the domino theory. The Gospel, faith, grace, and Jesus Christ could not tell us if the South Vietnamese regime was corrupt or if the domino theory was true.

The Catholic position of mediation finds itself between two extremes. On one hand, some people say that Christians and churches have no competence in specific issues because they involve political science or economic expertise that the church obviously does not possess. On the other hand, some people maintain that Christians and churches can readily, quickly, easily, and with great certitude discern what God is doing in the world. Some years ago I was asked to evaluate a one-page handout from a Catholic justice and peace commission. This handout had two paragraphs. The first paragraph quoted the last judgment scene in Matthew 25: "... when I was hungry, naked, thirsty. ..." The second paragraph then maintained that multinational corporations are immoral. I responded that if this commission were going to get into a discussion with the then-president of General Motors, Thomas Aquinas Murphy, it had better have some knowledge of economics and not rely only on Matthew 25! Often one hears the complaint that church people are "do-gooders" who do not understand all the complexities involved. There is some truth in this complaint, although at times it has been used to say that the church has no business whatsoever in these areas.

Authoritative teaching that is binding on all Catholics (to use the juridical terminology) by its very nature must be somewhat general and cannot be specific. The more complex and specific the issue, the more factual and scientific data and analysis are needed; as a result, there can be no single Catholic approach or answer. For example, even people who agree that distributive justice calls for a progressive scale of taxation can disagree on the specifics of a tax policy. Precisely because the documents of Catholic social teaching come from the hierarchical teaching office, they remain more general and avoid particular judgments about very specific issues. For example, the recent documents do not propose specific structures for the political and economic order between the extremes of liberalism and collectivism; instead they present principles and values that can guide our actions and criticize other approaches.[19]

Further Questions

Two further refining questions arise with regard to the authoritative teaching aspect of these documents: What precise response do Catholics owe to such teaching? How general or specific should such teaching be?

With regard to the first question, in accord with Catholic ecclesiology the documents deal with the category of authoritative, noninfallible teaching—to which Catholics owe the religious assent of intellect and will. In the past forty years, the issue of the possibility and feasibility of dissent from noninfallible teaching has centered on issues of personal and sexual morality such as contraception, divorce, homosexual acts, and abortion.[20] I agree with the majority of theologians who recognize the possible legitimacy of such dissent.[21] The first public discussion in the United States about legitimate dissent, however, came from the objection of William F. Buckley, editor of the *National Review*, to *Mater et magistra*'s teaching on socialization. Buckley claimed that the encyclical's approach denied the fundamental importance of the individual and justified too large a role for the state. The *National Review* described the reaction of Catholic conservatives to the encyclical under the heading *"Mater, si, magistra, no."* Catholics can dissent from such encyclical teaching.[22] There has been little or no debate since that time about dissent from papal social teaching, despite extensive discussion about dissent from papal sexual teaching.

The absence of controversy about the response to authoritative papal social teaching seems to derive from four different sources. First, the social teachings themselves are general; disputes tend to arise on more specific issues. In North America, Gregory Baum gives a socialist interpretation to these documents; Michael Novak, Richard Neuhaus, and George Weigel propose neoconservative understandings.[23] Neither side claims to dissent from the papal teaching. Second, the hierarchical magisterium itself has not made an issue of dissent in this area as it has in the area of sexual morality. Third, the hierarchical magisterium in social matters has been more open to change and development on many issues, such as the role of government, the forms of government, religious liberty, and human rights. A similar development and change has not transpired in sexual issues. Fourth, the greater fascination with sexual issues on the part of the church and society has brought more attention to these issues than to the issues involved in social teaching.

The second question pushes the issue of "how general is general and how specific is specific?" Obviously a continuum exists from the more general, to the less general, to the less specific, to the more specific. Recall that the U.S. bishops distinguished between formal church teaching, universal moral principles, and application of these moral principles to particular issues. The bishops recognized that their application of principles involved prudential judgments that can be interpreted differently by people of good will and by Catholics within the same faith community. I accept the basic approach of the U.S. bishops but disagree with their specific formulation. Sometimes formal church teaching can be specific, as in the recent teaching of John Paul II and the *Catechism of the Catholic Church* maintaining that capital punishment for all practical purposes should be abolished.[24] This teaching involves many prudential judgments and cannot claim a certitude that excludes the possibility of error. I personally maintain the position opposing capital punishment, but I can see how people who share my Christian faith could come to a different conclusion. The fact that many Catholics today still accept capital punishment illustrates the diversity that can exist on this issue even within the church.

Likewise, moral principles can have different degrees of generality and specificity. The moral principle that murder is always wrong is general and can be accepted by everyone. The moral principle that the direct killing of the innocent on one's own authority is always wrong is more specific because it incorporates into its norm the philosophical notion of direct and indirect. Catholics can rightly disagree with the philosophical notion of what constitutes direct and indirect because this judgment is based on only one philosophical analysis, which cannot claim certitude. Thus, it is too simple to draw the lines as the U.S. bishops have done. The general principle holds, however—the more specific a teaching is, the harder it is to claim certitude and to deny the possibility of difference or even dissent within the Catholic Church.

Tensions and Problems Connected with Authoritative Teaching

In the preceding section I show that the nature of authoritative church teaching very much colors the approach taken in Catholic social teaching. In this section I consider six tensions or problems arising from the authoritative nature of these documents.

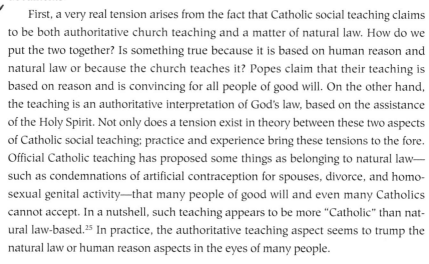

First, a very real tension arises from the fact that Catholic social teaching claims to be both authoritative church teaching and a matter of natural law. How do we put the two together? Is something true because it is based on human reason and natural law or because the church teaches it? Popes claim that their teaching is based on reason and is convincing for all people of good will. On the other hand, the teaching is an authoritative interpretation of God's law, based on the assistance of the Holy Spirit. Not only does a tension exist in theory between these two aspects of Catholic social teaching; practice and experience bring these tensions to the fore. Official Catholic teaching has proposed some things as belonging to natural law— such as condemnations of artificial contraception for spouses, divorce, and homosexual genital activity—that many people of good will and even many Catholics cannot accept. In a nutshell, such teaching appears to be more "Catholic" than natural law-based.[25] In practice, the authoritative teaching aspect seems to trump the natural law or human reason aspects in the eyes of many people.

What should be the proper relationship between these two aspects? Aquinas, borrowing from Greek philosophers, raised the significant question of whether something is morally good because it is commanded or is it commanded because it is morally good. Aquinas came down firmly on the side of what has been called intrinsic morality: Something is commanded because it is morally good. The command of the legislator or the ruler cannot make something true or good. Authority must conform itself to what is true and good.[26]

The important methodological developments that I analyze in part I and the substantive changes in part II prove that in practice the church has learned from the experience of others and from history. Recall that a more historically conscious methodology gives greater importance to inductive reasoning and learning from lived experience. In these cases, authoritative teaching has rightly conformed itself to the morally true and good.

What about the Catholic teaching that the pope and bishops are authoritative teachers in the church who are given the assistance of the Holy Spirit to carry out their God-given function of teaching God's law? Vatican II reminded us that the hierarchical magisterium itself is not superior to but subject to the word of God.[27] The hierarchical magisterium is subservient to the ultimate criterion of truth.[28] In addition, in these cases we are dealing not with revealed truths of faith but with teachings that the hierarchical magisterium itself insists are reasonable and convincing to all people of good will.

What does the Holy Spirit give, then, to the hierarchical magisterium in its search for the morally true and good? In keeping with the Catholic emphasis on mediation, the Holy Spirit does not provide any way to avoid the human processes of arriving at moral truth. The Holy Spirit helps the hierarchical magisterium in its attempt to discern the morally true and good. The work of the Holy Spirit is mediated in and through the human processes of knowing; it does not provide a magical shortcut.[29] Too often we have the impression that authoritative teaching makes something morally true or good. The best Catholic tradition insists, however, that moral truth and goodness constitute the ultimate criterion.

A second related tension exists between the authoritative nature of Catholic social teaching and the shift away from a triumphalistic church with the answers to all the problems of the world to a church in dialogue with all others working for a better human society. I have cited some of the more triumphalistic statements in Catholic social teaching about the church and the magisterium having at their disposal the deposit of faith by which they can answer the pressing problems of the world. If the emphasis continues to be on "authoritative church teaching," however, the impression is that the church alone has the answers to these problems. Even in *Centesimus annus,* John Paul II continues to speak of the "church's doctrinal patrimony" and "our responsibility . . . to show the way to proclaim the truth, and to communicate the light which is Christ" (n. 3, O-S, pp. 440–41).

Such an approach, however, stands in contrast with some of the understandings I develop in this volume. First, we are dealing with moral truths that are based on human reason and are accessible to all people of good will. Second, as indicated by the significant developments in the teaching, the hierarchical magisterium has learned moral truth along the way. The hierarchical magisterium is not only an authoritative teacher in this matter; it also is a learner. This hierarchical office does not simply possess the necessary moral truths in its "sacred patrimony." It is searching continually for the moral truth regarding the problems of peace and justice in our world and testing this truth in broader dialogue with all human sources of moral wisdom and knowledge and all people of good will. The teaching office of the church, with the assistance of the Holy Spirit, speaks authoritatively to its members, but it still must be open to learn from all human sources of wisdom and all people of good will.

A third tension derives from the danger that insisting on the authoritative nature of Catholic social teaching distorts and constricts the teaching role of the hierarchical magisterium in social issues. Such an emphasis distorts the role of the teaching office and the church because it tends to downplay and even deny the fact that the teaching office in the church also has a very important learning function. The teaching office has to learn the moral truth before it can teach it. The concept of authoritative teaching also constricts the notion of teacher to one who gives authoritative answers to others. A good teacher has a much more expansive role, however. Documents and principles are not the only way of teaching—or even the most influential. The good actions of the whole Christian community, including the hierarchical magisterium, are much more significant in terms of teaching than written documents. Actions speak louder than words. In addition, a good teacher does not necessarily have answers for students; a good teacher raises challenging questions that help students reflect more deeply on their own lives and their own situations. Imparting knowledge from a superior to an inferior is an impoverished notion of teaching.

The documents of Catholic social teaching can and should expand their own teaching role. The documents themselves could highlight the witness of various people and communities who have struggled on behalf of social justice. The documents also could raise some significant questions for all of us to grapple with rather than simply proposing "answers." Unfortunately, the concept of authoritative teaching has affected and restricted the teaching role of the hierarchical magisterium.

Fourth, the authoritative nature of the documents, along with the fact that they often were issued to commemorate earlier documents, tends to emphasize their continuity and does not give enough importance to the discontinuities that have occurred. The emphasis on these disparate documents as one corpus of Catholic social teaching, especially in the encyclicals of John Paul II, also downplays the inherent discontinuities. Although many of the later documents justify their own need by calling to mind the historical and cultural changes that have occurred since the previous document was issued, the emphasis remains on continuity with regard to methodology and substance.

John Paul II exemplifies this approach. He wrote *Sollicitudo rei socialis* to commemorate the twentieth anniversary of *Populorum progressio*. *Sollicitudo rei socialis* seeks to achieve two objectives: to affirm the continuity and renewal of Catholic social teaching—both of which are proof of its perennial value. The constant elements are its "fundamental inspiration," its "principles of reflection," its "criteria of judgment," and its basic "directives for action." Its newness derives from the fact that the teaching "is subject to the necessary and opportune adaptations suggested by the changes in historical conditions" (n. 3, O-S, p. 396). Later John Paul II writes of applying the earlier encyclical to the present historical moment (n. 4, O-S, p. 396). He fails to recognize any methodological or substantive discontinuity and downplays change by limiting it to new historical and cultural conditions.

In reality, significant discontinuities exist in the body of Catholic social teaching. Recall the fundamental changes that have occurred in the theological, ethical, and ecclesial methodologies in these documents. In chapters 5, 6, and 7 of this volume I also point out changes that have occurred on important content issues such as human rights, religious freedom, and the role of the state. This overemphasis on continuity with "our predecessors of happy memory" and failure to recognize significant discontinuities lend some credence to Chenu's thesis that Catholic social teaching has become an ideology. The credibility of Catholic social teaching would only increase if popes were to openly recognize their differences with their predecessors. The authoritative nature of these teachings and the tendency to regard them as constituting a unified whole prevent explicit recognition of very evident discontinuities and changes within them. In fact, the hierarchical magisterium must go further and recognize not only discontinuities but also error in its past teaching. The teaching on religious liberty was true long before Vatican II changed the official teaching. Leo XIII denied many human rights that the Catholic Church today accepts. (I develop this point in greater detail in chapter 7.)

Fifth, defensiveness about the authoritative teaching nature of these documents also comes through in their failure to cite sources other than the Scriptures, the fathers of the church, Thomas Aquinas, documents from "predecessors of happy memory," and previous documents from the pope who is writing. The impression seems to be that citations to other works would reduce the authoritative nature of such teaching. Paul VI made a move in this direction in *Populorum progressio* (1967) by citing other authors: L. J. Lebret, a French Dominican scholar and activist; Jacques Maritain, the French philosopher (twice); Oswald von Nell-Breuning, the German social ethicist who drafted *Quadragesimo anno*; Chenu, the French Dominican theologian who later challenged the understanding of an unchanging body of Catholic social teaching; Colin Clark, an English demographer; and even Blaise Pascal. John Paul II has not followed Paul VI in this approach, however, although he occasionally cites United Nations documents in *Centesimus annus* (e.g., fn. 26, 30, 52, 63). If Catholic social teaching is truly in dialogue with all sources that tell us about human existence and the experience of all people of good will, the documents should illustrate such dialogue.

A sixth problem arising from the authoritative nature of these documents concerns the way in which they are composed. The papal documents have been released in the name of the pope, with no record of any consultation. Often the identity of the principal drafter becomes known (e.g., Oswald von Nell-Breuning for *Quadragesimo anno*).[30] No one really knows the process that leads to the final document. Apparently, authoritative papal teaching demands that it come from the pope alone, without public consultation.

Rather than detracting from the authoritative nature of the document, a more open and consultative process would ensure the truly authoritative nature of the teaching and also more effectively carry out the teaching function itself. As I explain in the following section, input from the church in all parts of the world can compensate for the danger of a universal perspective and help the church live out its own catholicity.

The process that the U.S. bishops followed in issuing their pastoral letters on peace and the economy could serve as a model. Before writing the letters, the bishops invited experts and others to give them their input on the issues. The drafts of the documents ultimately were not only sent to the bishops but were made public, and responses were welcomed. Such a process encouraged public debate and made many more people conscious of the issues involved and what the bishops were trying to teach and communicate.[31]

Papal documents could and should follow a similar process. A broad public consultation involving regional and national conferences of bishops—who, in turn, would involve local churches and all people involved in them—could begin the process. On the basis of this consultation, a drafting committee and the pope would put together a first draft, which would then be sent back to the bishops' conferences and made public for further debate and discussion. In light of the feedback from this discussion, the pope could issue the final document.

Perspective, Audiences, and Focus

Papal social teaching by definition is intended for the worldwide Catholic community and for the whole world. Thus, it recognizes and strongly supports the possibility of a universal morality meant for all human beings. As I point out in chapter 2, however, Catholic tradition in general and Catholic social teaching in its development have overemphasized universality and have not given enough importance to the diversity that exists in our world.

Universal Perspective

By definition, documents coming from the papal teaching office or any form of the universal magisterium will have a universal perspective. At minimum, such a universal perspective must be conscious of the dangers in such an approach and always strive to be self-critical. An ecclesiology of communion, with its acceptance of the principle of collegiality, helps to overcome the inherent limitations of a universal perspective.[32] The principle of collegiality refers to the college of bishops throughout the world in union with the bishop of Rome. Together they constitute an important official teaching role in the church. Dialogue among all bishops of the world, together with all the people of God and all people of good will, by nature contributes to overcoming the limitations in a universal perspective. Four practical steps in preparing these documents would help to overcome the inherent pitfalls in a universal perspective.

First, the college of bishops or a representative group of them collaborates in writing a document. This approach was used in 1971 with *Justitia in mundo*. This institution of the World Synod of Bishops by definition has some protection against the limitations of the perspective of one person trying to be universal. Unfortunately, the international synods have not operated as effectively as they should. Since 1971 these synods have not written their own final documents; they have merely presented propositions to the pope, who writes the final document.

Even more important, the world synod does not have authority on its own. These synods are merely advisory to the pope. They should be more than advisory, however, precisely because they represent the collegiality of the church universal.[33] The synods could and should play a stronger role in the life of the church in general and particularly in preparing documents of Catholic social teaching.

Second, the papal and universal documents could build on documents issued by national and international conferences of bishops throughout the world. This process has not occurred. In general, the papacy of John Paul II has been very unwilling to give due recognition to the magisterial authority of national and international conferences of bishops. The papal documents and Catholic social teaching have no footnote references to documents coming from Episcopal conferences. Thus, Catholic social teaching loses out on a very important way of making sure that the documents speak to the concerns found in different areas.

Third, at minimum all documents—universal and local—should result from a consultation with the entire church universal. The U.S. bishops publicly and formally consulted specific experts and made their drafts public to encourage the broadest possible discussion. John Paul II claims to have consulted the cardinals and bishops in writing his 1995 encyclical *Evangelium vitae*.[34] One has the feeling, however, that the consultation was *pro forma* and was not taken seriously.

Fourth, these documents must make a special effort to represent the voices that too often have been silenced in the church and in the world. In its own life of learning and teaching, the church itself should carry out a preferential option for the poor. The perspective of poor people should be privileged in these documents.[35] Furthermore, it is well known that the Catholic Church in general and its social teaching in particular have been and continue to be patriarchal.[36] The voices of women in all their diversity must speak in these documents.

With regard to the voices of women, the Catholic Church faces a huge structural problem: Women have no real leadership positions in the church and have played no role in the formation of the papal documents of Catholic social teaching. Without doubt, this structural defect has alienated many Catholic women. For some women, the Catholic Church and its teaching office have lost all credibility. This huge dark cloud hangs ominously over all official Catholic teaching, including the documents of Catholic social teaching.

Two Audiences and a Narrow Focus

In chapter 2 I point out the unresolvable tensions that arise from the fact that these documents of Catholic social teaching address two different audiences—members

of the church and all people of good will. A very important shortcoming from an ecclesial perspective in these documents that are addressed to two audiences is their
failure to connect liturgy with social justice and daily life. The documents make little or no reference to liturgy. The Second Vatican Council, however, insisted that
"the liturgy is the summit toward which the activity of the church is directed; it is
also the source from which all power flows."[37] An essential connection exists between liturgy and life, but the documents of Catholic social teaching pay no attention to it. In fairness, most Catholic theologians who have dealt with social justice
also have tended to neglect the important connection between liturgy and social
justice.[38] One cannot fault only Catholic social teaching for not developing this aspect. In fact, Catholic social teaching can be more readily excused for not developing this aspect precisely because of its narrow focus and its two different audiences.

The narrow focus of Catholic social teaching—which is limited to the structures and institutions of a just society—also influences the fact that the documents
do not develop all of the moral aspects of life in this world. The focus on institutions and structures means that the documents pay little or no attention to the person who is living and working in the world and within structures and institutions.
The proper role of the lay person in the church and in the world tends to be downplayed. Vatican II insisted on the universal call of all baptized people to holiness
and recognized that the call to holiness is lived out in the daily responsibilities of
family, community, work, and play.[39] These documents, precisely because of their
narrow focus and their audience of all people of good will as well as Catholics, generally fail to develop this call of all baptized people to strive for holiness in the
midst of their daily responsibilities in the world.

The narrow focus of the documents of Catholic social teaching means that they
give little or no importance to the subjective aspect of morality. The person constitutes the subject pole of morality. The biblical metaphor reminds us that the good
tree brings forth good fruit. Good persons will do good deeds, and bad persons will
do bad deeds. Considerations that are aimed primarily at a church audience, with
a broader focus on life in the world, would have to give much greater importance to
conversion of heart and the basic virtues that should direct the actions of the
Christian person in this world. In many ways, the virtues are much more significant than the acts that come from them precisely because they are permanent and
tend to have a greater influence over a longer period of time.

The nature of the Catholic Church and its papal teaching office clearly have
colored the approach of Catholic social teaching.[40] As with the theological and ethical aspects of methodology, the church's self-understanding and its impact on
Catholic social teaching have evolved from the time of Leo XIII to the present. I

have proposed the need for further changes. This consideration concludes the methodological section of this book. In the following chapters I develop the substance of Catholic social teaching in a systematic way.

NOTES

1. Ernst Troeltsch, *The Social Teaching of the Christian Church*, vol. 2 (New York: Harper Torchbook, 1960), 691–729.

2. Pius XI, *Non abbiamo bisogno*, n. 8, in McLaughlin, *The Church and Reconstruction of the Modern World*, 303.

3. Jeremiah Newman, *What is Catholic Action? An Introduction to the Lay Apostolate* (Westminster, Md.: Newman, 1958).

4. Gérard Philips, "History of the Constitution," in *Commentary on the Documents of Vatican II*, ed. Herbert Vorgrimler, vol. 1 (New York: Herder and Herder, 1966), 110.

5. Dogmatic Constitution on the Church, nn. 1–29, in Flannery, *Vatican Council II*, 1–43.

6. Ibid., 72–79.

7. Pope Paul VI, "Opening Address to the Second Session of Vatican II," in Xavier Rynne, *The Second Session* (Farrar, Straus, 1964), 358.

8. *Gaudium et spes*, n. 43, in O'Brien and Shannon, *Catholic Social Thought*, 193; Pope John Paul II, *Tertio millennio adveniente*, nn. 133–36, *Origins* 24 (1994): 401ff.; *Incarnationis mysterium*, n. 11, *Origins* 28 (1998) : 450–51; "Jubilee Characteristic: The Purification of Memory," *Origins* 29 (2000): 649–50.

9. See Francis A. Sullivan, "The Papal Apology," *America* 182, no. 12 (April 8, 2000): 17–22.

10. Constitution on the Church, nn. 12, 35, in Flannery, *Vatican Council II*, 16, 52.

11. Declaration on Religious Liberty, n. 1, in Flannery, *Vatican Council II*, 551.

12. For the older position on religious freedom and its refutation by John Courtney Murray, see Donald E. Pelotte, *John Courtney Murray: Theologian in Conflict* (New York: Paulist, 1976).

13. Declaration on Religious Liberty, n. 13, in Flannery, *Vatican Council II*, 563–64; see also John Paul II, *Sollicitudo rei socialis*, n. 41, in O'Brien and Shannon, *Catholic Social Thought*, 424–25.

14. Thomas Sieger Derr, *Barriers to Ecumenism: The Holy See and the World Council of Churches on Social Questions* (Maryknoll, N.Y.: Orbis, 1983); Ronald H. Preston, *Confusions in Christian Social Ethics: Problems for Geneva and Rome* (Grand Rapids, Mich.: William B. Eerdmans, 1994).

15. Aquinas, *IaIIae*, q. 104.

16. The term "prophetic shock-minorities" originally was used in a different sense by Jacques Maritain, *Man and the State* (Chicago: University of Chicago Press, 1956), 139–46.

17. *Populorum progressio*, n. 13, in O'Brien and Shannon, *Catholic Social Thought*, 243; *Sollicitudo rei socialis*, n. 41, in O'Brien and Shannon, *Catholic Social Thought*, 424.

18. Jan Schotte, "Rome Consultation on Peace and Disarmament: A Vatican Synthesis," *Origins* 12 (1983): 691–95.

19. See, e.g., John Paul II, *Sollicitudo rei socialis*, n. 41, in O'Brien and Shannon, *Catholic Social Thought*, 424–25.

20. Richard B. Gaillardetz, *Teaching with Authority: A Theology of the Magisterium in the Church* (Collegeville, Minn.: Liturgical, 1997); André Naud, *Un aggiornamento et son éclipse: La liberté de la pensée dans la foi et dans l'Église* (Montreal: Fides, 1996); Charles E. Curran and Richard A. McCormick, eds., *Readings in Moral Theology No. 6: Dissent in the Church* (New York: Paulist, 1988).

21. Charles E. Curran, *The Catholic Moral Tradition Today: A Synthesis* (Washington, D.C.: Georgetown University Press, 1999), 197–234.

22. "The Week," *National Review* 11 (July 29, 1961): 38; "For the Record," *National Review* 11 (August 12, 1961): 77. For an in-depth defense of this position taken at that time, see Gary Wills, *Politics and Catholic Freedom* (Chicago: Henry Regnery, 1964). At the time Gary Wills was associated with *National Review*.

23. For representative articles of these authors and others dealing with the social teaching of John Paul II, see Charles E. Curran and Richard A. McCormick, eds., *John Paul II and Moral Theology: Readings in Moral Theology No. 10* (New York: Paulist, 1998), 237–375.

24. John Paul II, *Evangelium vitae*, n. 56, in *Origins* 24 (1995): 709; Cardinal Joseph Ratzinger, "Vatican List of Catechism Changes," *Origins* 27 (1997): 262.

25. John Coleman, "A Possible Role for Biblical Religion in Public Life," *Theological Studies* 40 (1979): 706.

26. Aquinas, *IaIIae*, q. 90–96.

27. Dogmatic Constitution on Divine Revelation, n.10, in Flannery, *Vatican Council II*, 103.

28. Yves Congar, "A Brief History of the Forms of Magisterium and Its Relations with Scholars," in *Readings in Moral Theology No. 3: The Magisterium and Morality*, ed. Charles E. Curran and Richard A. McCormick (New York: Paulist, 1982), 328; see also John P. Boyle, *Church Teaching Authority: Historical and Theological Studies* (Notre Dame, Ind.: University of Notre Dame Press, 1995).

29. Richard A. McCormick, *Notes on Moral Theology 1965–1980* (Washington, D.C.: University Press of America, 1981), 262–66.

30. Oswald von Nell-Breuning, "The Drafting of *Quadragesimo anno*," in *Readings in Moral Theology No. 5: Official Catholic Social Teaching*, ed. Charles E. Curran and Richard A. McCormick (New York: Paulist, 1986), 60–68. Unknown to Nell-Breuning, however, others also were involved in the drafting process of this encyclical. See Paul Droulers, *Politique sociale et Christianisme: Le père Desbuquois et l'Action populaire*, vol. 1 (Paris: Éditions Ouvrières, 1969–81), 152–62.

31. For the historical development of the pastoral letter on peace, see Jim Castelli, *The Bishops and the Bomb: Waging Peace in a Nuclear Age* (Garden City, N.Y.: Image, 1983).

32. Richard B. Gaillardetz, "An Ecclesiology of Communion and Ecclesiastical Structures: Toward a Renewed Ministry of the Bishop," *Église et théologie* 24 (1993): 175–203.

33. Patrick Granfield, "The Collegiality Debate," in *Church and Theology: Essays in Memory of Carl J. Peter*, ed. Peter C. Phan (Washington, D.C.: Catholic University of America Press, 1995), 88–110.

34. John Paul II, *Evangelium vitae*, n. 5, in *Origins* 24 (1995): 692.

35. Stephen J. Pope, "Proper and Improper Partiality and the Preferential Option for the Poor," *Theological Studies* 54 (1993): 242–71.

36. Christine E. Gudorf, "Encountering the Other: The Modern Papacy on Women," *Social Compass* 36 (1989): 295–310; Maria Riley, "Feminist Analysis: A Missing Perspective," in Curran and McCormick, *John Paul II and Moral Theology*, 276–90.

37. Constitution on the Liturgy, n. 10, in Flannery, *Vatican Council II*, 122.

38. In the United States, Virgil Michel (1890–1938) attempted to bring together the liturgy and social justice. See Paul B. Marx, *The Life and Work of Virgil Michel* (Washington, D.C.: Catholic University of America Press, 1957), and R. W. Franklin and Robert L. Spaeth, *Virgil Michel: American Catholic* (Collegeville, Minn.: Liturgical, 1988).

39. Dogmatic Constitution on the Church, nn. 39–42, in Flannery, *Vatican Council II*, 58–66.

40. For a perceptive analysis of the relationship

between ecclesiology and the broader social role of the church, see Richard P. McBrien, "The Future of the Church in American Soci-ety," in *Religion and Politics in the American Milieu,* ed. Leslie Griffin (Notre Dame, Ind.: University of Notre Dame Press, 1986), 87–101.

PART II

Content

CHAPTER 4

Anthropology

In part II of this volume I analyze the content of Catholic social teaching. The documents of Catholic social teaching focus primarily on the economic order, with some attention to the political order. As I have indicated in part I, the very fact that these papal documents propose authoritative teaching for Catholics means that they are general and avoid specific positions on complex issues.

This book reflects on Catholic social teaching from the perspective of the thematic, systematic, and academic discipline of moral theology. Catholic social teaching implicitly involves a systematic approach, but its authors have a very different primary purpose—the teaching of general perspectives for a just social order. A systematic, thematic, critical, and reflexive study attempts to show how different aspects of the teaching relate to one another and compares and contrasts Catholic social teaching with other approaches.

The logical grounding and starting point for a systematic social ethics is anthropology. One's understanding of the human person influences, grounds, and directs one's understanding of how human society should function.

Without developing a systematic social ethics, Catholic social teaching recognizes the fundamental importance of anthropology as the basis for its teaching. In *Centesimus annus* (1991) John Paul II maintains, "[T]he main thread, and in a certain sense, the guiding principle of Pope Leo's encyclical, and of all the church's social doctrine, is a correct view of the human person and of the person's unique value..." (n. 11, O-S, p. 447). *Centesimus annus* later insists that the human person is "the principle which inspires the church's social doctrine.... Her sole purpose has been care and responsibility for the human person who has been entrusted to her by Christ himself . . ." (n. 53, O-S, p. 479). In *Quadragesimo anno* (1931) Pius XI makes the same basic point: "But reason itself clearly deduces from the nature of things and from the individual and social character of human beings what is the end and object of the whole economic order assigned by God the Creator" (n. 42, O-S, p. 51). The whole structure of *Gaudium et spes* (1965) shows that anthropology is the key to understanding Catholic social teaching. The more theoretical first part of the document first considers the human person, followed by human community, and then human action (nn. 12–39, O-S, pp. 172–89). Only then does the second part discuss five problems or issues of special urgency.

ANTHROPOLOGY IN LIGHT OF METHODOLOGY

The methodological considerations I discuss in part I of this volume clearly color the anthropological perspectives of Catholic social teaching. The shift to a greater emphasis on the person and the freedom, equality, and participation of the person have great importance for anthropology. The shift to historical consciousness, as well as John Paul II's hesitancy about historical consciousness, also influences the anthropology of contemporary Catholic social teaching. The later documents tend to view the human person in the context of the relationality-responsibility model. In *Mater et magistra* (1961) John XXIII recognized, "One of the principal characteristics of our time is the multiplication of social relationships, that is a daily more complex interdependence of citizens, introducing into their lives and activities many and varied forms of associations . . ." (n. 59, O-S, p. 93). The ethical methodology I discuss in chapter 2 clearly influences the anthropology found in the documents of Catholic social teaching.

The theological methodology I describe in chapter 1 also affects the anthropology of Catholic social teaching. As I point out, however, the theological aspects of anthropology are not consistently developed and applied in the documents because of the twofold audience of Catholic social teaching. The anthropology applied in these documents tends at times to be too optimistic. The Catholic tendency to downplay the power of sin and the emphasis on human reason and its dialogue with all people of good will contribute to the danger of downplaying the existence of sin in the human arena.

The limited subject matter of Catholic social teaching also results in a limited anthropology that tends to overlook the person as the subjective pole of morality with its emphasis on the change of heart and the virtues that should characterize the person. Catholic social teaching is interested primarily in achieving just social structures. Very little is said about how people should live their lives within existing social structures. John Paul II's discussion of a spiritually of work in *Laborem exercens* (1981) constitutes an exception to this general approach (nn. 24–27, O-S, pp. 384–90). Thus, in addition to the aspects of anthropology in Catholic social teaching I describe in part I of this volume, other aspects of anthropology more directly affect the specific content of Catholic social teaching.

GENERAL ANTHROPOLOGY

In keeping with the Catholic tradition, *Populorum progressio* (1967) insists that

> [in] the design of God, every human person is called upon to develop and fulfill oneself, for every life is a vocation. . . . Endowed with intelligence and freedom, the human being is responsible for one's fulfillment as for one's salvation. . . . Thus it is that human fulfillment constitutes, as it were, a summary of our duties (nn. 15–16, O-S, p. 243).

In this section, *Populorum progressio* recognizes four aspects that have been characteristic of Catholic anthropology. First is the emphasis on human fulfillment, development, and happiness. From a theological perspective, the Catholic approach has insisted that the glory of God and human fulfillment are intimately related and not opposed to one another. The purpose of God in creating and redeeming human beings is the glory of God and human fulfillment. Here the Catholic emphasis on mediation plays a significant role. In the words of an early patristic writer, the glory of God is the human person come alive.[1] God's glory and grace are mediated in and through human fulfillment and happiness.

Second, the danger of optimism in Catholic theology also affects the anthropology described here. Human fulfillment and happiness will come only in the next life. Human beings will never be fully happy in this world. Although we are called to fulfillment and happiness, only the fullness of the reign of God will bring true human happiness and fulfillment. In the meantime, we live the eschatological tension between the now and the then. Human beings in this world will always face the daunting theological and personal problem of the existence of evil and the reality of suffering.

Third, Catholic inclusiveness and mediation have insisted on the need for both faith and works. *Populorum progressio* emphasizes that human beings are responsible for their own salvation. The Catholic tradition has rightly insisted on the importance of human responsibility and human works, but the tendency sometimes has been to take for granted the reality of salvation as God's gracious gift. The context of a document calling people to work for human fulfillment in this world helps to explain to some degree why the role of faith as God's gracious gift is not mentioned in this particular document. *Populorum progressio* does well to recognize the importance of human works, but salvation as God's gracious gift remains the fundamental reality.

Fourth, morality is intrinsic, not extrinsic. Extrinsic morality regards the moral norm as something imposed on the human being from outside. Intrinsic morality regards morality as coming from within the human person and contributing to her or his fulfillment and happiness. Despite some lapses in practice, the best Catholic theory has always insisted on intrinsic morality: Something is commanded because it is good, not the other way around. Thus, human fulfillment and happiness constitute the summary of our duties.

Christian anthropology has regarded the human person as composed of body and soul or spirit. Despite occasional dualistic approaches downplaying or even degrading the bodily and the material, the best Christian tradition has insisted on the unity and basic goodness of the individual human person. There is a hierarchical ordering, however, of the different human goods or levels of human existence. Within the documents of Catholic social teaching, Paul VI's *Populorum progressio* has offered the most sustained analysis of the different goods and levels of human existence. John Paul II, writing *Sollicitudo rei socialis* (1987) on the twentieth anniversary of *Populorum progressio,* points out again the hierarchical ordering of the goods that constitute authentic human development (n. 28, O-S, p. 413).

Populorum progressio develops the concept of a new humanism—an integral or transcendent humanism that recognizes all aspects of anthropology and the hierarchical relationship among them. Authentic human development involves a movement from less human conditions to those that are more human. Every human being needs the basic material necessities for a decent human existence; victory over social and political structures that are oppressive; development of knowledge and culture, esteem for the dignity of others, cooperation for the common good, and the will and desire for peace; recognition of supreme values, with God as their source; and the gift of faith by which we come to our fullest humanity, sharing in the life of the living God (n. 21, O-S, pp. 244–45). In such an understanding, the basic material goods are important, but they are subordinated to the more spiritual goods of human anthropology. Material goods are necessary, but they are not the ultimate source of human happiness and fulfillment.

In *Sollicitudo rei socialis* John Paul II insists that being is more important than having because having goods does not in itself perfect the human subject. In this context, John Paul II strongly condemns the materialism and consumerism that are so prevalent in our world. Mere accumulation of material goods leaves the person with a radical dissatisfaction because the human being is called to grow and develop with the higher goods. Material goods are important and necessary, but they must be subordinated to the person's true being and vocation (nn. 29–30, O-S, pp. 413–15). In this light, *Laborem exercens* points out that Catholic social teaching has insisted that workers need more than a just wage; they also should share in management and ownership (n. 14, O-S, p. 372). This true, authentic, or transcendent humanism recognizes the need for a basic level of material goods but warns against material goods becoming the be-all and end-all of human existence, smothering the more spiritual goods of authentic human development.

Because Catholic social teaching focuses primarily on economic questions, this teaching spotlights material goods and does not fully develop higher human goods. On one hand, the teaching deals with the minimum and the just distribution of material goods for all. The social teaching also emphasizes the dangers of materialism and consumerism that are so prevalent in the more wealthy nations of the world, however.[2] Material goods are not the most important goods and cannot ultimately satisfy the human desire for higher goods and often can get in the way of the pursuit of higher human values.

ANTHROPOLOGICAL BASIS OF SOCIAL, POLITICAL, AND ECONOMIC ORDERS

Catholic social teaching rests on two fundamental anthropological principles: the dignity or sacredness of the human person and the social nature of the person. *Gaudium et spes*, the most systematic treatment of the foundations of Catholic social teaching, insists on these two bases (n. 3, O-S p. 167; n. 12, O-S, p. 173).

Human Dignity

The dignity or sacredness of the human person in the larger Catholic tradition rests on the understanding from Genesis that the human person is created in the image and likeness of God. After treating God in the first part of his *Summa*, Thomas Aquinas opens the second part of the *Summa* by describing the human being as made in the image and likeness of God because like God the human being has intellect, free will, and the power of self-determination.[3]

Gaudium et spes likewise appeals to the human person as the image of God. According to Genesis, God made the human person as master of all earthly creatures to subdue them and use them for God's glory. Note that such a personalism does not give enough importance to the other created realities; it regards them only as instrumental with regard to the human person.[4] *Gaudium et spes* also cites Psalm 8:5-6 to show that God made the human person a little less than the angels, crowned the human with honor and glory, and has subjected all things to the human (n. 12, O-S, p. 173). In keeping with its theological methodology, *Gaudium et spes* goes on to say that only in the mystery of the Incarnate Word does the mystery of the human person take on light. The Christian person, conformed to the likeness of Christ the Son, the firstborn of many brothers and sisters, receives the first fruits of the Holy Spirit and is renewed and redeemed. In keeping with its Catholic universality, however, this document goes on to say, "All this holds true not only for Christians, but for all people of good will in whose hearts grace works in an unseen way." Through this participation in the Paschal Mystery of Jesus, the riddles of human sorrow and death become meaningful (n. 22, O-S, p. 179).

The God-given dignity of the human person (although the terminology "human being" was used before Vatican II's turn to the person as subject) has been a central point in Catholic social teaching. Leo XIII based the fundamental rights of the worker on this dignity. *Centesimus annus* (1991) has an entire chapter on "The Person as the Way of the Church" and insists on the fundamental importance of human dignity (nn. 53–62, O-S, pp. 479–84). Human dignity comes from God's free gift; it does not depend on human effort, work, or accomplishments. All human beings have a fundamental, equal dignity because all share the generous gift of creation and redemption from God. Such an approach runs counter to what people often think in our capitalistic and competitive society. Many people believe that human dignity is something we earn on our own and create for ourselves, but that is not the case. Consequently, all human beings have the same fundamental dignity, whether they are brown, black, red, or white; rich or poor; young or old; male or female; healthy or sick. In practice, we often tend to act as if certain more prestigious or influential or wealthy people have more dignity than poor people and others. That is not true because God's gift is the basic source of human dignity for all.

Social Nature

The second anthropological tenet of Catholic social teaching concerns the social nature of human beings, who live in relationship with all other human beings and with everything that God has made. From the beginning, Catholic social teaching has insisted on the social nature of human beings. *Rerum novarum* (1891) recognizes the natural propensity of human beings to live in the public society of the state and to enter into private societies such as labor unions (nn. 37–38, O-S, p. 33). *Gaudium et spes,* in the second chapter of part one, insists on the communitarian and social nature of human beings. The social aspect of human existence is not something added on to the person but an essential part of the human reality. Human beings need the social ties of family, associations, and political community for their proper development (nn. 24–25, O-S, p. 180).

Catholic social teaching recognizes that the whole of the Catholic tradition testifies to the social nature of human beings. Through creation we are all brothers and sisters who have the same God as our Creator. The documents tend to use the exclusive term "brotherhood" to explain the relationship of all human beings based on creation (e.g., *Gaudium et spes,* n. 88, O-S, p. 227; *Populorum progressio,* n. 43, O-S, p. 250; *Octogesima adveniens,* n. 12, O-S, p. 269; *Centesimus annus,* n. 40, O-S, p. 423). The twofold commandment of love of God and neighbor illustrates the fact that we are brothers and sisters who belong to the same human family, with moral obligations toward one another (*Gaudium et spes,* n. 24, O-S, p. 180). John Paul II points out in *Centesimus annus* that in addition to the "fatherhood of God" and the "brotherhood of all" Christian faith presents a new model of the unity of the human race—a communion of all based on the supreme model of the communion of the Trinity with three persons in one God (n. 40, O-S, p. 423).

Catholic social teaching alludes to the Catholic philosophical tradition's insistence on the social nature of human beings. Thomas Aquinas—who was shaped by the Christian tradition and by Aristotelian philosophy—insisted that the human being is social and political by nature. By our God-given nature we are called to live in political society with one another. The state is natural and necessary for human beings.[5] *Rerum novarum,* as one might expect, explicitly cites Aquinas with regard to the public society of the state and the private societies to which human beings are called by nature (n. 37, O-S, p. 33). *Mater et magistra* (n. 219, O-S, p. 120) and *Pacem in terris* (n. 23, O-S, p. 134) repeat the older Thomistic and Catholic teaching that human beings are by nature social.

Beginning with John XXIII in *Mater et magistra,* recent popes have recognized the growing human interrelatedness that underscores the importance of the relationship among all human beings (n. 130, O-S, p. 151). In *Populorum progressio* Paul VI insists on "the development of the human race in the spirit of solidarity" (n. 42, O-S, p. 250). John Paul II has made solidarity a central theme in his social teaching. His use of "solidarity" also shows the influence of the Solidarity movement in Poland, though his usage is much broader than that.[6]

> When interdependence becomes recognized in this way, the correlative response as a moral and social attitude, as a "virtue," is solidarity. This then is not a feeling of vague compassion or shallow distress at the misfortunes of so many people, both near and far. On the contrary, it is a firm and persevering determination to commit oneself to the common good; that is to say to the good of all and of each individual because we are all really responsible for all (*Sollicitudo rei socialis,* n. 38, O-S, p. 421).

This insistence on the fact that all human beings are sisters and brothers who are called to live and to work together in solidarity flies in the face of the rampant individualism in the United States that regards the individual as the be-all and end-all. The self-made person remains a strong mythic and iconic figure even in contemporary American culture. The self-made person is able to do whatever he or she wants if he or she works hard enough. Many commentators have pointed out the danger of individualism in American society.[7] The anthropology developed in Catholic social teaching opposes an individualism that emphasizes the person as a self-made individual. None of us is self-made. We are obviously dependent on God but also on many other human beings—family, friends, teachers, various associations, and the political community.

The social and communitarian nature of human existence shows itself in many ways. As *Gaudium et spes* and the Catholic tradition point out, social relationships and social structures are necessary for the development of the individual person—as illustrated first by the family (n. 25, O-S, p. 180). A moment's reflection reminds us that we are not self-made persons; we have received so much from our families. Families give us love, nurture, and hope; they educate us, sustain us, and accept us for who we are and not for what we do. People in the United States today lament the loss of strong family ties that often leave children thwarted in their development.[8]

Team efforts remind us that greater human fulfillment comes about when we work together with others to accomplish something we could never do on our own. Think, for example, of a symphony orchestra. By coming together with many other musicians under a leader, we can produce a sound that infinitely surpasses what any of us could do on our own. Some people might object that as a result I have lost my freedom to play my drums whenever I want to: I must obey the director and play only when called to by the music and the director. By being part of the whole and accepting such cooperation and the discipline connected with it, however, I can achieve much more than I could ever achieve on my own.

Team sports often illustrate that we are social by nature and more than isolated monads. The five best individual basketball players do not necessarily make the best team. Individuals must learn to interact with one another and work together for the good of the team to be successful. Someone who is not a team player is not really wanted. Here, too, however, great fulfillment and satisfaction come from participating in a successful team effort. In the United States today, sports often are threatened by the dangers of individualism—as the salaries and the ways in which sports idols are treated demonstrate. Even in the midst of this ethos, however, many athletes still appreciate the greater importance of team success. Even today, one still hears an athlete say that he would rather have a Super Bowl ring or a World Series championship than be named most valuable individual player. Team success is more humanly satisfying and fulfilling.

Education—especially higher education—also emphasizes the social nature of human beings. The language of higher education is very communitarian. We speak of the college or university community. The word "college" itself has communitarian undertones that refer to people who are bound together or read together. One might argue that education would be easier and certainly much cheaper if everyone went to the library and learned on her or his own. We claim that education is better ordered, however, in a community setting where we can learn from and teach one another. The good college or university professor is the one who also learns from her or his students and colleagues. We are a community of learners.

Despite the American myth of the self-made person, experience reminds us of the anthropological truth that we are social by nature and find fulfillment and true development only in and through social relationships and social structures.[9] This perspective does not oppose individual fulfillment and happiness, but it recognizes that individuals come to fulfillment only in and through social relationships. The Catholic approach, as usual, appeals to reason and experience for verification.

This anthropological grounding for the social, political, and economic orders, with its twofold bases, avoids the opposite dangers of individualism and collectivism. Individualism regards the person as an isolated monad—the self-made person with no binding relationships with others or the ecosystems of the earth. On the other hand, collectivism so emphasizes the collectivity that it fails to give enough importance to the dignity of the individual. By recognizing both the dignity of the human person and humans' social nature, Catholic social teaching positions itself between these two extremes. Anthropology directs and guides the way in which Catholic social teaching understands the origin of the state, its purpose and limits, the opposing systems of Marxism and capitalism, justice, private property, and human rights. In all of these areas, Catholic social teaching finds the greatest opposition in the United States from the perspective of an individualistic ethic that does not give enough importance to the social nature of the human person.

NOTES ———

1. Mary Ann Donovan, "Alive to the Glory of God: A Key Insight in St. Irenaeus," *Theological Studies* 49 (1988): 283–97.

2. Lothar Roos, "The Message of *Centesimus annus*: Focus on Communism, Capitalism, and Consumerism," *Tripod*, no. 65 (1991): 4–13.

3. Aquinas, *IaIIae*, Prologue.

4. Daniel M. Cowdin, "John Paul II and Environmental Concern: Problems and Possibilities," *Living Light* 28 (1991): 44–52.

5. Aquinas, *Ia* q. 96, a. 4; *IaIIae*, q. 61, a. 5; *IaIIae*, q. 72, a. 4; *IaIIae*, q. 95, a. 4; *IIaIIae*, q. 109, a. 3, ad 1; *IIaIIae*, q. 114, a. 2, ad 1; *IIaIIae*, q. 129, a. 6, ad 1; *III*, q. 65, a. 1. Aquinas cites Aristotle's *Nichomachean Ethics*, n. 1169, and *Politics*, n. 1253.

6. See Gregory Baum, *Compassion and Solidarity: The Church for Others* (New York: Paulist, 1990); Marie Vianney Bilgrien, *Solidarity: A Principle, an Attitude, a Duty? or the Virtue for an Interdependent World?* (New York: P. Lang, 1999).

7. Robert N. Bellah et al., *Habits of the Heart: Individualism and Commitment in American Life*, rev. ed. (Berkeley: University of California Press, 1996). For a criticism of American individualism by Catholic authors, see Donald L. Gelpi, ed., *Beyond Individualism: Toward a Retrieval of Moral Discourse in America* (Notre Dame, Ind.: University of Notre Dame Press, 1989).

8. There is an abundance of Catholic literature on the family. See, e.g., Lisa Sowle Cahill, *Family: A Christian Social Perspective* (Minneapolis: Fortress, 2000). Two helpful collections are Lisa Sowle Cahill and Dietmar Mieth, eds., *The Family* (Maryknoll, N.Y.: Orbis, 1995), and Michael G. Lawler and William F. Roberts, eds., *Christian Marriage and Family: Contemporary Theological and Pastoral Perspectives* (Collegeville, Minn.: Liturgical, 1996). For a study of how Catholic social teaching views the family in its broader relationship to the common good and human solidarity, see Julie Hanlon Rubio, "Does Family Conflict with Community?" *Theological Studies* 58 (1997): 597–617.

9. A communitarian school has developed in opposition to liberalistic individualism in the United States. For a complete bibliography, see the website of the Communitarian Network (www.communitariannetwork.org).

CHAPTER 5

The Political Order

Catholic social teaching puts special emphasis on the structures and institutions that bring about a just society. The most important institution is the political community, the government, or the state. The Catholic tradition generally has referred to the political community as the "state." In this chapter I discuss the nature and purpose of the state, developments in the understanding of the state, the shift from authoritarianism to democracy, developments in the content of the common good, and peace and war.

NATURE AND PURPOSE OF THE STATE

Catholic social teaching is not interested in developing a theoretical understanding of the origins, nature, and purpose of the state. These documents deal primarily with the role of the state in bringing about social justice. The understanding of the state in these documents is derived from and based on the theory of the state developed over the centuries in Catholic social ethics.[1]

Rerum novarum (1891) confirmed the need for the state to intervene to protect workers and poor people. The first duty of the state "is to make sure that the laws and institutions, the general character and administration of the commonwealth shall be such as to produce of themselves public well-being and private prosperity" (n. 26, O-S, p. 26). In Quadragesimo anno (1931), Pius XI commented on Rerum novarum, noting, "Leo XIII boldly passed beyond the restrictions imposed by liberalism and fearlessly proclaimed the doctrine that the civil power is more than the mere guardian of law and order..." (n. 25, O-S, p. 47). In addition to condemning individualistic liberalism, Leo XIII and Pius XI strongly opposed socialism, which gives too great a role to the state (e.g., *Quadragesimo anno,* nn. 111–26, O-S, pp. 66–70).

In the Catholic understanding, the state is a natural society that is based on the social nature that the Creator has given to human beings. *Gaudium et spes* (1965) offers a more theoretical view of the human person and in this context recognizes the natural, God-given character of the state or political order:

> Human beings' social nature makes it evident that the progress of the human person and the advance of society hinge on one another.... This social life is not something added on to the human being.... Among those social ties which the human being needs for one's own development, some, like the family and political community, relate with greater immediacy to one's innermost nature (n. 25, O-S, p. 180).

Later the same document concludes, "It is therefore obvious that the political community and public authority are based on human nature and hence belong to an order of things divinely foreordained" (n. 74, O-S, p. 216). The economic pastoral makes the same point: "What the Bible and Christian tradition teach, human wisdom confirms. Centuries before Christ, the Greeks and Romans spoke of the human person as a 'social animal' made for friendship, community, and public life" (n. 65, O-S, p. 594). Thus, Catholic social teaching understands the state or the political order (no matter what form it may take) as natural, necessary, and good but also limited—avoiding the extremes of liberalistic individualism and totalitarian socialism. This understanding must be developed in the context of the whole Catholic tradition.

The State as Natural, Necessary, and Good

What does it mean to say that the state or political order is natural, necessary, and good? What is the basis for such an understanding?

Human beings are social by nature, according to Catholic social teaching. The Creator has made us this way so that we need to live in various structures and associations such as the family and political community to achieve our own fulfillment and happiness. God's design for human beings reveals itself in the social nature that is ours. No person is an island. Because the state owes its existence to creation and human nature, it is not only natural and necessary but also good. The state or the political community, as the aforementioned texts point out, has a positive function to promote public well-being and private prosperity.

Such a Catholic understanding of the state differs from other approaches. From a theological perspective, the Catholic concept of the state differs from the Lutheran conception. The Lutheran approach regards the state in terms of the Noachic Covenant: God's promise to Noah that God would never again destroy the world. How did God carry out this promise? What means are used?[2]

Lutheran theology has always taken the reality of sin and its effects very seriously. Genesis and the Pauline letters strongly emphasize the role of sin. (It is no coincidence that Luther was a Pauline scholar.) Sin came into the world, and with sin came death. The earliest pages of Genesis show the all-encompassing power of death, beginning with Cain's killing of Abel. If sin were to run its "natural" course, death would follow for all. Sin by its very nature leads to death. Sinful human beings will kill one another. To prevent this, God instituted the state as an order of preservation to keep sinful human beings from killing one another. In the classical Lutheran understanding, the political use of civil law involves the coercive power of the state to keep sinful human beings from harming and killing one another.[3]

The state is not based on creation and human nature; it comes into being as a dyke against the power of sin. The state is not sinful in itself but owes its origin to God's promise to preserve human beings in existence after sin has occurred. The function of the state in this understanding is minimal and negative—preserving order and keeping human beings alive. Such a view emphasizes the coercive nature of the state, which uses its power to prevent human beings from self-destruction. Karl Barth—perhaps the foremost Protestant theologian of the twentieth century—claimed that the Lutheran understanding of the state helped to keep Hitler in power in Germany. The basis for such a claim rests on the role of the state to keep order and prevent disorder. An imperfect and even harmful order is better than no order at all. Without any political order chaos ensues.[4] Others have disputed Barth's thesis, but such a thesis illustrates the role and function of the state in Lutheran thought.[5]

The Roman Catholic understanding of the state differs from the classic Lutheran conception in important ways.[6] The Catholic approach regards the state as based on creation, not as an order of preservation to contain the power of sin. Thus, the Catholic view gives a more positive role to the state: pursuing justice, public well-being, and personal prosperity. The Lutheran understanding regards the state primarily in terms of preserving order. The Lutheran concept emphasizes the coercive power of the state, whereas the Catholic understanding conceives the state in terms of directing people to the common good and their own good.

Long ago Thomas Aquinas raised what many people today might think is an irrelevant question: Would there have been civil authority and a state if Adam and

Eve had not sinned? This question actually has great practical importance because Aquinas was asking whether the political order is based on creation or comes about only in response to sin. Aquinas maintains that there would have been political authority even if there were no sin because the role of political authorities is to direct people to the common good of the group as well as to their own good. Without sin, human beings would still live in society and need direction for the common good. Notice that authority is primarily directive, not coercive. In keeping with such an understanding, Aquinas regards human law not as an act of the will of the legislator but as an act of reason that orders things to the common good. Aquinas then offers a clinching argument: Even the angels have political community and authority. Notice the different orders of angels that exist. Someone has to direct the angelic choir to the good of all. Wherever individuals are gathered together into a group, it is necessary for someone to direct them to the common good.[7]

In the Catholic tradition the state is natural, necessary, and good, with a positive purpose and function. Yet although the Catholic concept rightly emphasizes the positive role of the state, based on creation and human nature, it ignores the sinful reality that also affects the state in our world. At times the state's function will be felt not as directive but as coercive. The notion that the state is not primarily coercive finds support in human experience. Revolution occurs when citizens perceive the state as coercive and oppressive. The well-functioning state, despite its shortcomings, is not primarily coercive and oppressive. All regimes seek to serve the needs of the people and claim to do so even if in reality they do not.

The Catholic approach strongly differs from the individualistic and liberalistic approach of the *laissez-faire* state. In such a philosophical view, the person is not social by nature but is an isolated individual. By necessity, however, individuals find themselves living with other individuals and must come to some type of *modus vivendi*. Individuals want and need some greater power to protect their basic rights and goods, which other people are only too prone to interfere with. Thus, individuals come together to work out a contract that gives them as much as possible for themselves and allows their basic individualistic rights and goods to be protected. By definition, such an approach is fearful of state power and tries to restrain it or restrict it as much as possible.[8]

This individualistic understanding associated with liberalism is quite common in the United States today. The ultimate difference inherent in the Catholic approach rests on anthropology; the Catholic emphasis is on the social nature of the person, who is more than a self-governing and self-made human being. By definition the Catholic approach regards the state as good and gives it a more positive role and function. Recall that *Rerum novarum* insists, "Whenever the general interest or any particular class suffers, or is threatened with evils which can in no other way be met, the public authority must step in to meet them" (n. 28, O-S, p. 28). Forty years later, Pius XI perceptively pointed out, "Leo XIII boldly passed beyond the restrictions imposed by liberalism and fearlessly proclaimed the doctrine that the civil power is more than the mere guardian of law and order..." (n. 25, O-S, p. 47). Thus, the state is natural, necessary, and good and has a positive function.

The State as Limited

The state also is limited, however. Here the Catholic approach is distinguished from totalitarianism in general and socialism in particular, which suggest a much greater role for the state than does Catholic social teaching. The limited role of the state is based on an anthropology that upholds the dignity of the human person. From the very beginning of Catholic social teaching, *Rerum novarum* insisted that "the human being is older than the state" (n. 6, O-S, p. 16). In addition, "[S]ince the domestic household is anterior both in idea and in fact to the gathering of human beings into a commonwealth, the former must necessarily have rights and duties which are prior to those of the latter, and which rest more immediately on nature" (n. 10, O-S, p. 18). The human being and the family are prior to the state in ontological importance, and in God's plan they come before the state and cannot be subordinated to the state. Thus, the person and the natural society of the family constitute strong limits on the role and function of the state.

The basic theory explaining the limitations of the state and its proper role has remained more or less constant in Catholic social teaching. However, significant changes have occurred in the practical understanding of the role of the state. In this section I deal with the continuing theory that *Quadragesimo anno* described as the "principle of subsidiarity."

> [O]ne should not withdraw from individuals and commit to the community what they can accomplish by their own enterprise and industry. So, too, it is an injustice and at the same time a grave evil and a disturbance of right order to transfer to the larger and higher collectivity functions which can be performed and provided for by lesser and subordinate bodies (n. 79, O-S, p. 60).

The principle of subsidiarity directing and guiding the role and function of the state comes from the Catholic understanding of the totality of human society itself.[9] Society is broader than the state and includes much more. A well-functioning society must recognize and employ all of the different actors in society. *Quadragesimo anno* refers to lesser and subordinate bodies, which today often are called mediating institutions or structures. The basic Catholic view of society looks something like this: At the very basis of society stands the human person, with God-given dignity and rights. The person is prior to the state and cannot be subordinated to the state or the collectivity, although the person is still social by nature. Next comes the family, which is the basic unit of society for the development of human beings. As a natural society, the family comes before the state and cannot be absorbed by the state. On the next level are institutions or structures such as neighborhoods or extended families. We live in and through these realities. Then come somewhat independent structures and institutions that are necessary for any society. Think, for example, of the role of the press and the media. Cultural institutions of all kinds abound for the development of the higher goods of the individual. Educational groups of great variety exist to foster the education of people. Religious groups, synagogues, mosques, and churches bring people together for religious purposes. Professional societies and labor unions work for the good of their members. Such groups that people freely join are called voluntary groups; in the Catholic understanding, we need such groups to achieve our fulfillment. Only then come the different levels of government: local, state, and national.

The social nature of human beings refers to all of these different realities, not just to the level of the government. Some commentators today assert that the problem in the United States often is the lack of mediating institutions between the government and the individual.[10] In a well-organized society, all of these persons, organizations, structures, and institutions have roles to play. Without all of them carrying out their proper function, society is missing something important and even necessary. Such an understanding recognizes that social living requires much more than just the political order. The public or societal order embraces many realities beside the political—social, cultural, educational, associational, and so forth. The government or political order is not the whole social order. This principle shows why the Catholic tradition opposes totalitarianism—which makes the state supreme and takes away the basic rights and roles of individuals, families, and all other mediating institutions.

The principle of subsidiarity comes from the Latin word *subsidium* ("help"). Higher levels are not to annihilate or absorb the lower or more basic levels. Voluntary associations should do all they can to help individuals and families do what they can and should only do what individuals and families cannot accomplish. Likewise, government should intervene to help voluntary associations and groups and do only what the voluntary groups cannot do on their own. Government itself should start with what is closest to the people at the grassroots level and the state and federal governments should help the local government to do all that it can do taking over only what the lower level cannot do.

The way we fund higher education in the United States is a good example of the principle of subsidiarity at work. Primary responsibility rests with individuals and families; voluntary and other institutions also have roles to play, but the state also must play a role to provide all of its citizens with the opportunity for higher education. Recall that higher education in the United States originally began as an enterprise under the auspices of the church. Gradually, private institutions also developed. Even in the nineteenth century, however, individual states came into the work of higher education in many ways—especially through land-grant universities. The states felt the need to educate their farmers and miners. As time passed, and especially in the twentieth century, the states saw the need to train teachers for elementary and high schools. Existing private institutions were not able to produce enough teachers, so the states started what often were called normal schools. Meantime, states also had started other public universities.

Higher education took a giant step forward after World War II. The government provided returning GIs with money to attend any college they wanted. This funding mechanism was a boon to existing public and private colleges and a stimulus for the development of new colleges.

As time passed, however, it became evident that the existing institutions, including the mix of private and public institutions, could not provide for higher education for everyone. Community colleges came into existence to offer basic training beyond high school and prepare some of their students ultimately to enter four-year colleges.[11]

Today we have a system of public and private education. The state has not wanted to do away with private institutions. In fact, the vast majority of private and religious educational institutions could not continue to exist today without government help. Governments provide grants and money to many students. Government provides low-interest loans and other types of help to private institutions. Government grants are offered for many different projects. As a result, the government works to promote and help private colleges; it also sees the need, however, to establish public colleges and universities because private and religious institutions cannot meet the evident need.

Some people in our society want to argue that voluntary groups such as churches and others share the primary responsibility for dealing with the problem of poverty in our country. Everyone should admit that churches have an important role to play, but the problem is so vast that churches and voluntary associations alone cannot solve it. The government must become involved. When the government becomes involved, however, it should not do away with intermediate and voluntary associations such as churches that also do what they can to help poor people. Today, for example, groups such as the Lutheran Social Service and Catholic Charities receive about two-thirds of their budgets from government funds. If they are willing to help all people regardless of race, creed, or color, the government is willing to fund them to help them work with poor people.[12] The government does not try to do away with mediating institutions such as churches; it uses them precisely because mediating institutions are closer to the grassroots level and can deal effectively with some aspects of the problem of poverty.

Common Good as Purpose of the State

Catholic social teaching regards the end or purpose of the state or government as the pursuit of the common good. *Rerum novarum* recognizes that the commonwealth or state serves the common good and cites Aquinas: "As the part and the whole are in a certain sense identical, the part may in some sense claim what belongs to the whole" (n. 27, O-S, p. 26). Whenever the early documents of Catholic social teaching mention the state or government in any detail, they always mention the common good. In justifying state intervention to help poor people, *Rerum novarum* refers to the purpose of the common good (nn. 28–29, O-S, pp. 27–28). *Quadragesimo anno's* treatment of the authority of the state insists on the common good as the end of the state (n. 49, O-S, pp. 52–53). Later documents continue this insistence on the common good as the end or purpose of the state. *Gaudium et spes* repeats the refrain that "the political community exists for that common good" (n. 74, p. 216). The economic pastoral frequently refers to the common good (e.g., n. 79, O-S, p. 597; n. 117, O-S, p. 606; n. 325, O-S, p. 653).

Catholic social teaching is aware of the difficulty of determining exactly what the common good is because its descriptions of the common good tend to be general and vague. *Mater et magistra* describes the common good as "the sum total of those conditions of social living, whereby human beings are enabled more fully and more readily to achieve their own perfection" (n. 65, O-S, p. 94). *Gaudium et spes* understands the common good in the same general way as "the sum of those conditions of social life by which individuals, families, and groups can achieve their own fulfillment in a relatively thorough and ready way" (n. 74, O-S, p. 216).

The economic pastoral cites *Gaudium et spes* and goes on to fill out this general understanding with more details. (I consider this further elaboration later in this chapter.) Not only is the description of the common good in *Mater et magistra* vague; the document also recognizes that the common good itself progresses and develops over time (n. 65, O-S, p. 94).

The concept of the common good again illustrates how the Catholic approach avoids the extremes of individualism and collectivism. For individualism there are only individual goods that each person pursues as best she or he can. There is no concern for the good of the society or the totality. For collectivism there is only the good of the collectivity; there is no concern for the good of the individual. By definition, the common good ultimately flows back to the good of the individual and thus brings together the good of the community and the good of the individual.[13] What is good for the community also is good for the individual. What is good for the orchestra as a whole is good for the individual musician. What is good for the team redounds to the good of the individual player. In societal terms, everyone benefits from clean air and the availability of public transportation. Because we truly are a political community in solidarity with all other members, elimination of poverty is good for the entire community as well as for individual poor people. The good of the person is bound up with the good of the community.

In the traditional Catholic understanding, no conflict exists between the good of the community and the good of the individual. Again, however, the problem of failing to recognize the existence of conflict and the effects of sin appears. Experience reminds us that it is very difficult for people—especially in more heterogeneous settings—to agree on a definition of the common good. In the short term, conflicts between individual goods and the common good are inevitable. In practice, the tendency for each person or group to pursue narrow individual or group interests makes working for the common good very difficult. The theory of the common good in the Catholic tradition runs into some obstacles and problems that have not been recognized.

Catholic social teaching understands the state as a reality that is natural, necessary, and good but limited, as determined by the principle of subsidiarity. The common good is the end or purpose of the state. Although the skeletal aspects of the theory of the state have remained essentially constant throughout the course of Catholic social teaching, there have been significant developments in the understanding of the state.

Developments in the Understanding of the State

Significant changes have occurred in the role and understanding of the state since 1891, but the social teaching documents themselves have not explicitly recognized these changes. Such changes relate above all to the role of the state, the form of the state, and the contents of the common good. These changes are closely interrelated.

Role of the State

Leo XIII clearly had a very authoritarian or at best paternalistic view of the state. He refers to the rulers (*principes*) of the state (e.g., *Rerum novarum*, nn. 25 ff, O-S, pp. 26*ff*). With regard to the authority of rulers, *Rerum novarum* claims, "The gift of authority is from God, and is, as it were, a participation of the highest of all sovereignties; and it should be exercised as the power of God is exercised—with a fatherly solicitude which not only guides the whole but reaches to details as well" (n. 28, O-S, pp. 27–28). Recall that Leo XIII often referred to the people as "the illiterate multitude." Thus, rulers participate in the authority of God in ruling the illiterate multitude.

Quadragesimo anno understands the role of the ruler in the context of the accepted Catholic teaching on law.

> To define in detail these duties, when the need occurs and when the natural law does not do so, is the function of the government. Provided that the natural and divine law be observed, the public authority, in view of the common good, may specify more accurately what is licit and what is illicit . . . (n. 49, O-S, pp. 52–53).

The Catholic neoscholastic tradition recognized different types of law: eternal law, divine law, natural law, and human law. Eternal law is the plan for the world in the mind of God. All other laws mediate that law. Divine positive law contains prescriptions that God has revealed to human beings. Natural law is the participation of eternal law in the rational creature. Human law either repeats the natural law or makes specific what is generic in the natural law. For example, according to natural law people should drive their cars carefully and in an orderly way. Human law determines which side of the street everyone should drive on.

Thus, human law is always in accord with eternal law and natural law. Such an understanding sees the human ruler (to use Leo XIII's and Pius XI's term) as promulgating and enforcing eternal law and natural law. If the human legislator makes a law that goes against natural or eternal law, the human law is unjust and does not oblige in conscience. Thus, the human legislator or ruler and human law are regarded as mediations of the divine legislator and the eternal law and are always to act in accord with these considerations.[14]

In chapter 2 I detail how Catholic social teaching moved from Leo's authoritarian view of the state to a participatory state in a free society. This transition occurred in the context of the church's struggle against totalitarianism, especially in the form of communism. The Catholic Church gradually came to be a strong defender of the freedom and rights of the individual person and advocated a lesser role for the state and civil law. The state no longer has the paternalistic function of directing the "illiterate multitude" to moral and religious truth.

During this same period, however, Catholic social teaching moved toward greater involvement by the state in social justice. Here the opponent was not communism but the continuing influence of *laissez-faire* liberalism and individualism that resisted state intervention in these areas. Again, Catholic social teaching sees itself in the middle, in opposition to both totalitarianism and individualism. There is no contradiction between an expanding role for government in the area of justice and a lesser role for government in the area of religion and private morality. Recall that *Dignitatis humanae* recognized the need for government intervention to safeguard justice. In the course of its development, Catholic social teaching has called for a greater role by government precisely in the area of social justice.

From the very beginning, *Rerum novarum*—in opposition to *laissez-faire* liberalism—called for government intervention to protect workers. The state should intervene not only for the good of all but for the good of a particular class. *Quadragesimo anno* correctly saw this call for government intervention as opposed to the individualistic liberalism of the time (n. 25, O-S, p. 47). In the United States, the Administrative Committee of the National Catholic War Council (the name of the National Conference of Catholic Bishops at that time) issued its Program of Social Reconstruction in 1919 in response to the challenge facing the country's effort for reconstruction at the end of World War I. This document called for long-range reforms and short-term reforms, including government checks on monopolies and perhaps even governmental competition for monopolies; continuation of the National War Labor Board; enactment of a legal minimum wage; provision by the state for insurance against illness, unemployment, old age, and other disabilities; and laws regulating working conditions.[15] This document was identified with a progressive American tradition; many of its proposals became law only years later under the New Deal. The need for government intervention to protect the rights of workers was a part of Catholic social teaching from its inception.

In *Mater et magistra,* however, John XXIII added to this tradition by insisting on a greater role for government in light of the growing interdependence of human existence. *Mater et magistra* introduced what has been called "the principle of socialization."[16]

> Indeed, as is easily perceived, recent developments of science and technology provide additional reasons why, to a greater extent than heretofore, it is within the power of public authorities to reduce imbalances whether these be between various sectors of economic life, or between different regions of the same nation, or even between different peoples of the world as a whole. . . . Consequently it is requested again and again of public authorities responsible for the common good, that they intervene in a wide variety of economic affairs, and that, in a more extensive and organized way than heretofore, they adapt institutions, tasks, means, and procedures to this end (n. 54, O-S, pp. 92-93).

This greater role for governmental intervention results from "the multiplication of social relationships, that is, a daily more complex interdependence of citizens . . ." (n. 59, O-S, p. 93). John XXIII still insisted on the principle of subsidiarity, however, to limit government involvement.

Gaudium et spes embraces the same teaching. "Because of the increased complexity of modern circumstances, government is more often required to intervene in social and economic affairs, by way of bringing about conditions more likely to help citizens and groups freely attain to complete human fulfillment with greater effect" (n. 75, O-S, p. 217). The pastoral constitution recognizes, however, the tension between socialization, on one hand, and personal independence and development on the other (n. 75, O-S, p. 217).

Subsequent documents continued to recognize this need for government intervention because of the increased complexities of human existence. Two specific illustrations of such government involvement are the concept of the indirect employer, with the state playing a major role, and the need to plan for the public good.

John Paul II developed the concept of the indirect employer in *Laborem exercens.* The concept of the indirect employer recognizes the social aspect of the employer-employee relationship and contract. Most people think that the employment contract involves just two parties—the employer and the employee. Not so, according to John Paul II. In some situations—especially in poor countries, though not only there—the chief employer might not be able to pay a living wage for a variety of reasons, especially the international factors—

for instance in the import and export process, that is to say, in the mutual exchange of economic goods, whether raw materials, semimanufactured goods, or finished industrial products. These links also create mutual dependence, and, as a result it would be difficult to speak in the case of any state, even the economically most powerful, of complete self-sufficiency or autarky. . . . It is easy to see that this framework of forms of dependence linked with the concept of the indirect employer is enormously extensive and complicated (n. 17, O-S, pp. 375–76).

The concept of the indirect employer is applicable to every society and in the first place to the state. "For it is the state that must conduct a just labor policy" (n. 17, O-S, p. 375). The indirect employer involves

all the agents at the national and international level that are responsible for the whole orientation of labor policy. . . . In order to meet the danger of unemployment and to insure employment for all, the agents defined here as 'indirect employer' must make provision for overall planning with regard to the different kinds of work by which not only the economic life, but also the cultural life of a given society is shaped; they must also give attention to organizing that work in a correct and rational way (n. 18, O-S, pp. 376–77).

The indirect employer involves the individual state and the particular ministries within it, but it also involves other groups and associations. On the international level, the indirect employer also includes other states and individual actors that affect the world economy. In a sense, one sees the principles of socialization and subsidiarity at work here with regard to the employment contract, which seems to involve only the employer and the employee. Note how such an approach can involve everyone who shares responsibility for unjust labor conditions in countries. The social aspect of employment and the roles played by the individual state and foreign states involved in trade, together with all other actors, broaden the understanding of and responsibility for just labor contracts and conditions. Note the need for planning among all these involved to work for structures that respect the

objective rights of the worker . . . that must constitute the adequate and fundamental criterion for shaping the whole economy, both on the level of the individual society and state and within the whole of the world economic policy and of the systems of international relationships that derive from it (n. 17, O-S, p. 376).

Laborem exercens's appeal for the need for planning involving the state and all other economic actors is the basis for the fourth chapter of the economic pastoral of the U.S. bishops, "A New American Experiment: Partnership for the Public

Good" (1986). The bishops recognize that our nation deserves credit for introducing participation into the political process, but "similar steps are needed today to expand economic participation, broaden the sharing of economic power, and make economic decisions more accountable to the common good" (n. 297, O-S, p. 646). This partnership involves cooperation within firms and industries, local and regional cooperation, the development of national policies, and partnerships at the international level.

With regard to the call for partnerships, the U.S. bishops cite a passage from *Laborem exercens* (n. 18, O-S, p. 377) in which John Paul II deals precisely with the indirect employer. "In the final analysis, this overall concern weighs on the shoulders of the state, but it cannot mean one-sided centralization by the public authorities" (n. 315, O-S, p. 651). Thus, the bishops insist on the need for economic planning, with the state playing an important role in the process. Again, however, the bishops do not deal with the pivotal practical question of how all this planning can be brought about. Thus, the papal insistence on the indirect employer and the bishops' call for partnership and planning involving the state and all others illustrate the need for greater involvement by the state in light of the growing complexities and interdependencies of our day.

Understanding of the State

Not only did the shift to the person as subject in Catholic social teaching affect the role of the state; it also affected the understanding of the state. Leo XIII and Pius XI clearly understood human society on the basis of the organic metaphor of the human body. In discussing capital and labor, Leo XIII argues,

> Just as the symmetry of the human body is the result of the disposition of the members of the body, so in a State it is ordained by nature that these two classes should exist in harmony and agreement, and should, as it were, fit into one another, so as to maintain the equilibrium of the body politic (n. 15, O-S, p. 20).

Leo XIII also argues in favor of the need for inequalities in society:

> There naturally exist among humankind innumerable differences of the most important kind; people differ in capability, in diligence, in health, and in strength; and unequal fortune is a necessary result of inequality in condition. Such inequality is far from being disadvantageous either to individuals or to the community; social and public life can only go on by the help of various kinds of capacity and the playing of many parts, and each individual, as a rule, chooses the part which peculiarly suits one's case (n. 14, O-S, p. 20).

Quadragesimo anno maintains that "human society forms a truly social and organic body" (n. 69, O-S, p. 58). Recall that the corporatist theory in that document is grounded in such an organic understanding of society.

The consideration of the state in *Gaudium et spes* does not invoke the organic concept of society (nn. 74–76, O-S, pp. 216–19). The word "community" is used most frequently to describe society. In an organic body, each part has its given role to play. In a community, however, the individuals are to participate freely. The role of "authority must dispose the energies of the whole citizenry toward the common good, not mechanically or despotically, but primarily as a moral force which depends on freedom and the conscientious discharge of the burdens of any office which has been undertaken" (n. 74, O-S, p. 216).

Octogesima adveniens—which emphasizes the aspirations of equality and participation that make themselves felt more persistently today as forms of human dignity and freedom—likewise moves decisively away from the organic body metaphor and replaces it with a community responding in freedom to the call for the common good.

> Political power...is the natural and necessary link for insuring the cohesion of the social body.... To take politics seriously...is to affirm the duty of the individual, of every individual, to recognize the concrete reality and the value of the freedom of choice that is offered to the human being to seek to bring about both the good of the city and of the nation and of humankind.... The passing to the political dimension also expressed a demand made by the people of today: a greater sharing in responsibility and in decision making (nn. 46–47, O-S, pp. 282–83).

Subsequent documents have continued in the same vein.

Why this change? Understanding the state through the metaphor of the organic human body fit well with Leo XIII's understanding of a hierarchical social order, complete with many inequalities, in which authority from on high had to direct the illiterate multitude to fulfill its God-given tasks. With the emphasis on freedom, equality, and participation, such a metaphor can no longer be accepted. The metaphor of the organic body was a firm foundation for regarding the social order as a true society, with all of the different parts working together for the common good. The emphasis on freedom, equality, and participation makes it more difficult to have a social and political community.

Leo XIII opposed freedom, equality, and participation precisely because they seemed to threaten the possibility of true human political community. These values were associated with individualistic liberalism. Everyone has to acknowledge that it is harder to achieve community in light of the greater diversity and heterogeneity today. *Octogesima adveniens* rightly points out what is needed to achieve true political community while respecting the freedom and equality of all: "Without a renewed education in solidarity, an overemphasis on equality can give rise to an individualism in which each one claims one's own rights without wishing to be answerable for the common good" (n. 23, O-S, p. 274). Thus, solidarity for the common good has replaced the organic human body metaphor as the basis for political community, which recognizes the importance of freedom and equality.

Thus, solidarity becomes a central concept in Catholic social teaching. *Centesimus annus* makes the point:

> In this way what we nowadays call the principle of solidarity, the validity of which both in the internal order of each nation and in the international order I have discussed in the encyclical *Sollicitudo rei socialis,* is clearly seen to be one of the fundamental principles of the Christian view of social and political organization (n. 10, O-S, p. 446).[17]

Solidarity, for example, determines the proper balance between subsidiarity and socialization. In chapter 6 I explore the implications of this solidarity for our understanding of material goods and the proper distribution of material goods within a society. Although contemporary Catholic social teaching recognizes the legitimate demands of liberalism for freedom and equality, it still insists on the social and communitarian dimensions of the human person. Solidarity is not easily achieved in this world, however—especially in light of its complexity, diversity, sinfulness, and egoism. Again, contemporary Catholic social teaching fails to recognize the many conflicts in human society today and the difficulty of having true solidarity and true political community in these conditions.

FROM AUTHORITARIANISM TO DEMOCRACY

The Catholic Church in the nineteenth century strongly opposed all forms of liberalism and regarded democracy as political liberalism. By the end of the twentieth century, however, the Vatican had become a world leader in advocating the cause of democracy throughout the world. George Weigel, the self-proclaimed neoconservative Catholic,[18] calls strong Catholic support for democracy the second twentieth-century revolution; the first was the Russian Bolshevik revolution in 1917. The Roman Catholic Church transformed itself from a bastion of the *ancien régime* to a leading supporter of democracy.[19]

Recall that in the Catholic understanding, political liberalism makes the human individual and human reason supreme; there is no relationship to God or God's law and no room for the church or religion in society. Separation of church and state relegated religion to the private sphere; secularization of marriage and education denied the God-given role of the church. The nineteenth-century Catholic Church strongly opposed all forms of liberalism, including political liberalism.[20]

Although Leo XIII had an authoritarian or at best paternalistic understanding of government and opposed modern freedoms, he did not explicitly condemn democracy. In fact, in his encyclical *Immortale Dei* (1885), which dealt with the constitution of the state, he maintained that "no one of the several forms of government is in itself condemned, inasmuch as none of them contains anything contrary to Catholic doctrine and all of them are capable, if wisely and justly managed, to insure the welfare of the state."[21] In the same paragraph, however, he repeats the Catholic opposition to religious freedom but invokes the thesis (ideal)-hypothesis (real) distinction. "The church does not on that account condemn those rulers who, for the sake of securing some great good or of hindering some great evil, allow patiently custom or usage to be a kind of sanction for each kind of religion having its place in the state."[22] Thus, in certain situations—especially when it was in the minority—the Catholic Church could tolerate religious freedom as the lesser of two evils.

Until recently Catholic scholars referred to the "indifference" of the church to forms of government. References to government were in terms of function rather than form. Rulers, whoever they were—kings, emperors, elected presidents—had to govern justly.[23] Historically the church has had to deal with all types of governments. A primary concern for the church has always been its freedom to carry out its mission and function. In chapter 7 I mention the compromises that the Catholic Church has made even in contemporary times with suspect governments to protect the church's freedom.

The transformation of the popes and Roman Catholicism into champions of democracy coheres with the methodological shift to the person as subject, with special emphasis on freedom, equality, and participation. In chapter 7 I show how, in the same context, the church accepted and strongly supported human rights. Opposition to totalitarianism and communism moved Roman Catholicism to champion democracy. The details of this development go well beyond the texts of Catholic social teaching and cannot be developed here.[24] The practical experience of Catholics in many countries, including the United States, confirmed the compatibility between Catholicism and democracy.[25] Even before World War II, the distinguished French neo-Thomist philosopher Jacques Maritain argued on Thomistic grounds for Christian democracy. Maritain exercised huge influence in the Catholic world.[26]

In terms of papal documents, it was only in the middle of World War II, in his Christmas message of 1944, that Pius XII gingerly recognized that "a democratic form of government appears to many people as the natural postulate imposed by reason itself."[27] This statement opened the door to further development in Catholic social teaching's strong support for democracy. *Pacem in terris* (1963) finally developed the full panoply of human rights and called for separation of the three functions of public authority—legislative, executive, and judicial—but recognized, "it is impossible to determine in all cases what is the most suitable form of government..." (n. 67, O-S, p. 142).

Dignitatis humanae (1965) marked a watershed in Catholic history. In this Vatican II document, Catholic teaching finally accepted the principle of religious freedom for all and endorsed the principle of the free society. This document (which I study in greater detail in chapter 7) clearly put Catholic teaching squarely on the side of democratic government. *Octogesima adveniens* maintains, "The two aspirations to equality and to participation seek to promote a democratic society" (n. 24, O-S, p. 274). *Sollicitudo rei socialis* calls for developing nations to follow the path to democracy: "Other nations need to reform certain unjust structures, and in particular their political institutions, in order to replace corrupt, dictatorial, and authoritarian forms of government by democratic and participatory ones" (n. 44, O-S, p. 427).

The Catholic Church, in the person of Pope John Paul II, strongly condemned authoritarian and dictatorial regimes in his many visits to all parts of the world. In South America, Asia, and Africa, John Paul II called for democratic regimes.[28] The Catholic Church was a major actor on the world scene and in countries such as Poland in the struggle against and ultimate collapse of communism behind the Iron Curtain; the church now faces challenges in making democracy work.[29] Strong evidence in the documents of Catholic social teaching and in the actions of the Catholic Church at all levels, including the papacy, supports the claim that Catholicism's transformation from an opponent of democracy to a firm supporter in the last half of the twentieth century truly ranks as "the other twentieth century revolution."

Have Catholicism in general and Catholic social teaching in particular now accepted the principles of liberalism? Much discussion centers on the relationship between Catholicism and liberalism today.[30] Subsequent analyses on the purpose of material goods, private property, criticism of Marxism and capitalism, and the social aspects of justice and human rights all point to the fact that Catholic social teaching cannot accept an individualistic liberalism. In keeping with its inclusive "both-and" tendency, Catholic teaching will accept what is good in liberalism and see the need for more. Undoubtedly, however, the Catholic tradition in the twentieth century learned from liberalism to appreciate the need for and importance of democratic forms of government. The form of government now greatly contributes to the justice of its functioning.

Centesimus annus recognizes a difference in the Catholic acceptance and support of democracy from liberalism in general and from some other approaches that exist today. Near the beginning of *Centesimus annus,* John Paul II quotes and explicitly mentions Leo XIII's encyclical *Libertas praestantissimum* (1888). In that encyclical, Leo XIII attacked modern liberties and democracy; John Paul II maintains, however, that the encyclical "called attention to the essential bond between human freedom and truth, so that freedom which refused to be bound to the truth would fall into arbitrariness and end up submitting itself to the vilest of passions, to the point of self-destruction" (n. 4, O-S, p. 442). John Paul II wants to see a connection between freedom and the truth, although Leo used this connection to deny the modern freedoms. *Centesimus annus* returns to this theme later and recognizes that the Catholic approach to democracy differs from some others:

> Those who are convinced that they know the truth and firmly adhere to it are somewhat unreliable from a democratic point of view, since they do not accept that truth is determined by the majority, or that it is subject to variation according to different political trends. It must be observed in this regard that if there is no ultimate truth to guide and direct political activity then the ideas and convictions can easily be manipulated for reasons of power. As history demonstrates, a democracy without values easily turns into open or thinly disguised totalitarianism (n. 46, O-S, p. 474).

Although John Paul II makes some good points in this passage, his remarks also raise questions. Contemporary philosophers disagree about how much agreement can be found with regard to the goods or values we hold in common. Many liberal thinkers today maintain that no particular society—let alone the global community—can agree on basic values that should be accepted by all of its members. In practice, many people act as if democracy means that the majority determines what is right. Relativists reject the possibility of coming to agreement within society. Others recognize the impossibility of agreement across different societies or traditions. Some philosophers hold to a thin concept of the good that limits the amount of substantive agreement. Others advocate a thick concept of the good.

There is no doubt that *Centesimus annus* argues for a very thick concept of the good: All human beings can and should agree on many goods or truths (e.g., the evil of abortion) that should guide a democratic society. One gets the impression from other papal encyclicals, such as *Veritatis splendor* (1993), that John Paul II has a very clear and certain idea of the truths that all people should embrace.[31]

In my judgment it is possible and necessary for states and societies to agree on certain basic truths and values. The Declaration of Independence in the United States proclaims that we hold these truths to be self-evident.[32] Our constitution proclaims a bill of rights for all citizens that the majority cannot deny. Many people today insist on certain human rights for all people around the globe. The World Parliament of Religions in 1993 called for a global ethic.[33] John Paul II seems to claim more certitude and more agreement than I think is possible, however. In chapter 7 I explore this question of truth and shared values, as well as the relationship between truth and freedom.

In 100 years papal social teaching changed considerably—perhaps even to the point of revolution in its support for democratic government. Yet papal teaching has not accepted the entire theory of individualistic liberalism, and John Paul II has a limited notion of pluralism in a democracy.

DEVELOPMENTS CONCERNING THE COMMON GOOD

Catholic social teaching consistently has appealed to the theory of the common good to explain the purpose of society and the state. In this section I discuss three significant changes in the content of the common good in the historical development of Catholic social teaching.[34] First, the most significant development in the understanding of the common good in Catholic social teaching involves the changing anthropology I describe in chapter 4. Contemporary documents stress the freedom, equality, and participation of persons. The earliest documents rejected such approaches as too individualistic and harmful to their understanding of the common good. In light of this changed anthropology, contemporary Catholic social teaching also has incorporated human rights into its understanding of the common good (as I develop in chapter 7).

Second, contemporary Catholic social teaching, in contrast to the earlier teaching, has come to recognize the important distinction and, to a degree, some practical separation between the temporal common good and the spiritual common good, which paved the way to recognize the right to religious freedom. In chapter 7 I discuss this development in greater detail, as well as the important distinction between the temporal common good and the public order that serves as the criterion governing the role of the limited state.

The recent documents of Catholic social teaching simply assume that these two new developments can fit into the older theory or concept of the common good. Such an approach is in keeping with the fact that these documents by definition do not go into the finer points of theoretical moral theology.

In reality, however, these newer developments in the content of the common good also affected the basic understanding and theory of the common good. Beginning in the 1940s, Jacques Maritain recognized that his more personalist approach to the content of the common good also affected the very concept and theory of the common good. Maritain considered human political society to be analogous to the divine society of the subsistent relations of the Trinity and animal society in which the individual animal is simply a part of the whole. Political society is neither exclusively personalist (like the divine life in the Trinity) nor exclusively communal (like animal society). The person is a part of political society and at the same time transcends it. Maritain still finds meaning, however, in the oft-repeated dictum of Thomas Aquinas (based on Aristotle) that the good of the city is more noble and more divine than that of the individual. For many Thomists, this pivotal text provided the basis for common good theory. Maritain, however, refers this saying to the supernatural reality and to its ultimate consummation whereby the person is raised to share as a pure personality in the uncreated society of divine persons, thus entering into the kingdom of God and the light of glory.[35]

Thus, Maritain interprets the famous saying that the good of the city is nobler and more divine than that of the individual as fully true only in the eschatological reign of God. In political community in this world, the person is a part in relationship to the whole in the order of terrestrial values, although the person—by reason of personhood—transcends the political common good. Not all Thomists of the 1940s were willing to accept Maritain's approach; some saw it as a move away from Aquinas and a denial of the primacy of the common good in the political order.[36] We should not be surprised that significant changes in the content of the political common good call for some change in the concept and theory of the common good.

Third, Catholic social teaching has recognized the worldwide nature of the social question. From the 1960s on, these documents have addressed the social question from the worldwide perspective, with special attention to the problems of developing countries (e.g., *Populorum progressio* and *Sollicitudo rei socialis*). As early as 1963, *Pacem in terris* directed its fourth part to the relationship of human beings and political communities within the world community. In light of this global interrelatedness, there is a universal common good that is more than the common good of a particular society or a particular state. *Pacem in terris* wisely recognizes the problem existing in the contemporary world because there is no universal worldwide authority to direct all to the universal common good. "Therefore, under the present circumstances of human society, both the structure and form of governments as well as the power which public authority wields in all the nations of the world must be considered inadequate to promote the universal common good" (n. 135, O-S, p. 152). In light of the needs of the universal common good, "the moral order itself demands" the existence of "public authority endowed with a wideness of powers, structure and means of the same proportions: that is, of public authority which is in a position to operate in an effective manner on a worldwide basis" (n. 137, O-S, p. 153).

Thus, *Pacem in terris* recognizes the existence of a worldwide common good that calls for a worldwide authority as a demand of the moral order to solve the structural problems in our world. In keeping with its natural law optimism, *Pacem in terris* does not appreciate the problems and even the pitfalls in such a world authority. The problems are huge. Experience shows that the powerful nations of the world will not give up their power or sovereignty to a world order. How is this worldwide structure to come about? Who will bring it into existence? How exactly will it be structured? The pitfall always remains that in the context of human limitation, human sinfulness, and the lack of eschatological fullness, such a situation will benefit the powerful and exclude the powerless and the marginalized. The only worldwide political order today is the United Nations—which is quite weak and needs constant strengthening. I seriously doubt if a just and effective global political structure will ever come into existence in the real world.

John Paul II frequently cites and supports the work of the United Nations. Here too, however, in *Centesimus annus* an overly optimistic tone emerges: "The United Nations, moreover, has not yet succeeded in establishing, as alternatives to war, effective means for the resolution of international conflicts. This seems to be the most urgent problem that the international community has yet to resolve" (n. 21, O-S, p. 454). Moreover, there are many other urgent problems, such as economic justice, that the international community has not been able to solve. We will never solve all of our urgent problems in this world. We have to try to do better, however. We all must admit the global interdependence of our world and the need to recognize and work for a global common good. Global treaties (e.g., the Law of the Sea Treaty) constitute a significant development. Agreeing on a global common good will be difficult at best, however, and authoritative political structures to promote and safeguard that global common good will never be adequate.

PEACE AND WAR

Peace and war are perennial topics in political ethics. The earlier documents of Catholic social teaching focused primarily on economic issues and did not discuss peace and war. Since the 1960s, however, Catholic social teaching has addressed these issues. The entire 1983 pastoral letter of the U.S. bishops considers this important issue in great depth.

Traditionally the Catholic Church has espoused what has been called the just war tradition.[37] The historical origins of the just war tradition go back to Augustine, with subsequent developments by Thomas Aquinas, sixteenth-century Spanish scholastics, and Francisco Suarez (d. 1617). The just war tradition attempts to justify war as a last resort in certain circumstances but to limit war in its inception and its execution.

The just war approach in the Catholic tradition requires many conditions to justify going to war (*ius ad bellum*): legitimate authority, just cause, last resort, declaration of war, reasonable hope of success, proportionality, and right intention. A second set of limits concerns the execution or practice of war itself. Two conditions limit what is acceptable in war (*ius in bello*): the principle of discrimination forbids the direct attack on noncombatants and the principle of proportionality maintains that the good to be attained outweighs the evil involved in the tactics employed.

Papal and Conciliar Teaching

Several twentieth-century popes have addressed the issues of peace and war. Pope Benedict XIV proposed a seven-point peace plan during World War I.[38] During and after World War II, Pius XII often raised the issues of peace and war.[39] Pius XII discussed the possible justification for going to war in light of the need for a more adequate international political structure that could curtail the recourse to war. On the basis of increasingly destructive military technology, Pius XII condemned wars of aggression and reduced the just causes of going to war from three (defense against aggression, avenging evil, and restoring violated rights) to one (defense against unjust attack). In addition, Pius XII recognized—in accordance with the principle of proportionality—that the evils of war could outweigh some unjust aggression. He saw no place for pacifism, however, and opposed conscientious objection once the government has decided that war is necessary as a last resort in self-defense.[40] Catholic social teaching in subsequent decades of the twentieth century continued some of the emphases of Pius XII (e.g., the need for international political organization, the legitimacy of defense against aggression) but also introduced significant changes.

JOHN XXIII

Pacem in terris (1963) was the first document in Catholic social teaching that addressed the issues of peace and war. The encyclical stresses the need to protect and promote peace, but only a small part of the encyclical deals with force and war. The encyclical does not explicitly acknowledge the right to defense against aggression. Only one sentence deals with the concept of just cause in going to war: "Therefore, in an age such as ours which prides itself on its atomic energy it is contrary to reason to hold that war is now a suitable way to restore rights which have been violated" (n. 127, O-S, p. 151). This sentence, especially in light of previous and subsequent hierarchical teaching, agrees with Pius XII in eliminating what had previously been one of the causes justifying the use of force. An earlier erroneous translation asserted, "It is hardly possible to imagine that in the atomic era war could be used as an instrument of justice." Such an assertion would have denied any just cause for going to war.[41]

John XXIII recognizes a role for deterrence but does not explicitly defend it. "[E]ven though the monstrous power of modern weapons acts as a deterrent, there is nevertheless reason to fear that the mere continuance of nuclear tests, undertaken with war in mind, can seriously jeopardize various kinds of life on earth" (n. 111, O-S, p. 149).

The arms race impedes social and economic progress. Justice demands that "the arms race should cease, that the stockpiles which exist in various countries should be reduced equally and simultaneously by the parties concerned, that nuclear weapons should be banned, and finally that all come to an agreement on a fitting program of disarmament, employing mutual and effective controls" (n. 112, O-S, p. 149). The approach here is primarily one of exhortation, but the pope does not call for unilateral disarmament and insists on the need for mutual and effective controls of disarmament.

VATICAN II

Gaudium et spes devotes the last chapter of its second part to "The Fostering of Peace and the Promotion of a Community of Nations" (nn. 77–90, O-S, pp.

219–29). The pastoral constitution accepts some pacifist perspectives but does not abandon the just war theory.

The horror of modern war "compels us to undertake an evaluation of war with an entirely new attitude" (n. 80, O-S, p. 222). This new attitude or approach, with its pacifist leanings, brought two changes in Catholic teaching. First, *Gaudium et spes* praises and thus accepts the pacifist position of "those who renounce the use of violence in the vindication of their rights" and use only nonviolent means. Thus, *Gaudium et spes* for the first time accepts nonviolence as a legitimate position for individual Catholics—but with the caveat "that this can be done without injury to the rights and duties of others or of the community itself" (n. 78, O-S, p. 220).

A second change in *Gaudium et spes* is that it calls for the acceptance of conscientious objection—a position opposed by Pius XII. "Moreover, it seems right that laws make humane provisions for . . . those who for reasons of conscience refuse to bear arms, provided, however, that they accept some other form of service to the human community" (n. 79, O-S, p. 221). The document makes no distinction between conscientious objection to all wars and selective conscientious objection to particular wars.

In keeping with the eschatological tension I discuss in chapter 1, the pastoral constitution recognizes, "Insofar as human beings are sinful, the threat of war hangs over them, and hang over them it will until the return of Christ" (n. 78, O-S, p. 220). In this context, the document follows the just war tradition. First, the pastoral constitution recognizes the right to legitimate defense as a last resort. "As long as the danger of war remains and there is no competent and sufficiently powerful authority at the international level, governments cannot be denied the right to legitimate defense once every means of peaceful settlement has been exhausted" (n. 79, O-S, p. 221). Second, the pastoral constitution condemns total war by using— without explicitly saying so—the just war principle of discrimination or noncombatant immunity. "Any act of war aimed indiscriminately at the destruction of entire cities or of extensive areas along with their population is a crime against God and humankind. It merits unequivocal and unhesitating condemnation" (n. 80, O-S, p. 222). This is the strongest condemnation in all of Vatican II.

The treatment of the arms race and deterrence is similar to that of *Pacem in terris*. Although many people regard nuclear deterrence "as the most effective way by which peace of a sort can be maintained," the resulting so-called balance is not a "sure and authentic peace." "[T]he arms race is an utterly treacherous trap for humanity, and one which injures the poor to an intolerable degree" (n. 81, O-S, pp. 222–23). The constitution does not call for unilateral disarmament, however.

"Hence everyone must labor to put an end at last to the arms race, and to make a true beginning of disarmament, not indeed a unilateral disarmament, but one proceeding at an equal pace according to agreement and backed up by authentic and workable safeguards" (n. 82, O-S, p. 223). *Gaudium et spes* insists on the duty of all people to work for the time when war can be outlawed by international consent. The document recognizes that such an outlawing of war "requires the establishment of some universal public authority acknowledged as such by all, and endowed with effective power to safeguard, on the behalf of all, security, regard for justice, and respect for rights" (n. 82, O-S, p. 223). *Gaudium et spes* does not say how this agreement can ever be achieved, however.

PAUL VI

Populorum progressio develops the Catholic teaching on peace and war in two ways. First, building on his primary emphasis on the need for development, Paul VI ends his discussion with a section titled "Development is the New Name for Peace." He writes, "Excessive economic, social, and cultural inequalities . . . are a danger to peace." Peace involves a more perfect form of justice among human beings and is not simply the absence of war or the result of an ever-precarious balance of power (n. 76, O-S, p. 258). In the urgent work for development by all individuals and institutions, the peace of the world and the future of civilization itself are at stake (n. 80, O-S, p. 259).

Paul VI also left the door ajar for the possibility of legitimate revolution, although his tone was very cautious. "We know, however, that a revolutionary uprising—save where there is manifest, long-standing tyranny which would do great damage to fundamental personal rights and dangerous harm to the common good of the country—produces new injustices, throws more elements out of balance and brings on new disasters" (n. 31, O-S, p. 247). In *Evangelii nuntiandi* (1975), however, Paul VI seems to take a different approach.

> The church cannot accept violence, especially the force of arms—which is uncontrollable once it is let loose—and indiscriminate death as the path to liberation, because she knows that violence always provokes violence and irresistibly engenders new forms of oppression and enslavement . . . (n. 37, O-S, p. 316).

Does this statement contradict Paul VI's earlier position in *Populorum progressio*? Perhaps not. The proposed position might be more hortatory in form, as the next sentence in the document seems to suggest. In addition, violence is linked with indiscriminate death. What if the deaths are not indiscriminate, as the just war theory would require? There also are several judgments of facts here. Is violence always uncontrollable? Does it always engender new forms of oppression and slavery? Is the proposal here only an ideal? Thus, although some ambiguity remains, Paul VI seems to recognize the possibility of a justified revolution.

Paul VI—like John Paul II—wrote about and addressed issues of justice and peace outside the context of Catholic social teaching. Paul VI's 1965 address to the United Nations contained the very moving appeal, "No more war, war never again![42] In the same speech, however, he also recognized that as long as human beings remain weak, vacillating, and to some extent evil, defensive arms unfortunately will be necessary.[43]

In 1968 Paul VI inaugurated the World Day of Peace on January 1 to focus the attention of the church and the world on the important issue of peace. He delivered important addresses on the subject of peace on each succeeding January 1st.[44] John Paul II has carried out the same approach.

JOHN PAUL II

Nowhere in his three encyclicals regarding Catholic social teaching does John Paul II deal in depth with the questions of peace and war. His references to peace and war are incidental and do not involve a new ethical analysis. For example, building on *Populorum progressio*'s emphasis that "development is the new name for peace," *Sollicitudo rei socialis* insists on justice in the world to overcome the temptation among victims of injustice to respond with violence. In this context of working for justice, John Paul II condemns the arms race: "[W]ar and military preparations are the major enemy of the integral development of peoples" (n. 10, O-S, p. 400).

Centesimus annus refers to peace and war in several places. John Paul II extols the peaceful and nonviolent opposition that brought down the Iron Curtain despite all the violence used against people (n. 23, O-S, p. 455). The post–World War II situation in Europe was really "a situation of non-war rather than genuine peace." True peace never results from military victory. This precarious peace fueled an insane arms race that swallowed up many resources. In the context of the East-West divide, extremist groups found ready support for their recourse to violence. Thus, fratricidal conflicts afflicted many Third World countries. "Moreover, the whole world was oppressed by the threat of an atomic war capable of leading to the extinction of humanity." In such a war, there are no winners or losers but the suicide of humanity. John Paul II ends this section by condemning "total war" (n. 18, O-S, pp. 452–53). Although the tone is very strong, the condemnation of total war is in keeping with just war principles—even though the right to defense against aggression is not mentioned here. John Paul II acknowledges this right elsewhere, however.

Centesimus annus subsequently reiterates John Paul II's negative reaction to the war in the Persian Gulf: "Never again war!" Again, however, he describes war as that "which destroys the lives of innocent people. . . ." There is a collective responsibility not only to avoid war but also to promote development, justice, and peace (n. 52, O-S, pp. 478–79). John Paul II's general opposition to war and the arms race and the need to increase solidarity and justice are clear. There is no detailed analysis beyond the statement of general approaches, but even his language indicates that he would not condemn all resorts to limited use of violence against unjust aggression—although he does not explicitly develop this thesis.

John Paul II has addressed peace and violence in many other forums and speeches on his many trips, his comments on contemporary events, and especially his messages every year for the World Day of Peace on January 1. Anything more than a summary of his position is beyond the scope of this book. John Paul II frequently deplores the arms race, especially its effect on poor people. He gives the impression that nuclear war could never be limited, but he has never called for unilateral nuclear disarmament. In Ireland, Latin America, and Africa, he has condemned violence in fighting injustice. These condemnations deal with injustice within a country and seem to be shutting the door on any possibility of just revolution—a position that Paul VI left slightly ajar.[45] Perhaps, however, such remarks are limited to the specific contexts or propose exhortations and goals rather than absolute principles or norms.

There is no doubt that John Paul II maintains that we have resorted to violence too often. He strongly condemned the Gulf War,[46] although in that very context he felt compelled to point out that he is not a pacifist.[47] Many of his World Day of Peace messages emphasize the need to work for peace and the evils of violence. For example, John Paul II's 2000 World Day of Peace message insists:

> Wars generally do not resolve the problems for which they are fought and therefore, in addition to causing horrendous damage, they prove ultimately futile. War is a defeat for humanity. Only in peace and through peace can respect for human dignity and its inalienable rights be guaranteed.[48]

In the same address, however, John Paul II allows humanitarian intervention of a military kind: "Clearly when a civilian population risks being overcome by the attacks of an unjust aggressor and political efforts and nonviolent defense prove to be of no avail, it is legitimate and even obligatory to take concrete measures to disarm the aggressor."[49]

U.S. Bishops' Pastoral Letter

The 1983 pastoral letter of the U.S. bishops, *The Challenge of Peace: God's Promise and Our Response*, constitutes the most systematic and in-depth discussion of the peace and war issue, with special attention to deterrence. The bishops insisted from the beginning that their teaching would be more specific and concrete than the general papal and conciliar teaching. They also insisted, however, that the pastoral would be based on that teaching and not opposed to it. Their specific pruden-tial judgments and conclusions do not have the same authoritative teaching force as the restatement of universal moral principles and the more general teaching of the universal hierarchical magisterium (nn. 7–12, O-S, pp. 493–94).

The bishops recognize that individual Christians can follow a pacifist approach or a just war approach (nn. 111–121, O-S, pp. 517–18). They go further than earlier universal documents by insisting that from the earliest days of the church, moved by the example of Jesus' life and by his teaching, some Christians committed them-selves to a nonviolent lifestyle. The letter refers to an ongoing tradition of nonvio-lence in the church, despite some hesitancy from the Vatican about such an asser-tion.[50] The letter cites *Gaudium et spes* to support its position but leaves out the condition for nonviolence in the Vatican II document—"provided that this can be done without injury to the rights and duties of others or of the community itself" (n. 78, O-S, p. 220). The bishops also reiterate their call, which they first made in 1968, for the acceptance of selective conscientious objection in the United States.

The pastoral claims that the approaches of pacifism and just war are interde-pendent and complementary (nn. 120–21, O-S, p. 518). They are complementary from an ecclesiological perspective in that both positions can and should exist within the church. I do not see, however, how the two positions are complementa-ry from an ethical perspective. There is some overlap, but the two positions are ethically opposed.[51]

The letter spells out in detail the conditions of just war theory (nn. 80–110, O-S, pp. 510–17), but it focuses on the use of nuclear weapons and nuclear deter-rence—which was the primary debate in the United States at the time. Thus, the bishops' whole concern is the *ius in bello* aspects of the just war theory.

With regard to the use of nuclear weapons, the letter develops its position in three steps. Step one condemns the use of nuclear weapons or any weapon used against population centers or predominantly civilian targets—what has been called countercity warfare. The bishops reiterate the teaching of *Gaudium et spes* that is based on the principle of discrimination or noncombatant immunity (nn. 147–49, O-S, p. 524).

The second step maintains, "We do not perceive any situation in which the deliberate initiation of nuclear warfare, on however restricted a scale, can be morally justified" (n. 150, O-S, p. 524). Here the bishops condemn the first use of smaller or tactical counterforce nuclear weapons on the basis of the principle of proportionality. The chances of keeping such a nuclear use limited are remote because escalation will be inevitable. Thus, the danger of an all-out nuclear war is disproportionate to the potential good to be achieved by the first use of limited counterforce nuclear weapons. This position logically calls for the need for a defense system that is based on conventional weapons (nn. 150–56, O-S, pp. 524–26).

The third step deals with what is called retaliatory (as distinguished from first use), counterforce (as distinguished from countercity) use. The letter recognizes that the "issue at stake is the *real* as opposed to the *theoretical* possibility of a 'limited nuclear exchange'" (n. 157, O-S, p. 526). In light of all of the problems in keeping such a war limited, the letter insists that the "burden of proof remains on those who assert that meaningful limitation is possible" (n. 159, O-S, p. 527). This position amounts to a reluctant noncondemnation of the retaliatory use of counterforce nuclear weapons. The bishops do not absolutely close the door on such use.

The reason the bishops leave open the possibility of retaliatory counterforce nuclear use has to do with their position on deterrence. With regard to deterrence, the bishops—following John Paul II—propose "a strictly conditioned moral acceptance of nuclear deterrence," which is not adequate as a long-term basis for peace (n. 186, O-S, p. 533). The general conclusion of some limited deterrence remains fundamentally the same throughout the different drafts of the letter, although these drafts contain different rationales for this conclusion.[52] In the final document, two fundamental considerations guide the approach. First, the bishops remain essentially in accord with John Paul II's position in his message to the special session of the United Nations in 1982: "In current conditions 'deterrence' based on balance certainly not as an end in itself but as a step on the way toward a progressive disarmament, may still be judged morally acceptable" (n. 173, O-S, p. 530). Throughout the process, the bishops were opposed to unilateral nuclear disarmament. Second, the bishops accept the moral principle that one cannot threaten to do what is morally wrong because it involves an evil intention to do the morally wrong. Thus, one cannot threaten or deter with counterpopulation and countercity weapons. Nuclear use and deterrence are clearly linked because one cannot threaten to do what is morally wrong (n. 178, O-S, p. 531).

Deterrence is a complex and difficult issue not only in itself but also with regard to its ethical grounding. The bishops have ruled out a bluff strategy that claims that countercity deterrence does not necessarily involve the intention to do evil. They have tied use and deterrence closely, with the result that they could not condemn all use if they still wanted to allow some deterrence. This approach helps to explain their noncondemnation of retaliatory counterforce nuclear use.[53] First use of counterforce nuclear weapons is excluded on the likelihood of disproportionate and unlimited war following from it. Retaliatory counterforce use seems to involve the same problems and dangers, however. Note how the papal and conciliar statements avoid these problems by never explicitly condemning countercity deterrence and by not explicitly accepting the principle that countercity deterrence involves the immoral intention to do what is morally wrong.

The pastoral letter then spells out three basic consequences for deterrence—which, like their condemnation of any first use of counterforce nuclear weapons, challenged official U.S. policy. First, counterforce deterrence has the limited goal of preventing the use of nuclear weapons, not prevailing in a nuclear war. Second, sufficiency to deter rather than nuclear superiority remains the basic criterion. Third, nuclear deterrence is a step on the way to progressive disarmament and must be judged accordingly. Further casuistry in the letter develops other prudential judgments about counterforce deterrence (nn. 187–99, O-S, pp. 533–35). Parts 3 and 4 of the letter insist on the need for all people to work for peace and call for changes of heart and education on a personal level and structural changes in the political and international orders. The letter acknowledges the problem, however, that there is no international public authority with the capacity to shape and ensure our mutual interdependence today (nn. 241–44, O-S, pp. 544–45).

Critics disagreed with the U.S. bishops' pastoral letter from the left and the right. From the left, some critics advocated a strongly pacifist position and unilateral nuclear disarmament.[54] The ethical school headed by Germain Grisez and John Finnis argued for the need for unilateral nuclear disarmament on moral grounds.[55] On the right, Catholic neoconservatives such as Michael Novak and George Weigel argued that the bishops' letter was too critical of U.S. defense policies and did not fully appreciate the serious threat of communism.[56]

Despite some ethical and methodological differences, the main lines of official Catholic teaching on peace and war today are clear. Individuals may support pacifism or a limited just war approach. All people are called to work for peace that involves a change of heart as well as a change of political and international structures, although the documents never indicate how these effective structures are to come into existence. A strong presupposition against violence has become even stronger in the past half-century. In this imperfect world, however, nations—as a last resort—can use limited violence in defense against aggression. Nations and people today too readily and quickly resort to war and violence, however. War and violence can never bring about true peace; at best they can only eliminate in a negative way one of the problems standing in the way of true peace.

NOTES

1. For the classical neoscholastic work on the state in Catholic social thought, see Henrich A. Rommen, *The State in Catholic Thought: A Treatise in Political Philosophy* (St. Louis: B. Herder, 1947). For an influential mid–twentieth-century approach to the state, see Jacques Maritain, *Man and the State* (Chicago: University of Chicago Press, 1951).

2. For the concept of the Noachic covenant and its ramifications, see Helmut Thielicke, *Theological Ethics*, vol. 1, *Foundations* (Philadelphia: Fortress, 1966), 147, 349, 439–40, 570–72, and 656; Helmut Thielicke, *Theological Ethics* vol. 2, *Politics* (Philadelphia: Fortress, 1969), 16, 165–66, and *passim*.

3. Thielicke, *Theological Ethics: Foundations*, 141–46, 272–73, 277–78.

4. Karl Barth, *Eine Schweizer Stimme, 1938–1945* (Zurich: Evangelischer Verlag, 1948), cited in William H. Lazareth, "Luther's 'Two Kingdoms' Ethic Reconsidered," in *Christian Social Ethics in a Changing World*, ed. John C. Bennett (New York: Association, 1966), 119–20.

5. Lazareth, *Christian Social Ethics in a Changing World*, 119–31.

6. Contemporary Lutheranism, like contemporary Roman Catholicism, has evolved somewhat different understandings of the state. See, e.g., Karl H. Hertz, ed., *Two Kingdoms and One World: A Sourcebook in Christian Ethics* (Minneapolis: Augsburg, 1976).

7. Thomas Aquinas, *Ia*, q. 96, a. 4; on law as an ordering of reason, see *IaIIae*, q. 90.

8. For a Catholic opposition to such individualism, see Johannes Messner, *Social Ethics:*

Natural Law in the Western World, rev. ed. (St. Louis: B. Herder, 1964), 125–27.

9. Messner and other Catholic thinkers associate such an individualistic approach with Thomas Hobbes, John Locke, David Hume, and Jean Jacques Rousseau. See Messner, *Social Ethics*, 209–17.

10. Robert N. Bellah et al., *The Good Society* (New York: Alfred A. Knopf, 1991), 79–81, 133–44.

11. John S. Brubacher and Willis Rudy, with new chapters by Willis Rudy, *Higher Education in Transition: A History of American Colleges and Universities* (New Brunswick, N.J.: Transaction, 1997).

12. Fred Kammer, "The Pluralism Diamond," *Social Thought* 14 (spring 1988): 23–36. For an analysis of faith-based initiatives, see Fred Kammer, "Public-Religious Partnerships," *America* 184, no. 11 (April 2, 2001): 6–10.

13. Messner, *Social Ethics*, 96–150.

14. Zalba, *Theologiae Moralis Summa*, vol. 1, 329–595.

15. For this statement and a book-length commentary on it by its primary author, see John A. Ryan, *Social Reconstruction* (New York: Macmillan, 1920).

16. For a survey of reactions to *Mater et magistra*, with special emphasis on socialization, see Donald R. Campion, "*Mater et magistra* and its Commentators," *Theological Studies* 24 (1963): 1–52.

17. For a study of the use and importance of solidarity in church documents, especially in the writings of John Paul II, see Bilgrien, *Solidarity*.

18. George Weigel, "The Neo-Conservative Difference: A Proposal for the Renewal of Church and Society," *Pro Ecclesia* 4, no. 2 (spring 1995): 190–211.

19. George Weigel, "Catholicism and Democracy: The 'Other Twentieth Century Revolution,'" in *Morality and Religion in Liberal Democratic Societies*, ed. Gordon L. Anderson and Morton A. Kaplan (New York: Paragon, 1992), 223–50.

20. Peter Steinfels, "The Failed Encounter: The Catholic Church and Liberalism in the Nineteenth Century," in *Catholicism and Liberalism*, 19–44.

21. Pope Leo XIII, *Immortale Dei*, n. 36, in Gilson, *The Church Speaks to the Modern World*, 177.

22. Ibid., n. 36, p. 378.

23. John F. Cronin, *Social Principles in Economic Life*, rev. ed. (Milwaukee: Bruce, 1964), 281; Heinrich A. Rommen, "The State," *New Catholic Encyclopedia*, vol. 13, 652–53.

24. Paul E. Sigmund, "Catholicism and Liberal Democracy," in *Catholicism and Liberalism*, 217–41.

25. Weigel, *Morality and Religion*, 223–50.

26. John P. Hittinger, "Jacques Maritain and Yves R. Simon's Use of Thomas Aquinas in Their Defense of Liberal Democracy," in *Thomas Aquinas and his Legacy*, ed. David M. Gallagher (Washington, D.C.: Catholic University of America Press, 1994), 149–72; Michael Novak, "Human Dignity, Human Rights," *First Things*, no. 97 (November 1999): 39–42; Michael Novak, "The Achievement of Jacques Maritain," *First Things*, no. 8 (December 1990): 39–44; Paul E. Sigmund, "Maritain on Politics," in *Understanding Maritain: Philosopher and Friend*, ed. Deal W. Hudson and Matthew J. Mancini (Macon, Ga.: Mercer University Press, 1987), 153–70.

27. Pope Pius XII, "1944 Christmas Message," in *The Pope Speaks: The Teachings of Pope Pius XII*, ed. Michael Chinigo (New York: Pantheon, 1957), 292–99.

28. Weigel, *Morality and Religion*, 238–46. For a more negative evaluation, see Peter Hebblethwaite, "The Vatican's Latin American Policy," in *Church and Politics in Latin America*, ed. Dermot Keogh (New York: St. Martin's, 1990), 49–64.

29. Nathalie Gagnere, "The Return of God and the Challenge of Democracy: The Catholic Church in Central Eastern Europe," *Journal of Church and State* 35 (1993): 859–84.

30. See Douglass and Hollenbach, *Catholicism and Liberalism*.

31. Pope John Paul II, "*Veritatis splendor*," *Origins* 23 (1993): 297–334. For my analysis and criticism of this encyclical, see Charles E. Curran, "*Veritatis Splendor*: A Revisionist Perspective," in the *Historical Development of Fundamental Moral Theology in the United States: Readings in Moral Theology No. 11*, ed. Charles E. Curran and Richard A. McCormick (New York: Paulist, 1999), 242–66.

32. John Courtney Murray made the American proposition the basis for his understanding of political society in the United States. See *We Hold These Truths: Catholic Reflections on the American Proposition* (New York: Sheed and Ward, 1960).

33. Hans Küng and Karl-Josef Kuschel, eds., *A Global Ethic: The Declaration of the Parliament of the World's Religions* (New York: Continuum, 1993). For my analysis of this declaration, see Charles E. Curran, "The Global Ethic," *The Ecumenist* 37, no. 2 (spring 2000): 7–10.

34. For some of the more significant contemporary studies of the content of the common good, see James Donahue and M. Theresa Moser, eds., *Religion, Ethics, and the Common Good*, annual publication of College Theology Society, vol. 41 (Mystic, Conn.: Twenty-Third Publications, 1996); David Hollenbach, "The Common Good Revisited," *Theological Studies* 50 (1989): 70–94; Michael Novak, *Free Persons and the Common Good* (Lanham, Md.: Madison, 1988); Brian Stiltner, *Religion and the Common Good:*

Catholic Contributions to Building Community in a Liberal Society (Lanham, Md.: Rowman & Littlefield, 1999); Oliver F. Williams and John W. Houck, eds., *The Common Good and U.S. Capitalism* (Lanham, Md.: University Press of America, 1987).

35. Jacques Maritain, *The Person and the Common Good* (Notre Dame, Ind.: University of Notre Dame Press, 1966), 47–89.

36. Charles de Koninck, *De la primauté du bien commun* (Quebec: Éditions de l'Université Laval et Montreal: Fides, 1943): Jules A. Baisnée, "Two Catholic Critiques of Personalism," *Modern Schoolman* 22 (1944–1945): 59–74; I. Th. Eschmann, "In Defense of Jacques Maritain," *Modern Schoolman* 22 (1944–1945): 183–208; Charles de Koninck, "In Defense of St. Thomas: A Reply to Father Eschmann's Attack on the Primacy of the Common Good," *Laval théologique et philosophique* 1, no. 2 (1945): 9–109; Yves R. Simon, "On the Common Good," *Review of Politics* 6 (1944): 530–33. For a contemporary discussion and defense of Maritain's position, see Stiltner, *Religion and the Common Good.*

37. For an overview of Catholicism and just war, see J. Bryan Hehir, "The Just War Ethic and Catholic Theology: Dynamics of Change and Continuity," in *War or Peace? The Search for New Answers*, ed. Thomas A. Shannon (Maryknoll, N.Y.: Orbis, 1980), 15–39.

38. John F. Pollard, *The Unknown Pope: Benedict XV (1914–1922) and the Pursuit of Peace* (London, Geoffrey Chapman, 1999).

39. Margherita Marchione, *Pope Pius XII: Architect for Peace* (New York: Paulist, 2000).

40. For an ethical analysis of Pius XII's position on just war, see Murray, *We Hold These Truths*, 249–73; see also J. Bryan Hehir, "The Just War," in *War or Peace?*, 17.

41. For a discussion of this erroneous translation, see Paul Ramsey, *The Just War: Force and Political Responsibility* (New York: Charles Scribner's Sons, 1968), 78.

42. Pope Paul VI, "Address to the General Assembly of the United Nations (October 4, 1965)," in *The Gospel of Peace and Justice: Catholic Social Teaching since Pope John*, ed. Joseph Gremillion (Maryknoll, N.Y.: Orbis, 1976), 383, n. 19.

43. Ibid., p. 384, n. 23.

44. All of the "World Day of Peace Messages" are available on the Vatican website at www.vatican/va/holy_father/paul_vi/messages/peace/index.

45. For an overview of John Paul II's teaching on peace and war before 1989, see J. Bryan Hehir, "Catholic Teaching on War and Peace: The Decade 1979–1989," in *Moral Theology: Challenges for the Future: Essays in Honor of Richard A. McCormick, S.J.*, ed. Charles E. Curran (New York: Paulist, 1990), 359–64.

46. Pope John Paul II, "Letter to President Bush Urging the Avoidance of War in the Persian Gulf," *Origins* 20 (1991): 534–35; *Centesimus annus*, n. 52, O-S, p. 478.

47. Pope John Paul II, "We Are Not Pacifists," *Origins* 20 (1991): 625.

48. Pope John Paul II, "World Peace Day Message: Peace on Earth to Those Whom God Loves," *Origins* 29 (1999), n. 3, p. 451.

49. Ibid., n. 11, p. 452.

50. Jan Schotte, "Rome Consultation on Peace and Disarmament: A Vatican Synthesis," *Origins* 12 (1983): 691–95.

51. See Kenneth R. Himes, O.F.M., "Pacifism and the Just War Tradition in Roman Catholic Social Teaching," in *One Hundred Years of Catholic Social Thought: Celebration and Challenge*, ed. John A. Coleman (Maryknoll, N.Y.: Orbis, 1991), 339–42.

52. For the different approaches to deterrence in the three drafts, see Charles E. Curran, *Critical Concerns in Moral Theology* (Notre Dame, Ind.: University of Notre Dame Press, 1984), 132–40; for differences between the pastoral letters of the U.S. and West German bishops,

see Charles E. Curran, *Tensions in Moral Theology* (Notre Dame, Ind.: University of Notre Dame Press, 1988), 138–61.

53. The majority of the bishops, near the end of their discussion, did not understand the intricate relationship between use and deterrence. The final meeting of the bishops at first passed an amendment opposed to any use of nuclear weapons. Later in the meeting they rescinded their amendment because logically they would have been forced to espouse unilateral nuclear disarmament. See Jim Castelli, *The Bishops and the Bomb: Waging Peace in a Nuclear Age* (Garden City, N.Y.: Image, 1983), 169–70.

54. Gordon Zahn, "The Church's 'New Attitude toward War,'" in *Questions of Special Urgency: The Church in the Modern World, Two Decades after Vatican II,* ed. Judith A. Dwyer (Washington, D.C.: Georgetown University Press, 1986), 203–20.

55. John Finnis, Joseph M. Boyle, Jr., and Germain Grisez, *Nuclear Deterrence, Morality, and Realism* (New York: Oxford University Press, 1987).

56. Michael Novak, *Moral Clarity in the Nuclear Age* (Nashville, Tenn.: T. Nelson, 1983); George Weigel, *Tranquillitas Ordinis: The Present Failure and Future Promise of American Catholic Thought on War and Peace* (New York: Oxford University Press, 1987), especially 257–85.

CHAPTER 6

The Economic Order

In this chapter I consider the economic aspects of Catholic social teaching. Again, the basic anthropology of the human person who is sacred and social influences all that is said about the economic order. Here, too, historical development has occurred within the body of Catholic social teaching, and occasions for the document (e.g., to refute socialism, to deal with the problems of the developing world, to commemorate the anniversary of a previous document) have colored the approach. In this chapter I discuss four aspects of the economic order: the meaning and purpose of material goods in relation to human possession and use, the preferential option for the poor, the understanding of justice, and Catholic social teaching's approach to the opposed economic systems of Marxism and capitalism.

MATERIAL GOODS AND WEALTH

John Paul II has summarized well the contemporary approach of Catholic social teaching to material goods and wealth. Chapter 4 of *Centesimus annus* (1991) is titled "Private Property and the Universal Destiny of Material Goods" (nn. 30–43, O-S, pp. 461–72). *Sollicitudo rei socialis* (1987) maintains,

> It is necessary to state once more the characteristic principle of Christian social doctrine: The goods of this world are *originally meant for all*. The right to private property is *valid and necessary*, but it does not nullify the value of this principle. Private property, in fact, is under a "social mortgage" which means that it has an intrinsically

social function, based upon and justified precisely by the principle of the universal destiny of goods (n. 42, O-S, p. 426).

Leo XIII on Private Property

John Paul II discusses the meaning and purpose of material goods and wealth in the context of private property because at the beginning of Catholic social teaching, Leo XIII strongly emphasized the right to private property. In his opposition to socialism, Leo XIII maintained at the very beginning of *Rerum novarum* (1891), "But all agree, and there can be no question whatever, that some remedy must be found, and quickly found, for the misery and wretchedness which press so heavily at this moment on the large majority of the very poor" (n. 2, O-S, p. 15). Leo XIII mentions and rejects the socialist solution's "endeavor to destroy private property, and maintain that individual possessions should become the common property of all, to be administered by the State or by municipal bodies. . . ." These proposals are emphatically unjust, make workers themselves suffer, and give too much power to the state (n. 3, O-S, p. 15).

PRIVATE PROPERTY IN RERUM NOVARUM

When a person engages in remunerative labor, the very reason and motivation of working is to obtain property—to have the power of disposal of it and to hold it as one's own: "Everyone has by nature the right to possess property as one's own" (n. 5, O-S, p. 16). This characteristic distinguishes human beings from animals. Human beings alone have reason and must provide for themselves and their families; to do so, human beings need stable and permanent possession of things.

> Now, when a human being thus spends the industry of one's mind and the strength of body in procuring the fruits of nature by that act the individual makes one's own that portion of nature's field which one cultivates—that portion on which one leaves, as it were, the impress of one's own personality, and it cannot but be just that one should possess that portion as one's own, and should have a right to keep it without molestation (n. 7, O-S, p. 17).

Again we have another proof that private ownership is in accord with nature's law.

Leo XIII insists that the principle of private ownership is "found in the study of nature and in the law of nature herself" (n. 8, O-S, p. 17). In dealing with the immediate problem of the plight of the worker, his argument makes sense. Possession of private property enables workers to provide for themselves and their families. There are some curious aspects to this line of argument, however. First, Leo XIII's argument is based heavily on an agrarian and preindustrial understanding of human existence.

> For the soil which is tilled and cultivated with toil and skill utterly changes its condition; it was wild before, it is now fruitful; it was barren, and now it brings forth fruit in abundance. . . . As effects follow their cause, so it is just and right that the results of labor should belong to the one who has labored (n. 8, p. 17).

The emphasis on agrarian labor does not deal with the reality of the situation in the midst of the Industrial Revolution.

Leo XIII's reasoning deals well with the problem of the plight of the individual worker. He does not directly address another aspect of the problem that is even greater, however: abuse of private property on the part of owners and capitalists.

Leo emphasizes labor as the title to acquire private property. Such an approach is altogether appropriate in dealing with the rights of workers. Again, however, he does not discuss the broader picture and the uses of private property. What about abuses connected with inheritance and unfair advantage in acquiring private property in other ways?

LEO XIII AND THOMAS AQUINAS

Perhaps the most curious aspect of Leo XIII's approach to private property concerns the relationship to the approach of Thomas Aquinas. Leo XIII called for the imposition of Thomistic philosophy and theology in the Catholic world, so one would expect his teaching on private property to be in accord with that of Thomas Aquinas. Such is not the case, however.

Aquinas discusses private property in two articles in the second part of the *Summa*. The first article asks whether it is rational for human beings to possess material goods. A twofold distinction follows. With regard to the nature of external or material goods, external goods depend on the God that created them and are not subordinate to human will or desire. God is the owner of everything that is created. With regard to their use, human beings have a natural dominion over external goods because as rational creatures made in the image and likeness of God, human beings must use external goods to achieve their own ends.[1]

A second question then asks, however, if human beings have the right to possess something as one's own with the power of procuring and disposing of it as one wants. Again Aquinas makes a distinction. With regard to the dominion or power of procuring and disposing of things as one's own, Aquinas offers three reasons to support this right. First, people are more solicitous to care for things if they own them than if they are common property. (I remember an older Dominican teacher making the point by saying that European students in the 1950s used to cover their textbooks to preserve them—but nobody ever thought to put a cover on a library book!) Second, a more orderly and less confusing human existence results if everyone owns property as their own. Third, human life will be more tranquil and peaceful because each person will be content with her or his own possessions. Then, however, Aquinas writes about the use of external or material goods, as distinguished from ownership. Human beings are to use their goods as though they are common and not proper because these goods should serve the needs of all. Thus, Aquinas clearly distinguishes between two kinds of dominion: a general dominion that belongs to all human beings to use external goods to achieve their needs and fulfillment and a specific type of dominion that we know today as the system of private property, which Aquinas accepts for the reasons given. Use of this right of private property is limited by the common aspect of material goods.[2]

In *Rerum novarum* Leo XIII recognizes that "God has given the earth to the use and enjoyment of the universal human race," but this assertion does not deny that there can be private property (n. 6, O-S, p. 16). Leo XIII strongly insists that private property in the strict sense is a postulate of human nature and natural law. Whereas Aquinas used the argument that the very nature of rational human beings means that they must provide for themselves through generic dominion of all to use external goods, Leo uses the same basic argument to make the more specific point of justifying a system of private property. Aquinas justified private property in the strict sense not on the basis of human nature as such but on the basis of historical conditions of human existence in this sinful world that make it better to have private property.

Aquinas says explicitly that private property or owning things as one's own is not against natural law but has been added to natural law by the requirements of human reason.[3] Why does he maintain that the specific form of private property is not based on natural law as such but has been added to it? Aquinas was very cognizant of the teaching of the early church that understood this specific notion of private property to be based primarily on human sinfulness, not on human nature as such. Elsewhere Aquinas approvingly cites Isidore of Seville's assertion that common possession of all things and the freedom of all human beings are matters of natural law. In Aquinas's day, however, both private property and slavery existed. Had natural law changed? No. Something can be said to belong to natural law in two ways: because nature inclines to it or because nature does not command the contrary. An example of the second type is the fact that by natural law, human beings were naked. Nature did not give human beings clothing, but human reason and artifice regarded clothing as more useful for human beings. In this context, Aquinas argues that natural law has been changed not by going against it but only by adding something to it.[4]

What is the ultimate reason, however, that Isidore claimed that common possession of all things and the human freedom of all persons were requirements of natural law? According to Isidore, private property and slavery came into existence not because of human nature but because of human sinfulness. Earlier in the *Summa*, Aquinas explicitly accepts this position. He had maintained that even without sin there would still have been a need for political authority and the state.[5] Aquinas held, however, that in the state of innocence there would have been no need for the right of private property in the strict sense. In the present, with the existence of sin, division of possessions is necessary because common possession would be an occasion of discord. In the state of innocence, however, human beings could live in perfect harmony in using common possessions. One can even see this possibility today among some good people.[6] The right of private property in the strict sense owes its origin to human sinfulness. The three reasons Aquinas proposes in his defense of the strict right to private property all result from human sinfulness. If there were no sin, these reasons would not be present.[7]

Thus, Leo XIII absolutizes the strict right to private property and sees only its use limited by what we call today the universal destiny of the goods of creation to serve the needs of all. On the other hand, Aquinas regards the strict right to private property not as an absolute based on human nature but as resulting from human sinfulness. This right is subordinate to and instrumental in the service of the universal destiny of the goods of creation to serve the needs of all. For this reason, Aquinas holds that a person in extreme necessity can legitimately take from another the material goods that he or she needs. This action is not theft because in necessity all things are common.[8] The strict right to private property is limited by the more generic intention that the goods of creation serve the needs of all. Not just the use of private property is limited by the universal common destiny.[9]

How did Leo XIII come to accept the changed understanding that absolutized the strict right to private property and defend it on the basis of human nature as such? Commentators point to the role of Italian Jesuit Luigi Taparelli d'Azeglio, one of the founders of the neoscholastic movement in Italy in the nineteenth century.[10] Taparelli was the first rector of the restored Jesuit Roman College in 1824, an influential contributor to the Jesuit journal *Civiltà Cattolica*, and the person who converted young seminarian Gioacchino Pecci—the future Pope Leo XIII—to the

Thomism that Leo XIII later championed in what is often called today neoscholasticism.[11] Taparelli d'Aezglio also was a mentor and collaborator of the Jesuit Matteo Liberatore, who wrote the first draft of *Rerum novarum*.[12] According to Léon de Sousberghe, it remains certain that the thesis of the natural right of private property in the strict sense made its solemn and definitive entry into neoscholastic literature and Catholic teaching with Taparelli. This is not the position of Aquinas, however.[13] Many commentators regard such a position as much closer to John Locke than to Aquinas.[14]

Robert E. Sullivan has proposed an intriguing thesis regarding *Rerum novarum*'s teaching on private property. Sullivan readily approves of the natural law argument for private property in *Rerum novarum* and regards this natural law right to property as an idea on which modern civil society and its freedoms depend. In keeping with the approach of much of official Catholicism at the time, Leo XIII actually accommodated himself to the present condition by asserting that this position already had been a part of the perennial Catholic tradition. Sullivan refers to the myth that there was a Catholic tradition whose theological and institutional coherence was free of discontinuity, tension, and ambiguity. This was the myth proposed by Leo in *Aeterni Patris* (1879) making Thomism *the* Catholic philosophy and theology with the power to renew civilization.[15]

In the United States context in the beginning of the twentieth century, John A. Ryan proposed an understanding of private property that was closer to the thought of Aquinas and emphasized the instrumental nature of private property in the strict sense. Ryan was the foremost proponent of Catholic social ethics in the United States in the first half of the twentieth century. His doctoral dissertation had dealt with the living wage.[16] His 1916 *Distributive Justice*, limiting discussion of private property to the ownership of land, begins by insisting that the goods of creation exist to serve the needs of all human beings. Ryan goes on to accept ownership of private property in a strict sense as a natural right of the third class. A right of the first class has as its object that which is an intrinsic good, such as the right to life. A right of the second class has as its object that which is directly necessary for the individual, such as the right to marry. A right of the third class has as its object not that which is directly necessary for the individual but what is indirectly necessary for the individual because it is necessary as a social institution providing for the general welfare. Ryan recognizes that his argument that private property best contributes to the general welfare of all is an empirical argument that is based on consequences, not an absolute demand of human nature as such. In Ryan's judgment, the right to private property is certainly valid against complete socialism but only probably valid against modified forms of common ownership. Ryan's approach is more in the spirit of Aquinas and his instrumental understanding that private property best serves the needs of all and the common welfare.[17]

Developments after Leo XIII

In *Quadragesimo anno* (1931) Pius XI introduces his discussion of private property by claiming to defend Leo XIII against the calumny that he upheld the wealthier class against the proletariat. Pius XI asserts that Leo did not deny the twofold character of property—individual and social—which thus avoids the opposite extremes of individualism and collectivism (nn. 44–46, O-S, pp. 51–52). Although Pius XI still regards private property in the strict sense as a right given to human beings by nature and the Creator and denies that the right to private property and its use are bound by the same limits, he recognizes "boundaries imposed by the requirements of social life upon the right of ownership itself or upon its use" (n. 48, O-S, p. 52). The latter concept opens the door to regarding ownership as somewhat instrumental and limited by the social aspect of property. Pius XI emphasizes the social dimension of property more than Leo XIII, who in the context of providing private property for all workers emphasized the individual aspect of property. Pius XI also goes on to discuss the titles of ownership, including first occupancy and work or industry, claiming that this is the teaching of tradition and of Leo XIII. Leo XIII emphasized only labor or industry in *Rerum novarum*, however. It is more than curious that Pius XI provides no footnote to where first occupancy as a title is found in Leo XIII (n. 52, O-S, pp. 53–54). Pius XI claims there is no difference between his approach to private property and that of Leo XIII. Such claims for absolute continuity and no discontinuity are not only defensive but they tend to undermine the credibility of Catholic social teaching.

In *Mater et magistra* (1961) John XXIII continues to affirm that private property, including ownership of the means of production, is permanently valid and rooted in the very nature of things (n. 109, O-S, p. 101). Earlier, however, the encyclical insisted that the right of every human being to use material goods for their own sustenance is prior to the right of private ownership (n. 43, O-S, p. 90). In addition, this encyclical brings the understanding of property into the context of industrial society by recognizing that social security and professional skills and training are most important for individuals (n. 104–108, O-S, p. 101). *Mater et magistra* also calls for effective distribution of private property through all ranks of citizenry (n. 113, O-S, p. 102). In keeping with the principle of socialization, the document recognizes an expanded role for the state and public ownership as demanded by the common good but limited by the principle of subsidiarity (n. 117, O-S, p. 103).

Gaudium et spes (1965) proposes a general and more theoretical discussion of material goods that does not address a particular problem, as did *Rerum novarum* and earlier documents. As a result, it could offer a more thorough discussion of its general understanding and not begin from a particular perspective. *Gaudium et spes* begins its discussion of socioeconomic life by recalling the twofold character of anthropology, pointing out some aspects of the present economic scene but then recognizing the dangers created by the many inequalities in our world today (with many people lacking the necessities of life). The situation calls for economic development that is based on certain principles governing socioeconomic life. Central among these principles is the common purpose of created things (nn. 63–66, O-S, pp. 208–11).

> God intended the earth and all that it contains for the use of every human being and people. Thus, as all people follow justice and unite in charity, created goods should abound for them on a reasonable basis. Whatever the forms of ownership may be, as adapted to the legitimate institutions of people according to diverse and changeable circumstances, attention must always be paid to the universal purpose for which created goods are meant. In using them, therefore, a person should regard one's lawful possessions not merely as one's own but also as common property in the sense that they should accrue to the benefit of not only oneself but of others. For the rest, the right to have a share of earthly goods sufficient for oneself and for one's family belongs to everyone (n. 69, O-S, pp. 212–13).

In accord with this document, the first and most important aspect of material goods is the common purpose of created goods to serve the needs of all. Although the document upholds private property as an expression of personality and an extension of human freedom, it makes no explicit claim for a natural law basis for private property. This right of private control or ownership is subject to the common purpose of created things. In this light, the document calls for the expropriation of large underdeveloped estates on the basis of the demands of the common good—but requiring just compensation (n. 71, O-S, pp. 214–15).[18]

Populorum progressio (1967) cites n. 69 from *Gaudium et spes* and immediately adds, "All other rights whatsoever, including those of property and free commerce, are to be subordinated to this principle. They should not hinder but on the contrary favor its application. It is a grave and urgent social duty to redirect them to their primary finality" (n. 22, O-S, p. 245). The next paragraph maintains,

"[P]rivate property does not constitute for anyone an absolute and unconditioned right" (n. 23, O-S, p. 245).

It is now clear that for contemporary Catholic social teaching, the first thing to be said about material goods is their common purpose and destiny to serve the needs of all. The absoluteness of private property is denied. In this life, private property must always be justified by how it relates to the destiny of the goods of creation to serve the needs of all. Private property is not the first and most important reality with regard to the understanding of material goods and wealth.

Since *Mater et magistra*, Catholic social teaching has recognized "the most pressing question of our day concerns the relationship between economically advanced commonwealths and those that are in process of development" (n. 157, O-S, p. 110). The concern of Catholic social teaching is now worldwide. In this worldwide context, the most fundamental principle insists that "the right to have a share of earthly goods, sufficient for oneself and one's family belongs to everyone" (*Gaudium et spes*, n. 69, O-S, p. 213).

A Problem

Contemporary Catholic social teaching grounds the universal and social destiny of the goods of creation in the doctrine of creation itself. God created the world to serve the needs of all of God's people, not just a few. God put into the world what is necessary to supply the basic needs of all who have been created. There is a significant problem, however, with such a grounding of the teaching that material goods exist to serve the needs of all. Such an approach betrays an older, more agriculturally based world and does not really deal with property and material goods as we know them today. The universal destiny of the goods of creation to serve the needs of all implies that the Creator put into the world natural resources that human beings could then tap into through their labor. These natural resources—such as earth, rain, and sun—provide the basic material that human beings use to produce food, clothing and shelter. Human beings cultivate the God-given natural resources to produce goods and wealth.

The production of material goods and wealth today, however, has little or no dependence on natural or created goods. The computer age only intensifies what has been happening in the past 200 years. The production of wealth depends primarily and to an overwhelming degree on human skills, creativity, and entrepreneurship, together with good old-fashioned hard work and discipline. Because the production of wealth and material goods does not depend on the natural goods of creation, the universal and social nature of material goods based on creation does not really apply to material goods and wealth produced today. With a greater emphasis on human creativity, co-creation, and entrepreneurship, it seems that the individual is more and more the source of what she or he makes or produces in terms of goods, services, and wealth.[19]

What can form the basis for the social aspect of the wealth and material goods that seem to be so much owed to individual initiative and creativity? An anthropology that highlights solidarity seems to be the best grounding for the social aspect of wealth. Such solidarity includes a threefold relationship with God; with other human beings, ultimately including all humanity; and with the world itself. Our relationship to God reminds us of our dependence on God. Life itself and even our talents are gifts from God. Think of our health. Yes, we are more conscious today of the responsibility to care for our health, but many aspects of our physical health are beyond our control. We did not make our bodies to our own specifications. Think of the fact that some people are born in developed countries and others in much poorer countries. Believers recognize that many of our talents come from God's gracious gifts. Even our creative actions participate in the creative act of God. We are co-creators. What seems to be our own creativity and initiative must be understood as dependent on God as well as our responsibility.

Solidarity also involves relationship with other human beings, which extends from the immediacy of the family to teachers, friends, fellow country people, and all people in the world. Again, believers regard themselves as sisters and brothers of all other human beings precisely because we are children of the one God who is mother and father of us all. We exist in solidarity with all those who, like us, bear in themselves the image of God. We recognize a special dependence on parents, spouses, families, friends, and others. Despite the significance of creativity and initiative, none of us can claim to be a self-made person. In solidarity we have received much from others.

Solidarity also reminds us of our union with and dependence on nature and the ecosystems of the world. There would be no life or possibility of creativity without the air we breathe. The earth and the world truly are the home where we live.

In the following section I develop our special solidarity with the poor and with the needy. Yes, most of the wealth and material goods produced today come from individual and group creativity and initiative, but because of who we are as sacred and social human beings, these material goods and wealth have a social dimension and continue to bear a relationship to God, neighbor, and the earth itself. In subsequent discussions of distributive justice and human rights I develop this basic reality of solidarity and strengthen the position that material goods and wealth have a social dimension to serve the needs of all.[20]

PREFERENTIAL OPTION FOR THE POOR

Solidarity from the Christian perspective involves solidarity with poor people. Contemporary Catholic social teaching considers this relationship to poor people in terms of a preferential option for the poor. In his rightly acclaimed book *Option for the Poor*, Donal Dorr uses this concept to describe the whole of Catholic social teaching, although he recognizes that the term itself came into common use only in the 1970s.[21] From the very beginning *Rerum novarum* maintains, "Still when there is question of protecting the rights of individuals, the poor and helpless have a claim to special consideration" (n. 29, O-S, p. 28).

The term itself first appeared in Catholic social teaching in the encyclicals of John Paul II. In *Sollicitudo rei socialis* he refers to "the option or love of preference for the poor" (n. 42, p. 425). Such usage shows a hesitancy to adapt the concept of the preferential option for the poor and the need to modify it by equating it with love for the poor. Preferential option and preferential love are not exactly the same thing. In *Centesimus annus* John Paul II insists that the teaching of *Rerum novarum* "is an excellent testimony to the continuity within the church of the so-called 'preferential option for the poor,' an option which I defined as a 'special form of primacy in the exercise of Christian charity'" (n. 11, O-S, p. 447). In a defensive way, John Paul II wants to offer his own understanding of the preferential option and to exaggerate the continuity in Catholic social teaching by claiming the preferential option for the poor as something always present in Catholic social teaching.

The U.S. bishops' economic pastoral regards the contemporary concept of the preferential option for the poor as having a basis in Scripture and the early church. This preferential option forms part of the biblical vision that guides economic life (n. 52, O-S, p. 591). In discussing the nation's priorities this pastoral letter asserts, "As individuals and as a nation, therefore, we are called to make a fundamental 'option for the poor'" (n. 87, O-S, p. 599). The bishops then discuss the question of the priorities of the nation on the basis of this option.

Origins of the Concept

Where does the phrase "option for the poor" come from, and what does it mean? The term arose in the context of liberation theology as developed originally in Latin

America and then in other parts of the world.[22] The concept of the option for the poor finds its roots and meaning in several different contexts.[23] First, a strong biblical base supports the option for the poor.[24] Here too, one sees that the option for the poor is not just a synonym for love for the poor. God has a special care and predilection for poor people. The Psalms and all of the literature of the Hebrew Bible constantly maintain that God hears the cry of poor people. God will protect poor people even though no one else seems to be concerned about them. God will defend poor people against the rich. The God of the Hebrew Bible stands up for poor people even if human beings trample them in the dust. Nowhere does the Hebrew Bible say that God hears the cry of the rich or protects them in a special way.

The preferential option for the poor also has strong Christological roots.[25] Jesus was a victim who was unjustly put to death on the cross. Jesus therefore identifies with all victims of marginalization, poverty, and injustice. The kenotic theory maintains that Jesus came down from heaven and even stripped himself of his divinity to become one with us. Thus, Jesus chose to be one with the poor and the outcast. In the scene at the synagogue in Nazareth in Luke's Gospel, Jesus proclaims the good news to poor people and liberation to captives.

Liberation theology's understanding of the option for the poor not only has Scriptural and Christological roots, it also has very strong epistemological roots.[26] Who is the best knower? Most of the Western tradition and the contemporary world of science and higher education have insisted that the ideal knower is a neutral, objective, and value-free observer who will be convinced only by facts. Prejudice and bias are totally negative. Even in the practical order, we recognize the need and importance of impartiality. Judges are to be impartial. Above all, jurors must be impartial. A partial juror who knows the accused or one of the attorneys will be dismissed. In theory and in practice, the ideal human knower is an objective, neutral, value-free, impartial observer of the human scene.

Liberation theologians of all stripes strongly criticize such an epistemological understanding.[27] We all bring our experience and our prejudices with us. A generation ago, history was thought to be an objective science that dealt only with historical facts. Today, however, we are conscious of the fact that history is written by the victors. If Native Americans were still the majority in this country, we would not be teaching that Columbus discovered America in 1492.

A moment's reflection indicates that no one can claim to be impartial, objective, neutral, and value-free. We all bring our own backgrounds and baggage with us. White males in this country claimed to be objective with a universal and all-embracing horizon. For a long time, however, they could not admit the humanity of black Americans. For the greater part of its existence, our country did not give women the right to vote.

Liberation theology begins with the recognition that God herself is prejudiced in favor of the poor. God is not neutral and value-free. We usually think that bias and prejudice are negative terms. The Judeo-Christian God, however, is prejudiced and biased in favor of poor people. So should Christians be prejudiced in favor of poor people. The obvious challenge of relating this prejudice or partiality to the larger epistemological issue of including all aspects of reality is analogous to the theological issue of reconciling God's preferential option for the poor with God's universal love for all.

Liberation theology's option for the poor is intimately connected with theological method. The primacy of praxis in liberation theology maintains that truth is obtained through reflection on liberating praxis.[28] Theological truth is not primarily derived from speculation and library research but from reflection on liberating praxis. The option for the poor also is the first step for theological method. Thus, liberation theology's method differs considerably from the traditional theological method of Christian and Catholic social ethics.

Liberation theology's option for the poor also involves commitment to a concrete way of social change. Too often in the past, change was regarded as occurring from the top down. Poor people now are to become subjects of their own history.[29] Juan Luis Segundo refers to people who are poor and oppressed as artisans of a new humanity.[30] Social change comes from the ground up, not from the top down. Poor people themselves will bring about the changes.

There can be no doubt that Catholic social teaching has learned the option for the poor from liberation theology. Yet the Vatican also has been critical of some aspects of liberation theology, such as too heavy a reliance on Marxism and politicization of faith brought about by a loss of transcendence and future eschatology. The second of the two documents issued by the Congregation for the Doctrine of the Faith in the 1980s was less critical of liberation theology than the first.[31] Liberation theologians have disputed these criticisms from the Congregation for the Doctrine of the Faith.[32] There have been not only theological tensions between the Vatican and liberation theology but also suspicion and criticism about what liberationists were doing in practice, especially in South America.[33] The myriad details of these tensions lie beyond the scope of this volume, however.

Everyone recognizes a great difference, however, between the method of Catholic social teaching and the method of liberation theology. By its very nature, Catholic social teaching employs a more universal approach addressed to a general worldwide audience, including all people of good will (or, in the case of the U.S. bishops, a particular country). The more theoretical approach and universalist perspective of Catholic social teaching differ greatly from the praxis approach and more particular perspective of liberation theology. Catholic social teaching also does not put as much emphasis on social change from the bottom up, with poor people as the bearers of social transformation. Again, the more universal approach will consider all of the agents involved in social change. Despite the manifest differences and even tensions between the two approaches, even many liberation theologians regard these differences and tensions as complementary and helpful rather than opposed.[34]

The pastoral letter on the economy implicitly recognizes the complementarity between the theoretical and universal approach of the document itself and a more practical grassroots approach with poor people being the agents of social transformation. In 1970 the U.S. bishops launched their Campaign for Human Development, which strongly supports community organizations that bring neighborhood groups together to improve their conditions and work for social justice on a local level. These organizations are ecumenical and interreligious, so they lack the spiritual and theological aspects of the base Christian communities involved in liberation theology. The approach of these community organizations is analogous, however, with the approach of liberation theology. The pastoral letter maintained, "Our experience with the Campaign for Human Development confirms our judgment about the validity of self-help and empowerment of the poor" (n. 357, O-S, p. 661).[35] Consequently, a methodology that emphasizes more theoretical and universal aspects can be compatible with a more praxis-oriented approach.

Further Elaboration

From theological, ethical, and epistemological perspectives, analogous questions arise about the option for the poor. Is such an option compatible with God's universal love for all people—even the sinner and the enemy (theological)? Does partiality in favor of poor people mean that ethics must treat people differently and no longer maintain an impartial respect for all (ethical)? Does the option for the poor deny other persons and aspects that must be considered by the knower (epistemological)? The general and preliminary answer to these three questions comes from the recognition in *Centesimus annus* and in the bishops' pastoral that we are dealing with a *preferential* option for the poor, not an exclusive option.

An exclusive option clearly raises problems on the theological, ethical, and epistemological levels. On the theological level, an exclusive option for the poor goes against the love of God for all, even sinners, but a preferential option would not. In biblical times, God loved all but still had a preferential option for the poor. On the ethical level, an exclusive option for the poor fails to recognize the intrinsic dignity and rights of all human beings—a universal aspect of all human beings, who must be treated the same way. A preferential option, however, does not deny the basic dignity and the rights of all. William O'Neill argues convincingly that the partiality of a preferential option for the poor is vindicated by the idea of impartiality itself. Impartiality or equal respect justifies preferential treatment for people whose rights are most in danger.[36] From an epistemological perspective, a preferential option does not necessarily exclude any aspects from consideration. There can be a danger that in starting with the experience of people who are poor and marginalized, one might not give enough consideration to other factors. A self-critical thinker, however, could overcome the possible dangers that would distort the epistemological reality. Although much work remains to be done in this area, the preferential option for the poor can be accepted from theological, ethical, and epistemological perspectives that are consonant with Catholic social ethics in general and Catholic social teaching in particular.[37]

The U.S. bishops recognize the theological, ethical, and especially epistemological or hermeneutical aspects of the preferential option in their pastoral letter on the economy. They point out the

> obligation to evaluate social and economic activity from the viewpoint of the poor and the powerless. . . . The "option for the poor," therefore, is not an adversarial slogan that pits one group or class against another. Rather it states that the deprivation and powerlessness of the poor wounds the whole community. . . . These wounds will be healed only by greater solidarity with the poor and among the poor themselves (nn. 87–88, pp. 599–600).

Thus, solidarity with poor people through a preferential option for the poor strengthens the true solidarity of all. Christians must look at the problems of the social order and their solutions primarily from the viewpoint of people who are poor and powerless.

On the basis of this preferential option for the poor, the U.S. bishops propose three priorities in economic decision making:

> a. The fulfillment of the basic needs of the poor is of the highest priority. . . . b. Increasing active participation in economic life by those who are presently excluded or vulnerable is a high social priority. . . . c. The investment of wealth, talent, and human energy should be specially directed to benefit those who are poor or economically insecure (nn. 90–92, p. 600).

In keeping with the bishops' approach, the first question we should ask when we consider any type of law or public policy is what effect will it have on poor people. Although this is not the only question that is to be asked—all other aspects must be considered—it is the first question. Think how greatly this attitude differs from the reality present in the United States today. Almost no one thinks of public policy primarily from the viewpoint of poor people. We have so many groups with their own political action committees who are concerned only with the good of their own profession or their own members. Unfortunately, there is no one to speak up for poor people. This is the role par excellence for the church and the community of the disciples of Jesus.

JUSTICE

Justice is an important value and principle for any society. Justice entails giving everyone their due.[38] How is justice determined, however, and what are the criteria of justice? One would expect Catholic social teaching to develop the meaning of justice in great length and detail. Surprisingly, however, these documents devote little attention to justice, its meaning, and its application. Although the documents of Catholic social teaching are not theoretical treatises written from a systematic perspective, one is still struck by the comparatively small discussion of justice found in these documents. Behind the few references to justice, however, stands the Thomistic and neoscholastic concept of justice, with its three different types: commutative, distributive, and legal.

General Approach to Justice

The early documents of Catholic social teaching are familiar with and obviously depend on this tradition in their few specific references to justice, although they do not deal in any detail with their understanding of justice. In a one paragraph discussion of justice, *Rerum novarum* specifically refers to distributive justice. This justice calls for rulers to be solicitous about the material welfare of all, especially poor people, so that they might be "housed, clothed, and enabled to support life" and thus share in the benefits they helped to create (n. 27, O-S, p. 27).

In *Quadragesimo anno* Pius XI refers to commutative justice as calling us "faithfully to respect the possessions of others, and not to invade the rights of another, by exceeding the bounds of one's own property" (n. 47, O-S, p. 52). This encyclical also refers to commutative justice as governing the relationship between capital and labor (n. 110, O-S. p. 66) and warns that commutative justice is absolutely necessary but not enough: Charity also is needed in society (n. 137, O-S, p. 74). *Quadragesimo anno* also develops the principle of just distribution (nn. 56–58, O-S, pp. 55–56). An innovation appears in *Quadragesimo anno*, however. On eight different occasions Pius XI introduces a new term: social justice. Following the encyclical, a cottage industry arose among Catholic scholars in an attempt to understand the exact meaning of social justice and its relationship to the neoscholastic understanding of justice.[39]

In the broadest sense, social justice includes all other social virtues that are demanded by the common good of society. It includes the three types of justice in the neoscholastic tradition: commutative, distributive, and legal. In the strict sense, social justice is the virtue that has as its formal object what is due to the common good in human society. Even Catholic commentators still do not agree, however, about the exact meaning of social justice as what is required by the common good. Some understand social justice as bringing together distributive and legal justice. Others regard it as a new type of justice that properly orders all societal institutions to facilitate the practice of commutative, distributive, and legal justice. The more common opinion identifies social justice with legal justice—what the individual owes to the common good.[40]

The documents of Catholic social teaching never become involved in this debate, and though the later papal documents often refer to justice, they never really explain what justice means or the different types of justice. *Justitia in mundo*, the 1971 document from the synod of bishops, might be expected to treat justice in great detail—in accord with its title and its first chapter on "Justice and World Society"—but it does not (O-S, pp. 289–92). The document seems to assume that all people can readily recognize the injustices in our world today. We are living in a very paradoxical situation. We are conscious of the basic equality and full human dignity of all human beings as the foundation of a just global society. Paradoxically, however, the forces of division and antagonism are gaining strength. The gap among people with regard to wealth, power, and decision making is growing—especially in the undeveloped world but even in the developed world. Human rights often are denied; many victims of injustice exist, and the environment is threatened by pollution and consumerism. *Justitia in mundo*, however, never develops any theoretical understanding of justice. A confirmatory recognition that Catholic social teaching has failed to develop an understanding of justice comes from the *New Dictionary of Catholic Social Thought*.[41] This rightly acclaimed reference work has no article on justice or any of the types of justice, such as distributive or social justice.

Only in the 1986 pastoral letter of the U.S. bishops do we find a brief theoretical consideration of the different types of justice and their requirements for society. The first of the ethical norms for economic life developed by the bishops concerns the responsibilities of social living, with special emphasis on the requirements of justice. Here the bishops' document develops the threefold aspect of justice—commutative, distributive, and social or contributive (nn. 68–76, O-S, pp. 595–96). The following analysis develops this threefold aspect of justice.[42]

This understanding of justice follows from a Catholic anthropology that recognizes the dignity and the social nature of the human person. There are three different types of justice, corresponding to three different types of relationships. Commutative justice involves the relationship between physical individuals or moral individuals such as corporations. In a sense, these are one-on-one relationships (although the "one" may be a corporation). Buying and selling of contracts or agreements among corporations illustrate commutative justice. The term "commutative" comes from *commutate,* the Latin word for exchange, and is Thomas Aquinas's word to describe Aristotle's position.[43]

Distributive justice governs the relationship of society or the state to the individual. How should society distribute its goods and burdens fairly among people? There is an obvious difference between society in general and the state, which in nontotalitarian societies is much less than the broader public society. This distinction is not important for the analysis here; I discuss it in greater depth in chapter 7.

Legal, social, or contributive justice governs what the individual owes to society. The older word "legal" referred primarily to the obligation to obey the just laws of society as the minimal requirement of the common good. The newer word "contributory" is in keeping with the present emphasis on the need for persons to actively participate in and contribute to the common good of society.

From a theoretical viewpoint, not everyone in the Catholic tradition agrees precisely with the foregoing understandings. Aquinas himself refers to legal justice not as a particular virtue governing the acts of the individual with regard to society and the common good but as a general virtue that directs all other virtues (e.g., social charity) to the good of society and the common good. In this broader understanding, legal justice has no particular acts of its own; it directs other virtues.[44] In practice, however, the differences are not great. Furthermore, in keeping with the most common opinion among Catholic commentators—though by no means the unanimous position—legal justice and social justice are used to describe the same relationship of the individual to society and the common good.

This theory of justice puts flesh on the anthropological skeleton of the human person as sacred and social. On the American scene—in keeping with the perennial danger of individualism—not enough attention is paid to distributive justice as will become evident in the next paragraphs.[45] The U.S. ethos often resists the demands of distributive justice and wants to understand all justice in terms of commutative justice.

Commutative justice deals with the private goods of individuals or groups, as in contracts of all kinds.[46] Commutative justice is blind, no respecter of persons, and involves arithmetic equality. For example, if I borrow $10 from you and $10 from Bill Gates, I owe each of you $10. It does not matter that he might have a little more money than you have! This justice is blind and does not consider the person. Arithmetic equality governs these transactions precisely because there is strict equivalence between the things considered, and the persons involved do not enter the equation. Ten dollars is $10 no matter whom I borrow it from. We often recognize that justice should be blind. Think of the traditional symbol of justice on the Supreme Court building in Washington—the blind woman holding the scale. Give this ancient symbol great credit for using a female figure to represent what often are legal and business transactions. Yet there also is a problem with this symbol. Commutative justice is blind, but other forms of justice are not. The blind person symbolizes only one aspect of justice and reminds us that the approach to justice in the United States, with its individualistic roots, wants to regard all of justice as blind. Distributive and legal justice are not blind.

Distribution of Goods

According to the traditional teaching, distributive justice differs from commutative justice and has different characteristics.[47] Distributive justice is not blind, does respect persons, and involves proportional rather than arithmetic equality. Because individual persons have their own identities, needs, and talents, society cannot be blind in distributing goods and burdens; it must consider the person in her or his particularity. Precisely because distributive justice regards the reality under consideration (e.g., medical care or amount of tax) in the context of the person and the common good, the quantity involved will differ from case to case. Thus, distributive justice involves proportional rather than arithmetic equality. Like legal or social justice, distributive justice presupposes the existence of the political community and the relationships of the community to citizens and members of the community.

Society in general distributes two things to its members: goods and burdens. I focus first on the distribution of material goods. What is a fair or just distribution of wealth or material goods in society? In the Catholic tradition, just distribution involves many different canons, norms, or titles. The fundamental canon of the distribution of material goods, however, is human need. *Centesimus annus* insists that "it is a strict duty of justice and truth not to allow fundamental human needs to remain unsatisfied . . ." (n. 34, O-S, p. 464). This basic criterion of human need rests on two foundations. First, in accordance with the dignity and sacredness of the human person, every human person by virtue of her or his humanity has the right to a minimally decent human existence. (I discuss human rights and their grounding in greater detail in chapter 7.) The second basis for the canon of need comes from the universal destiny of the goods of creation (now "material" goods) to serve the needs of all. The U.S. bishops' pastoral letter calls for "the establishment of a floor of material well-being on which all can stand. This is a duty of the whole of society and it creates particular obligations for those with greater resources" (n. 74, O-S, p. 596).

How this basic need and canon of distribution are fulfilled depends on many different persons and factors. The ordinary way for people to acquire material goods is through work. From the time of Leo XIII to the present, Catholic social teaching has insisted on a just wage—based on the demands of distributive justice, not commutative justice. "Wages, we are told, are fixed by free consent; and, therefore, the employer when he pays what was agreed upon has done his part . . ." (n. 34, O-S, p. 31). Leo XIII rejects such a position. Because work is personal and necessary, "It follows that each one has a right to procure what is required in order to live; and the poor can procure it in no other way than by work and wages" (n. 34, O-S, p. 31). In *Centesimus annus* John Paul II regards this teaching on a just wage as censuring the "thorough-going individualism" that considers the wage contract only in terms of the free consent of two individuals (n. 8, O-S, p. 444).

The pastoral letter of the U.S. bishops implicitly applies its understanding of distributive justice to its reform of the welfare system:

> (1) Public assistance programs should be designed to assist recipients wherever possible, to become self-sufficient through gainful employment. . . . (2) Welfare programs should provide recipients with adequate levels of support. . . . (3) National eligibility standards and a national minimum benefit level for public assistance programs should be established. . . . (4) Welfare programs should be available to two-parent as well as single-parent families . . ." (nn. 211–14, O-S, pp. 625–26).

By definition, these proposals are somewhat general and can be interpreted in different ways; nevertheless, they provide significant guidance, on the basis of distributive justice, for just welfare proposals.[48]

Need is the basic canon of distribution in the Catholic tradition, but there are other canons or titles of distribution. John A. Ryan, the foremost Catholic social ethicist in the United States in the first half of the twentieth century, mentions five canons: equality, needs, effort and sacrifice, productivity, and scarcity.[49] All persons have the right to a basic level of material goods for a minimally decent human life, but above and beyond this minimum, different people can have more and different amounts of wealth on the basis of the other canons.

The concept of distributive justice governing the distribution of wealth and material goods in society again condemns the extremes of individualism and collectivism. The individualistic approach to the distribution of material goods often limits justice primarily to procedural justice and frequently invokes the metaphor of the race. A just system calls for everyone involved to start at the same time and place; once the whistle is blown, however, all contestants are free to get for themselves whatever they can. The Catholic approach puts more substantial canons of distribution in place to determine what is just and ensures a basic minimum for everyone.[50]

The debate over affirmative action programs illustrates the difference between a distributive justice approach and an individualistic approach. The pastoral letter maintains, "Judiciously administered affirmative action programs in education and employment can be important expressions of the drive for solidarity and participation that is at the heart of true justice. Social harm calls for social relief" (n. 73, O-S, p. 596). Affirmative action programs have occasioned much discussion in our country, and the cautious language of the pastoral indicates that the bishops are well aware of the practical problems involved in working out such programs. In theory, however, distributive justice must take account of the common good in distributing goods such as education and employment. Individualism considers only the individual and his or her qualifications.[51]

On the other hand, the Catholic tradition of distributive justice stands in contrast to the collectivist insistence on total equality in wealth and material goods for all. Above and beyond the basic minimum, there can be differences in wealth, based on the other canons of distribution such as sacrifice, effort, and scarcity. In opposition to strict socialism, which regards labor as the only title to ownership, *Quadragesimo anno* insists, "They are wrong in thus attacking and seeking the abolition of ownership and all profits deriving from sources other than labor . . ." (n. 57,

O-S, p. 55). Again, although the documents of Catholic social teaching themselves do not develop a theoretical treatise on the canons of distribution for the basis of ownership, they recognize that labor is not the only title to ownership and wealth.

Catholic social teaching has insisted, however, that vast differences between rich and poor are wrong because they are counter to the solidarity that should unite people in a society—even in a global society. *Quadragesimo anno* points out, "For every sincere observer realizes that the vast differences between the few who hold excessive wealth and the many who live in destitution constitute a grave evil in modern society" (n. 58, O-S, p. 56). The economic pastoral regards "extreme inequality as a threat to the solidarity of the human community, for great disparities lead to deep social divisions and conflict" (n. 74, O-S, p. 596). Here the pastoral letter refers to a similar comment in *Gaudium et spes* (n. 29, O-S, p. 183). Note how the growing emphasis on equality in Catholic social teaching calls into question vast differences in wealth.[52]

Catholic social teaching could learn a helpful lesson and more specific criterion from American philosopher John Rawls, who specifically addresses this issue in his defense of political liberalism. Rawls' second principle of justice states, "Social and economic inequalities are to be arranged so that they are both: (a) to the greatest benefit of the least advantaged, consistent with a just savings principle, and (b) attached to offices and positions open to all under conditions of fair equality of opportunity."[53] If something similar were to become a part of Catholic social teaching, not only would poor people have a right to a basic minimum; inequalities above and beyond that minimum could be justified only if they are to the greatest benefit of the least advantaged. Such a criterion illustrates the preferential option for the poor.

Some observers have criticized Catholic social teaching for giving too much attention to the distribution of wealth and not enough to the creation of wealth. Such criticisms have come especially from Catholic neoconservatives in the United States such as Michael Novak, who rightly points out that John Paul II has tried to correct this imbalance.[54] There is some validity in these criticisms.

The primary focus of the documents of Catholic social teaching has been on the needs of poor people. Consequently, distribution has been their primary concern. The traditional Catholic concept of justice—with its three parts—does not consider creation of wealth to be involved in justice; only the just exchange and distribution of wealth is involved. The preindustrial roots of the Catholic tradition played a role in emphasizing distribution and not mentioning creation of wealth. In addition, the emphasis on freedom, creativity, and initiative have come to the fore only in the later documents of Catholic social teaching.

John Paul II, with his personalistic anthropological perspective, has recognized the importance of the creation of wealth. *Centesimus annus* insists,

> Organizing such a productive effort, planning its duration in time, making sure that it corresponds in a positive way to the demands which it must satisfy, and taking the necessary risks—all this too is a source of wealth in today's society. In this way, the role of disciplined and creative human work and, as an essential part of that work, initiative and entrepreneurial ability becomes increasingly evident and decisive (n. 32, O-S, p. 462).

Sollicitudo rei socialis defends "the right of economic initiative" (n. 15, p. 403). Human creativity and co-creation are very important in producing more wealth, but this wealth must be distributed in accord with the demands of human solidarity and distributive justice.

In the distribution of goods, Catholic social teaching has placed great emphasis on the distribution of material goods and the need of all people for a minimally decent human existence. Catholic anthropology, however, recognizes significant spiritual goods and a hierarchy of goods. This anthropological understanding also has influenced the attitudes of Catholic social teaching toward workers and their rights. Not only does the teaching insist on a just wage and just working conditions; *Quadragesimo anno* also calls for the work contract to be modified by a partnership contract, "for thus the workers and executives become sharers in the ownership or management, or else participate in some way in the profits" (n. 65, O-S, p. 57). In *Mater et magistra* John XXIII insists on the need for workers to participate in the enterprise because they are more than "mere servants" (nn. 91–96, O-S, pp. 98–100). This emphasis on participation, which later came to be an important part of Catholic social teaching, appeared first in the context of workers. John Paul II, with his personalist philosophy and his emphasis on the priority of the subjective aspect of work, strongly insists on participation across the board as well as in the workplace (*Laborem exercens*, n. 8, O-S, p. 362; *Centesimus annus*, n. 34, O-S, p. 465). Thus, justice for the worker insists on the fundamental importance of the material needs of the worker but calls for something in addition—active participation and sharing by the worker in the enterprise.

Distribution of Burdens

Distributive justice deals with the distribution not only of goods but also of burdens within society. In the eyes of many people, the biggest burden in political society is taxation. Politicians in this country hammer away at the need to cut taxes because everybody seems to feel that taxes are too burdensome. In reality, however, just taxation is the primary way of funding government and its positive role. This discussion cannot go into the many debates about bureaucracy and inefficiency; I concentrate on the theory of just taxation.

Papal documents have not given much attention to taxation. *Mater et magistra*, for example, teaches, "As regards taxation, assessment according to ability to pay is fundamental to a just and equitable system" (n. 132, O-S, p. 106). The economic pastoral is more specific and employs the principles of distributive justice:

> [T]he tax system should be structured according to the principle of progressivity so that those with relatively greater financial resources pay a higher rate of taxation. The inclusion of such a principle in tax policies is an important means of reducing the severe inequalities of income and wealth in the nation (n. 202, O-S, p. 624).

Distributive justice calls for the principle of progressivity. People who have more should not only pay arithmetically more than others; they also should pay a higher percentage of their income. Distributive justice involves not arithmetic equality but proportional equality. The virtue of solidarity within the political community calls for such progressivity. People who have more should contribute more to the common good. Thus, distributive justice opposes any flat tax system.

In the United States there is good news and bad news about our tax system in the context of principles of distributive justice and progressivity. Our federal income tax is progressive. There are different levels of taxation, depending on income. This is not true, however, of sales taxes or payroll taxes. There has been much discussion about the exact nature of social security,[55] but the Social Security tax is capped at an income level of less than $80,000. Note how over the years we have come to depend more and more on regressive forms of taxation. The economic pastoral points out, "Action should be taken to reduce or offset the fact that most sales taxes and payroll taxes place a disproportionate burden on those with lower incomes" (n. 202, O-S, p. 624).

One final example of just distribution in Catholic social teaching concerns the burden of military service. The United States today has an all-volunteer army. The very term appeals to the emphasis on freedom in our country. Is this system just, however? The all-volunteer army does not look like the population as a whole. Our soldiers tend to be poorer and less well educated than the mean, and the proportion of people of color is higher than in the society at large. Not many college graduates volunteer for the military. The principles of distributive justice call for all citizens to share in the burden of service to the nation. A more equitable system would require service from all, with provision made for other types of service for people who are conscientiously opposed to war.

The insistence on distributive justice as distinguished from commutative justice is characteristic of Catholic social teaching, with its emphasis on the social nature of human beings as well as their inherent dignity and sacredness. This particular emphasis in Catholic social teaching distinguishes it from an individualistic approach that reduces all justice to commutative justice. On the basis of distributive justice, the economic pastoral opposes free trade and supports reduction of international debt for poor nations. The pastoral letter claims that the preferential option for the poor "does not, by itself, yield a trade policy; but it does provide a frame of reference" (n. 267, O-S, p. 639). Basic ethical questions and norms apply to trade policy: "Who benefits from the particular policy measure? How can any benefit or adverse impact be equitably shared?" (n. 269, O-S, p. 639). The economic pastoral, even in 1986, pointed out that "growing external debt that has become the overarching economic problem of the Third World also requires systemic change to provide immediate relief and to prevent reoccurrence" (n. 277, O-S, p. 641).[56] One might argue on the basis of commutative justice that the contracts involved in both situations were not valid because the parties lacked true freedom. The Catholic approach, however, wants to consider these issues in terms of distributive justice rather than commutative justice.

Legal, Social, or Contributive Justice

Whereas distributive justice involves many economic issues, legal, social, or contributive justice emphasizes the political and social aspects. From the very beginning, legal justice referred to the obligation to obey society's just laws. Notice the requirement of *just* laws. Without going into great detail, the Catholic tradition in theory has always recognized the possibility of civil disobedience. The economic pastoral introduces the new name *contributory* justice, "for it stresses the duty of all who are able to help create the goods, services, and other nonmaterial or spiritual values necessary for the welfare of the whole community" (n. 71, O-S, p. 595). Such an emphasis followed the move to equality and participation of all in later Catholic social teaching.

In this context, active involvement and participation in the life of society should involve all the different structures and mediating institutions of society, as spelled out in the principle of subsidiarity. The political community depends greatly on all of these other forms of community and association if it is to be truly

participative. Corresponding to the duty of everyone to participate in the life of society is the right of all to participate. *Justitia in mundo* asserts, "Participation constitutes a right which is to be applied both in the economic and in the social and
political field" (O-S, p. 291). The economic pastoral insists,

> Recent Catholic social thought regards the task of overcoming these patterns of ex-
> clusion and powerlessness as a most basic demand of justice. Stated positively, jus-
> tice demands that social institutions be ordered in a way that guarantees all persons
> the ability to participate actively in the economic, political, and cultural life of socie-
> ty (n. 78, O-S, p. 597).

In summary, although one is surprised at how little explicit attention Catholic
social teaching gives to the theory and understanding of justice, there is no doubt
that the traditional Catholic understanding of the three types of justice and their
corresponding duties heavily informs Catholic social teaching.

MARXISM AND CAPITALISM

The meaning and purpose of material goods and wealth, the preferential option for
the poor, and the principles of justice—especially concerning the distribution of
wealth—all have a bearing on the further question of the proper economic system
or structure. Catholic social teaching has always recognized the importance of
structure and institutional systems.

Again, an anthropology that stresses both the dignity and the social nature of
the human person greatly influences judgments about the proper economic structures. As I develop in chapter 4, the Catholic position is a middle position between
the extremes of individual liberalism and collectivism. In the economic order as
well, Catholic social teaching logically maintains a similar middle position between
liberalistic capitalism, which fails to recognize the social aspects of the human person, and socialism or Marxism, which fails to recognize the dignity or sacredness
of the person.

In keeping with the recognition that Catholic social teaching develops the
moral aspects of the question rather than the technical and economic aspects, one
should not expect to find a full-blown economic system proposed in any of these
documents. As I have noted, however, *Quadragesimo anno's* long section on the reconstruction of society outlines a corporatist approach that is neither capitalistic
nor socialistic. As a result, some commentators have spoken of a "third way"
Catholic approach that is different from capitalism and socialism.[57] Subsequent

popes have moved away from such a position, however. *Sollicitudo rei socialis* specifically declares, "The church's social doctrine is not a 'third way' between liberal capitalism and Marxist collectivism, nor even a possible alternative to other solutions, less radically opposed to one another" (n. 41, O-S, p. 425).

Early Documents

This anthropological approach that avoids the two extremes developed and changed over time. *Rerum novarum* begins with a condemnation of socialism for its denial of private property (nn. 3-4, O-S, p. 15). Socialist proposals are futile even for the workers and give too great a role to the state (n. 3, O-S, p. 15). Using the metaphor of the organic body to describe society, the encyclical condemns the class struggle (n. 15, O-S, p. 20). Leo XIII insists "that the main tenet of socialism, the community of goods, must be utterly rejected . . ." (n. 12, O-S, p. 19). *Rerum novarum* contains no such discussion of liberal capitalism, although occasional remarks along the way are quite strong. For example, Leo XIII refers to "the cruelty of grasping speculators who use human beings as mere instruments for making money" (n. 33, O-S, p. 30).

In this context as well, *Quadragesimo anno* enlarges the perspective of *Rerum novarum* and interprets it as opposed to both liberalism and socialism (n. 10, O-S, p. 44). Recall that Pius XI had put greater emphasis on the social aspect of property than Leo XIII and consistent with such an approach points out the dangers of capitalism. "Capital, however, was long able to appropriate to itself excessive advantages . . . [but] the actual state of things was not always and everywhere as bad as the liberalistic tenets of the so-called Manchester School might lead us to conclude . . ." (n. 54, O-S, p. 54). For Pius XI, however—and, in his interpretation, for Leo XIII—capitalism "is not vicious of its very nature" but because of the abuses that forget about "the human dignity of the workers, the social character of economic life, social justice, and the common good" (n. 101, O-S, p. 64).

The treatment of socialism is longer and more precise. According to Pius XI, socialism has split into two camps—the more radical approach of communism and a more moderate form of socialism—but neither "has abandoned socialism's fundamental principles which do not accord with Christian belief" (n. 11, O-S, p. 66). Communism, the more radical form of socialism, pursues merciless class warfare and complete abolition of private ownership, espouses violent means, and is openly hostile to the church and God (n. 112, O-S, pp. 66–67). More moderate socialism condemns violence and moderates to some extent class warfare and the abolition of private property. Pius XI's conclusions are clear, however:

Whether socialism be considered as a doctrine, or as a historical fact, or as a 'movement,' if it really remains socialism, it cannot be brought into harmony with the dogmas of the Catholic Church. . . . "Religious socialism," "Christian socialism" are expressions implying a contradiction in terms. No one can be at the same time a sincere Catholic and a true socialist (nn. 117–20, O-S, pp. 68–69).

In the concepts of moral theology, socialism is intrinsically evil because it contravenes basic Christian teachings on private property and class relations, whereas capitalism is not intrinsically evil but often leads to abuses. Thus, the condemnations are not symmetrical. Socialism alone is intrinsically evil.

Six years later, Pius XI's encyclical *Divini redemptoris* (1937) dealt exclusively with atheistic communism. The Bolshevik regime in Russia, the communist threat to countries such as Mexico and Spain, and communist responses to the worldwide depression occasioned this condemnation of Godless and materialistic communism. Here Pius XI used the technical language of moral theology: "Communism is intrinsically wrong, and no one who would save Christian civilization may collaborate with it in any undertaking whatsoever."[58] From then on, Roman Catholicism was an implacable foe of communism. When the Communist Party in Italy was a strong threat in 1949, the Congregation of the Holy Office decreed that Catholics who freely and knowingly enlisted in or showed favor to the Communist Party could not be admitted to the sacraments, and that those who proposed and defended materialistic, anti-Christian communism would be excommunicated.[59]

Beginning in the late 1940s, Roman Catholicism played a leading role in the cold war.[60] Persecution of the church behind the Iron Curtain only increased Catholic anticommunism. The United States and the Vatican were the strongest opponents of communism in the world. Karl Barth, the Swiss Protestant theologian who had courageously condemned Hitler in Germany, saw no need to publicly excoriate communism because communism constitutes no temptation for most people. He was content to let "Mr. Truman and the Pope" do the condemning.[61] This collaboration of the Vatican and the United States against communism also brought about a much greater acceptance of U.S. Catholics by their fellow citizens. Of course, with that acceptance came the temptation of being too uncritical about the United States and its problems.

In the 1960s, however, the Vatican softened its anticommunism long before such a move became popular in the United States. At the beginning of the Second Vatican Council in 1962, Pope John XXIII insisted that there be no condemnations of any type. The spirit of the council was one of dialogue and persuasion, not condemnation.[62] In *Pacem in terris* John XXIII employed a clear distinction between false philosophical teachings regarding the nature, origin, and destiny of the universe and of human beings, and movements which have a direct bearing either on economic and social questions, or cultural matters or on the organization of the state, even if these movements owe their origin and inspiration to these false tenets (n. 159, O-S, p. 157).

These movements are subject to change and contain elements that are positive and deserving of approval. "For these reasons it can at times happen that meetings for the attainment of some practical results which previously seemed completely useless now are either actually useful or may be looked upon as profitable for the future" (n. 60, O-S, p. 157). Whereas Pius XI put together socialism as a doctrine, a historical fact, and a movement, John XXIII clearly distinguishes between false philosophical teachings and movements. In diplomatic and cumbersome language, John XXIII opens the door to dialogue. John F. Cronin, the most visible Catholic commentator on papal social teaching in the United States at the time, refers to John XXIII's approach as unprecedented.[63] The cold war was beginning to thaw.

Paul VI

Paul VI's social teaching developed even further the opening by John XXIII. Again, historical factors greatly influenced what the pope said. Ever since John XXIII, popes had recognized the worldwide nature of the economic and social problem. *Populorum progressio* addressed precisely this issue. The poverty of the Third World clearly showed that existing economic systems were not working and in many ways were even contributing to the problem. On the intellectual front, especially in Europe, an intense Christian-Marxist dialogue began among scholars from both sides after Vatican II.[64] On the practical front, especially in Latin America, some proponents of liberation embraced a Christian Marxism as the best way to deal with the injustices and economic problems in their countries.[65]

An ecclesiological factor also was at work. The papacy, as the central authority in Roman Catholicism, has always been concerned that the church in individual countries be free to carry out its mission. On the basis of this concern, the church has entered into concordats with governments to assure its freedom. In the first half of the twentieth century, the papacy made concordats with the governments of Italy and Germany to secure some freedom for the church. In the process, however, the church gave some respectability to these governments.[66] Some historians claim that this overriding concern of the church to protect its freedom was behind Pius XII's silence about the Holocaust.[67]

Paul VI was deeply interested in securing the freedom of the church to operate in countries behind the Iron Curtain. His strategy was two-pronged: secret ordinations of bishops and priests to work underground and attempts to work out agreements with communist countries. His dialogue with communist countries was called his *"ostpolitik."*[68] One poignant vignette from the 1970s illustrates the change in the Catholic Church's relationship with communism. In the late 1940s and 1950s, Józef Mindszenty, the primate of Hungary, was a Catholic hero who stood up to communism and was imprisoned for his stand. Mindszenty was a living martyr. During the Hungarian uprising in 1956, Mindszenty was freed; after the Soviet takeover he sought protection and housing in the American embassy in Budapest. Throughout this period, the Vatican and the United States worked together in opposition to communism. Later, however, when Paul VI wanted to normalize the relationship of the church with the government of Hungary, the Hungarian government insisted that Mindszenty had to go. The Vatican dragged the reluctant Mindszenty out of Hungary, essentially silenced him, and later removed him from his position as the Archbishop of Esztergom. The hero and martyr of the anticommunism of the 1940s and 1950s had become a problem in the détente of the 1970s.[69]

All of these factors help to explain Paul VI's approach to capitalism and Marxism in *Populorum progressio* and *Octogesima adveniens. Populorum progressio* deals primarily with the problem of Third World countries after colonialism. Paul VI calls for rich nations to assist the developing world and to recognize the injustices of free trade when there is such a discrepancy of power among countries. Development is the new name for peace. He condemns the system of unchecked liberalism "which considers profit as the key motive for economic progress, competition as the supreme law of economics, and private ownership of the means of production as an absolute right that has no limits and carries no corresponding social obligation" (n. 26, O-S, p. 246). Although the statement often is qualified (e.g., "supreme law," "absolute right"), there is no similar criticism of Marxism. The *Wall Street Journal* referred to the encyclical as "warmed-over Marxism."[70]

Octogesima adveniens gives more attention to Marxist and liberal ideologies. The Marxist ideology embraces atheistic materialism and violence, denies the transcendent, and absorbs the individual into the collectivity. Liberal ideology

> exalts individual freedom by withdrawing it from every limitation, by stimulating it through exclusive seeking of interest and power, and by considering social solidarities as more or less automatic consequences of individual initiatives, not as an aim and a major criterion of the value of the social organization (n. 26, O-S, pp. 275).

With regard to socialism, Paul VI quotes the famous distinction of John XXIII in *Pacem in terris* and points out "various levels of expression of socialism: a generous aspiration and a seeking for a more just society, historical movements with a political organization and aim, and an ideology which claims to give a complete and self-sufficient picture of human beings" (n. 31, O-S, p. 276).

Paul VI, in his cautious way, goes on to make even more distinctions in Marxism by referring to how different people understand Marxism. For some people Marxism is the class struggle; for others it is "the collective exercise of political and economic power under the direction of a single party"; for others it is a sociological ideology that is based on historical materialism.

> At other times, finally, it presents itself in a more attenuated form, one also more attractive to the modern mind: as a scientific activity, as a rigorous method of examining social and political reality, and as the rational link, tested by history, between theoretical knowledge and the practice of revolutionary transformation.

This type of analysis privileges "certain aspects of reality to the detriment of the rest . . ." but "it nevertheless furnishes some people . . . the claim to decipher in a scientific manner the mainsprings of the evolution of society." Paul VI goes on to caution against forgetting the links that bind all of these levels together (nn. 33, 34, O-S, pp. 376–77). Thus, Paul VI cautiously opened the door to Christians who use Marxism as a tool of sociological analysis.

Octogesima adveniens goes on to raise questions about the revival of the liberal ideology in light of totalitarian tendencies. People who propose such an approach easily forget "that at the very root of philosophical liberalism is an erroneous affirmation of the autonomy of the individual . . ." (n. 35, O-S, p. 277). The Christian with the gift of the Holy Spirit should go beyond every system and ideology such as "bureaucratic socialism, technocratic capitalism, and authoritarian democracy" and judge such ideologies in the light of utopias that provide a critical structure that "provokes the forward-looking imagination both to perceive in the present the disregarded possibility hidden within it, and to direct itself toward a fresh future. . . ." Thus, Christians should go beyond every system or ideology without failing to commit themselves to serving the needs of others (nn. 36–37, O-S, pp. 277–78).

Paul VI moves beyond the earlier teaching (communism as intrinsically evil and capitalism as subject to abuse) to condemn both ideologies and open the door to a Christian use of Marxist sociological analysis. Note, however, that the ideologies are defined in such absolute terms that very few people today would identify with either of them. Such narrow condemnations help to explain why many people of different persuasions can still appeal to papal social teaching to defend their positions. In this connection, recall the need on the part of the teaching itself to respect the freedom of the believer in the church. Paul VI clearly opened new ground, however.

John Paul II

John Paul II was less open to Marxism in his social teaching than Paul VI. Again, historical and personal factors influenced John Paul II's approach. Karol Wojtyla was a professional moral theologian. In his writings before becoming cardinal and later pope, he avoided—for political reasons—the terms communism or socialism, but he "appears to have located in the term *utilitarianism,* the roots both of Soviet-style materialistic communism and of the materialist consumerist capitalism of the West."[71] These two very different approaches spring from the same materialistic source. Wojtyla's philosophical personalism opposes both Marxism and capitalism.

As a member and leader of the church in Poland before becoming pope, John Paul II experienced the tensions and opposition between the church and its communist regime. The Polish church under Cardinal Stephan Wyszynski was always fearful that the Vatican in its *ostpolitik* policy failed to understand the local situation and would cut some type of deal with the Polish government. Wojtyla helped to lead a church in opposition to a communist government. After becoming pope, he was a central figure in supporting the Solidarity movement against the government, ultimately contributing to the collapse of Poland's communist government. In fact, he played a significant role in the collapse of communism in Eastern Europe in 1989.[72] The encyclical *Centesimus annus* concentrated on that collapse and its aftermath. In the meantime, John Paul II had strong reservations about aspects of liberation theology—especially its use of Marxism—although he came to accept and even use liberation concepts such as the preferential option for the poor and sinful structures.

LABOREM EXERCENS

This encyclical borrows from Wojtyla's earlier thought by regarding Marxism and capitalism as based on what he calls materialistic economism (n. 7, O-S, p. 360), which gives priority to the objective rather than the subjective aspect of workers. Early capitalism treated the worker "on the same level as the whole complex of the material means of production, as an instrument and not in accordance with the true dignity of one's work—that is to say, where the worker is not treated as subject and maker. . . ." This danger continues to exist (n. 7, O-S, pp. 360–61). Materialistic economism also lies behind dialectical materialism and Marxism.

> In dialectical materialism too the person is not first and foremost the subject of work and the efficient cause of the production process, but continues to be understood and treated, in dependence on what is material, as a kind of 'resultant' of the economic or production relations prevailing at a given period. . . . The same error, which is now part of history and which was connected with the period of primitive capitalism and liberalism, can nevertheless be repeated in other circumstances of time and place . . . (n. 13, O-S, p. 370).

The symmetry is not perfect in this text, however, because John Paul II refers to primitive capitalism.

The symmetry is perfect in the discussion of the Catholic approach to private property, which "diverges radically from the program of collectivism as proclaimed by Marxism. . . . At the same time it differs from the program of capitalism practiced by liberalism and by the political systems inspired by it." In the same paragraph, John Paul II maintains that "one cannot exclude the socialization, in suitable conditions, of certain means of production" (n. 14, O-S, p. 371). On the other hand, he explicitly rejects the class struggle of Marxism and insists on a struggle for justice. "Even if in controversial questions the struggle takes on a character of opposition toward others, this is because it aims at the good of social justice, not for the sake of 'struggle' or in order to eliminate the opponent" (n. 20, O-S, p. 380).

Thus, *Laborem exercens*'s personalistic understanding of work—emphasizing the priority of the subjective over the objective aspects—is critical of both Marxism and capitalism. Like Marx, John Paul II emphasizes the primacy of work, but he sees it in a broad sense covering all kinds of work and thus going beyond all classes and contributing to human flourishing and not human alienation.[73]

SOLLICITUDO REI SOCIALIS

This encyclical written to commemorate the twentieth anniversary of *Populorum progressio* discusses liberal capitalism and Marxist collectivism in light of the problems of the Third and even Fourth Worlds. Despite efforts by individual countries and international organizations such as the United Nations, the situation of the developing nations had worsened notably, and "the gap between the areas of the so-called developed North and the developing South" has increased (nn. 12–14, O-S, pp. 401–402). However, "modern underdevelopment is not only economic but also cultural, political, and simply human . . ." (n. 15, O-S, p. 403). In the economic arena specifically, the problems included housing, unemployment and underemployment, and growing international debt (nn. 17–19, O-S, pp. 404–406).

Although John Paul II recognizes the complexity of the picture, he concentrates on one political cause for the aggravated underdevelopment of the South: "the existence of two opposing blocks, commonly known as the East and the West." This political opposition of East and West derives from two different ideologies: "liberal capitalism" and "Marxist collectivism." These two ideologies are based on two different anthropologies and antithetical forms of the organization of labor and of the structure of ownership. "[T]he church's social doctrine adopts a critical attitude to both liberal capitalism and Marxist collectivism" (nn. 20–21, O-S, pp. 406–407). "Each of the two blocks harbors in its own way a tendency toward imperialism, as it is usually called, or toward forms of neo-colonialism . . ." (n. 22, O-S, p. 408).

This abnormal situation, which is the result of war and unacceptable exaggerated concern for security,

> deadens the impulse toward united cooperation by all for the common good of the human race, to the detriment especially of peaceful peoples who are impeded from their rightful access to the goods meant for all. Seen in this way, the present division of the world is a direct obstacle to the real transformation of conditions of underdevelopment in the developing and less advanced countries.

As a result, "The developing countries, instead of becoming autonomous nations concerned with their own progress toward a just sharing in the goods and services meant for all, become parts of a machine, cogs on a gigantic wheel" (n. 22, O-S, pp. 407–408).

Elsewhere *Sollicitudo rei socialis* affirms "the right of economic initiative" and the "creative subjectivity of the citizen" (n. 15, O-S, p. 403); the major thrust of the encyclical, however, remains a condemnation of both ideologies as major causes of the underdevelopment of the South.

CENTESIMUS ANNUS

This 1991 encyclical has an entirely different setting—a reflection on *Rerum novarum* 100 years later, especially in light of the fall of the Iron Curtain and the collapse of communist governments in the Soviet Union and the former Soviet bloc in 1989. In this encyclical John Paul II poses a very pointed question: "[C]an it perhaps be said that, after the failure of communism, capitalism is the victorious social system, and that capitalism should be the goal of the countries now making efforts to rebuild their economy and society?" Is capitalism the model for "the countries of the Third World which are searching for the path to true economic and civil progress?" (n. 42, O-S, p. 471).

> The answer is obviously complex. If by capitalism is meant an economic system which recognizes the fundamental and positive role of business, the market, private property and the resulting responsibility for the means of production, as well as free human creativity in the economic sector, then the answer is certainly in the affirmative, even though it would perhaps be more appropriate to speak of a business economy, market economy, or simply free economy. But if by capitalism is meant a system in which freedom in the economic sector is not circumscribed within a strong juridical framework which places it at the service of human freedom in its totality, and which sees it as a particular aspect of that freedom, the core of which is ethical and religious, then the reply is certainly negative (n. 42, O-S, p. 471).

In this context, John Paul II points out that Catholic social teaching presents no concrete models but "recognizes the positive value of the market and of enterprise, but which at the same time points out that these need to be oriented toward the common good" (n. 43, O-S, p. 471). "[O]wnership morally justifies itself in the creation, at the proper time and in the proper way, of opportunities for work and human growth for all." The integral development of the human persons who work means that business cannot be understood only as a "society of capital goods" but also "as a society of persons" (n. 43, O-S, pp. 471–72).

This somewhat extended discussion coheres with other remarks in the encyclical. On one hand, John Paul II affirms the importance of "initiative and entrepreneurial ability" (n. 32, O-S, p. 462) and recognizes "the legitimate role of profit" (n. 35, O-S, p. 465). On the other hand, the state "has the task of determining the juridical framework within which economic affairs are to be conducted" (n. 15, O-S, p. 450); the free market alone cannot satisfy fundamental human needs (n. 34, O-S, p. 464).[74] Although profit plays a legitimate role, other human and moral factors also have roles to play (n. 35, O-S, p. 465).

John Paul II regards the fall of communism as practical proof of his theoretical opposition to communism but recognizes that

> the sincere desire to be on the side of the oppressed and not to be cut off from the course of history has led many believers to seek in various ways an impossible compromise between Marxism and Christianity. Moving beyond all that was short-lived in these attempts, present circumstances are leading to a reaffirmation of the positive value of an authentic theology of integral human liberation (n. 26, O-S, p. 458).

One sees here John Paul II's strong opposition to the use of Marxism in liberation theology. In its place he proposes his new and authentic theory of liberation (n.26, O-S, p. 458).

On the other hand, in the context of the Third World question John Paul II answers his central question by claiming, "[I]t is unacceptable to say that the defeat of so-called 'Real Socialism' leaves capitalism as the only model of economic organization" (n. 35, O-S, p. 465). *Centesimus annus* warns, "The Western countries, in turn, run the risk of seeing this collapse as a one-sided victory of their own economic system, and thereby failing to make necessary corrections in that system" (n. 56, O-S, p. 481). The conclusion seems to be that John Paul II recognizes a place for the market, private property, human creativity, profit, and entrepreneurship, but these elements are always limited by the primary concern for the common good of all, the recognition that material goods exist to serve the needs of all, and the need for the state to play a role in protecting and promoting the common good.

The most controversial passage in this encyclical concerns the welfare state, which is addressed here for the first time. Excesses or abuses have produced harsh criticism of the "welfare state" or the "social assistance state."

> By intervening directly and depriving society of its responsibility, the social assistance state leads to a loss of human energies and an inordinate increase of public agencies, which are dominated more by bureaucratic ways of thinking than by concern for serving their clients and which are accompanied by an enormous increase in spending. In fact, it would appear that the needs are best understood and satisfied by people who are closest to them and who act as neighbor to those in need (n. 48, O-S, p. 476).

Here John Paul II appeals to the principle of subsidiarity, although he also has recognized the importance of the principle of socialization.

As might be expected, interpretations of this passage vary widely. From a Catholic neoconservative perspective, Michael Novak points out that Vatican II accepted the American idea of religious freedom, and "in *Centesimus annus* Rome has assimilated American ideas of economic liberty."[75] Donal Dorr recognizes the disappointment on the part of many Catholics caused by John Paul II's criticism of the welfare state, but he regards that criticism not as a retreat from previous statements but as a move beyond the welfare state. The state should not create dependency among poor people; it should empower them to take their own initiatives.[76]

At a minimum, one can conclude with David Hollenbach, "It would be a serious mistake to think that the pope has blessed the form of capitalism existing in the United States today. In fact the encyclical is a major challenge to much recent

U.S. economic and social policy."[77] The papal criticism of the social assistance state is based on John Paul II's emphasis on a participatory community. The state has an important role to play in bringing about such a participatory community, but its assistance should not be in the form of impersonal bureaucracies that foster passive dependence.

Thus, anthropology stands behind the major themes of the economic aspects of papal social teaching. A Christian anthropology recognizes God's special concern and option for the poor and the marginalized. The dignity and social nature of human beings insists on the need to provide all of God's people with a minimally decent human existence. Justice that involves not only one-on-one relationships but also social relationships insists on a fair and just distribution of the goods of creation and material wealth for all God's people.

As fundamentally important as material goods are, the anthropology of Catholic social teaching recognizes a hierarchy of values and goods, with the spiritual being higher and more important than the material. Materialism, consumerism, and economism are wrong precisely because they exaggerate or even absolutize material values.

In light of this anthropology, Catholic social teaching has criticized Marxist and capitalist ideologies and positions. Although different accents and emphasis have appeared in different historical circumstances, Catholic social teaching in light of its anthropology and its tradition will continue to insist on the Catholic "both-and"—the dignity of the individual human person and the social nature of the human person called to live in political, social, and economic communities.

NOTES ———————

1. Aquinas, *IIaIIae*, q. 66, a. 2.

2. Ibid.

3. Ibid., ad 1.

4. Aquinas, *IaIIae*, q. 94, a. 5, ad 3.

5. Aquinas, *Ia*, q. 96, a. 4.

6. Ibid., q. 98, a. 1, ad 3.

7. Aquinas, *IIaIIae*, q. 66, a. 2.

8. Ibid., q. 67, a. 7.

9. For a further development of positions similar to that developed in the text, see Abdon Ma. C. Josol, *Property and Natural Law in Rerum Novarum and ST. 2-2, q. 66, aa. 1, 2, 7: An Expository and Comparative Study* (Rome: Accademia Alfonsiana, 1985); J. Diez-Alegría, "La lettura del magistero pontificio in materia sociale alla luce del suo sviluppo storico," in *Magistero e morale: atti del 3o congresso nazionale dei moralisti* (Bologna, Italy: Edizioni Dehoniane, 1970), pp. 211-56. For a position that sees greater continuity between Leo XIII and Aquinas and disputes some of my earlier writing on this issue, see Matthew Habiger, *Papal Teaching on Private Property 1891–1981* (Lanham, Md.: University Press of America, 1990), 1–58, 346–57.

10. For his chief work, see Luigi Taparelli d'Azeglio, *Saggio teoretico di diritto naturale*

appogiato sul fatto, 5 vols. (Naples, Italy: Civiltà Cattolica, 1850).

11. Thomas J. A. Hartley, *Thomistic Revival and the Modernist Era* (Toronto: University of St. Michael's College, 1971), 18–30.

12. The various drafts of *Rerum novarum* can be found in Giovanni Antonazzi, ed., *Enciclica Rerum novarum: Testo autentico e redazioni preparatorie dai documenti originali* (Rome: Edizioni di storia e letteratura, 1957).

13. Léon de Sousberghe, "Propriété, 'de droit natural:' Thèse néoscholastique et tradition scholastique," *Nouvelle revue théologique* 72 (1950): 582–96; see also Richard L. Camp, *The Papal Ideology of Social Reform* (Leiden, Netherlands: E. J. Brill, 1969), 55–56; John Coleman, "What is an Encyclical? Development of Church Social Teaching," *Origins* 2 (1981): 35.

14. Jose María Díez-Alegría, "Ownership and Labour: The Development of Papal Teaching," in *Rerum Novarum: A Hundred Years of Catholic Social Teaching*, ed. John Coleman and Gregory Baum, (Philadelphia: Trinity Press International, 1991), 19; see also de Sousberghe, "Propriété, 'de droit natural,'" 580–81, 588–94; Coleman, "What is an Encyclical?" 35. For a defense of the teaching of *Rerum novarum* as that of Thomas Aquinas and not of John Locke, see Habiger, *Papal Teaching on Private Property*, 343–46.

15. Robert E. Sullivan, "Modernizing Tradition: Some Catholic Neo-Scholastics and the Genealogy of Natural Rights," in *Religion and the Authority of the Past*, ed. Tobin Siebers (Ann Arbor: University of Michigan Press, 1993), 184–208.

16. For a biography of Ryan, see Francis L. Broderick, *Right Reverend New Dealer: John A. Ryan* (New York: Macmillan, 1963). For my analysis and criticism of Ryan's thought, see Charles E. Curran, *American Catholic Social Ethics* (Notre Dame, Ind.: University of Notre Dame Press, 1982), 26–91.

17. John A. Ryan, *Distributive Justice: The Right and Wrong of our Present Distribution of Wealth* (New York: Macmillan, 1916), 56–60.

18. See Ermenigildo Lio, *Morale e beni terreni: La destinazione universale dei beni terreni nella Gaudium et spes* (Rome: Città Nuova, 1976).

19. Catholic neoconservatives in the United States have insisted on creation and creativity to justify their support of democratic capitalism as it exists in this country and their opposition to the economic pastoral of the U.S. bishops. See *Toward the Future: Catholic Social Thought and the U.S. Economy: A Lay Letter* (New York: Lay Commission on Catholic Social Teaching, 1984). The *Lay Letter* was an attempt to propose a more positive and favorable approach to the U.S. economy than the drafts of the bishops' pastoral letter. Part two of the *Lay Letter* (pp. 25–52) is titled "The Lay Task of Co-Creation."

20. For further discussion of the issue, see Daniel R. Finn, "Creativity as a Problem for Moral Theology: John Locke's 99 per cent Challenge to the Catholic Doctrine of Property," *Horizons* 27 (2000): 44–62.

21. Donal Dorr, *Option for the Poor: A Hundred Years of Catholic Social Teaching*, rev. ed., (Maryknoll, N.Y.: Orbis, 1992).

22. The literature on liberation theology is enormous. For significant documents, see Alfred T. Hennelly, ed., *Liberation Theology: A Documentary History* (Maryknoll, N.Y.: Orbis, 1990). For the best one-volume compendium from liberation theologians themselves, see Ellacuría and Sobrino, *Mysterium Liberationis*; see also Christopher Rowland, ed., *The Cambridge Companion to Liberation Theology* (New York: Cambridge University Press, 1999). For a sympathetic discussion from a U.S. perspective, see Arthur F. McGovern, *Liberation Theology and Its Critics* (Maryknoll, N.Y.: Orbis, 1989). For a negative evaluation from a U.S. perspective, see Michael Novak, *Will It Liberate? Questions about Liberation Theology* (New York: Paulist, 1986). For a bibliography, see Thomas J. Davis, ed.,

Liberation Theology: A Bibliography Selected from the ATLA Religion Database (Chicago: American Theological Library Association, 1985).

23. For the understanding of the option for the poor from the father of liberation theology, see Gustavo Gutiérrez, "Option for the Poor," in *Mysterium Liberationis*, ed. Ellacuría and Sobrino, 235–50; see also Leonardo Boff and Virgil Elizondo, eds., *Option for the Poor: Challenge to the Rich Countries* (Edinburgh: T & T Clark, 1986).

24. Norbert F. Lohfink, *Option for the Poor: The Basic Principle of Liberation Theology in the Light of the Bible* (N. Richland Hills, Tex.: Bibal, 1995).

25. Jon Sobrino, *Jesus the Liberator: A Historical-Theological Reading of Jesus of Nazareth* (Maryknoll, N.Y.: Orbis, 1993).

26. Clodovis Boff, "Epistemology and Method of the Theology of Liberation," in *Mysterium Liberationis*, ed. Ellacuría and Sobrino, 57–85.

27. For a feminist liberationist epistemology, see Lisa Sowle Cahill, *Sex, Gender, and Christian Ethics* (New York: Cambridge University Press, 1996), 14–72.

28. Gustavo Gutiérrez, "Theology, Spirituality, and Historical Praxis," in *The Future of Theology: Essays in Honor of Jürgen Moltmann*, ed. Miroslav Volf, Carmen Krieg, and Thomas Kucharz (Grand Rapids, Mich.: Eerdmans, 1996), 176–84; Clodovis Boff, *Theology and Praxis: Epistemological Foundations* (Maryknoll, N.Y.: Orbis, 1987).

29. Stephen J. Pope, "Christian Love for the Poor: Almsgiving and the 'Preferential Option,'" *Horizons* 21 (1994): 303–308.

30. Juan Luis Segundo, *Theology for Artisans of a New Humanity*, 5 vols. (Maryknoll, N.Y.: Orbis, 1973–1974).

31. Congregation for the Doctrine of the Faith, *Instruction on Certain Aspects of the "Theology of Liberation"* (Washington, D.C.: United States Catholic Conference, 1984); also in Hennelly, *Liberation Theology*, 393–414; Congregation for the Doctrine of the Faith, *Instruction on Christian Freedom and Liberation* (Washington, D.C.: United States Catholic Conference, 1986); also in Hennelly, *Liberation Theology*, 461–97.

32. Claretian Publications, compiler., *Liberation Theology and the Vatican Document*, 3 vols. (Quezon City, Philippines: Claretian Publications, 1985–1988).

33. Peter Hebblethwaite, "The Vatican's Latin American Policy," in *Church and Politics in Latin America*, ed. Dermot Keogh (London: Macmillan, 1990), 49–64.

34. Ricardo Antoncich, "Liberation Theology and the Social Teachings of the Church," in *Mysterium Liberationis*, ed. Ellacuría and Sobrino, 103–22.

35. James R. Jennings, ed., *Daring to Seek Justice People Working Together: The Story of the Campaign for Human Development, Its Roots, Its Programs, and Its Challenges* (Washington, D.C.: United States Catholic Conference, 1986); James R. Jennings, *Empowerment and Hope: 25 Years of Turning Lives Around* (Washington, D.C.: United States Catholic Conference, 1996); Lawrence J. Engel, "The Influence of Saul Alinsky on the Campaign for Human Development," *Theological Studies* 59 (1998): 636–61.

36. William R. O'Neill, "No Amnesty for Sorrow: The Privilege of the Poor in Christian Social Ethics," *Theological Studies* 55 (1994): 638–56.

37. Stephen J. Pope, "Proper and Improper Partiality and the Preferential Option for the Poor," *Theological Studies* 54 (1993): 242–71.

38. Aquinas, *IIaIIae*, q. 58, a. 1.

39. William Ferree, *The Act of Social Justice* (Washington, D.C.: Catholic University of America Press, 1943).

40. Zalba, *Theologiae Moralis Summa*, vol. 2, 453–61.

41. Judith A. Dwyer, ed., *New Dictionary of Catholic Social Thought* (Collegeville, Minn.: Liturgical, 1994).

42. This analysis follows the highly acclaimed work of Josef Pieper, *The Four Cardinal Virtues* (Notre Dame, Ind.: University of Notre Dame Press, 1966), 41–113.

43. Aquinas, *IIaIIae*, q. 61, a. 1. Aquinas here cites Aristotle, *Ethics*, Book 5, n. 1130, B, 31–33.

44. Aquinas, *IIaIIae*, q. 58, a. 5. For a strong defense of this position, see Jeremiah Newman, *Foundations of Justice* (Cork, Ireland: Cork University Press, 1954).

45. For an application of a Catholic understanding of justice to the American scene, see Daniel C. Maguire, "The Primacy of Justice in Moral Theology," *Horizons* 10 (1983): 72–85; Daniel C. Maguire, *A Case for Affirmative Action* (Dubuque, Iowa: Shepherd, 1992).

46. Pieper, *Four Cardinal Virtues*, 76–80.

47. Ibid., 81–103.

48. For a further in-depth discussion, see Thomas Massaro, *Catholic Social Teaching and United States Welfare Reform* (Collegeville, Minn.: Liturgical, 1998).

49. Ryan, *Distributive Justice*, 243–53.

50. For the distinction between procedural and substantive justice with a defense of the latter, see John Rawls, *Political Liberalism*, rev. ed. (New York: Columbia University Press, 1996), 421–33.

51. See Maguire, *A Case for Affirmative Action*.

52. Drew Christiansen, "On Relative Equality: Catholic Egalitarianism after Vatican II," *Theological Studies* 45 (1984): 651–75.

53. John Rawls, *A Theory of Justice* (Cambridge, Mass.: Belknap Press of Harvard University Press, 1971), 302.

54. Michael Novak, *Freedom with Justice: Catholic Social Thought and Liberal Institutions* (San Francisco: Harper & Row, 1984).

55. For an approach to social security on the basis of Catholic social teaching, see Charles F. O'Donnell, "The Social Encyclicals and Social Security," in *Things Old and New: Catholic Social Teaching Revisited*, ed. Francis P. McHugh and Samuel M. Natale (Lanham, Md.: University Press of America, 1993), 243–58.

56. For a more recent statement, see Administrative Board of the United States Catholic Conference, "A Jubilee Call for Debt Forgiveness," *Origins* 28 (1999): 793–800.

57. John F. Cronin, *Catholic Social Principles: The Social Teaching of the Catholic Church Applied to American Economic Life* (Milwaukee, Wisc.: Bruce, 1950), 200–253.

58. Pope Pius XI, *Divini redemptoris*, n. 58, in McLaughlin, *The Church and the Reconstruction of the Modern World*, 390.

59. Cited in Cronin, *Social Principles and Economic Life*, 104.

60. Anthony Rhodes, *The Vatican in the Age of the Cold War, 1945–1980* (Norwich, England: Michael Russell, 1992).

61. Karl Barth, *Against the Stream: Shorter Post-War Writings*, ed. Ronald Gregor Smith (New York: Philosophical Library, 1954), 116–18.

62. Pope John XXIII, "Opening Speech to the Council," in *The Documents of Vatican II*, ed. Walter M. Abbott (New York: Guild, 1966), 716.

63. John F. Cronin, *The Social Teaching of Pope John XXIII* (Milwaukee, Wisc.: Bruce, 1963), 20. Cronin was a strong anticommunist who was the acknowledged expert on the subject for the U.S. bishops; see John F. Cronin, *Communism: Threat to Freedom* (Washington, D.C.: National Catholic Welfare Conference, 1962). For Cronin's friendship with Richard M. Nixon, which began in their common struggle against communism, and his later work as the primary speech writer for Nixon when Nixon was vice president, see Gary Wills, *Nixon Agonistes* (New York: Signet, 1971), 34–39. See also John Timothy Donovan, "Crusader in the Cold War: A Biography of Fr. John F. Cronin, S.S. (1908–1994)" (Ph.D. diss., Marquette University, 2000).

64. Peter Hebblethwaite, *Christian-Marxist Dialogue: Beginnings, Present Status, and Beyond* (New York: Paulist, 1977); Paul Mojzes,

Christian-Marxist Dialogue in Eastern Europe (Minneapolis, Minn.: Augsburg, 1981); Nicholas Piediscalzi and Robert G. Thobaban, eds., *Three Worlds of Christian-Marxist Encounters* (Philadelphia: Fortress, 1985).

65. John Eagleson, ed., *Christians and Socialism: Documentation of the Christians for Socialism Movement in Latin America* (Maryknoll, N.Y.: Orbis, 1975).

66. Frank J. Coppa, ed., *Controversial Concordats: The Vatican's Relations with Napoleon, Mussolini, and Hitler* (Washington, D.C.: Catholic University of America Press, 1999).

67. For an indictment of Pius XII, see John Cornwell, *Hitler's Pope: The Secret History of Pius XII* (New York: Viking, 1999). For a defense of Pius XII, see Pierre Blet, *Pius XII and the Second World War: According to the Archives of the Vatican* (New York: Paulist, 1999).

68. Jonathan Luxmoore and Jolanta Babiuch, *The Vatican and the Red Flag: The Struggle for the Soul of Eastern Europe* (London: Geoffrey Chapman, 1999); Pedro Ramet, ed., *Catholicism and Politics in Communist Societies* (Durham, N.C.: Duke University Press, 1990).

69. Blahoslav S. Hruby, "Cardinal Mindszenty as a Casuality of Détente," *Worldview* 18 (January 1975): 13–18; see also Luxmoore and Babiuch, *Vatican and the Red Flag,* 42–46, 165–69.

70. "Review and Outlook," *Wall Street Journal* (March 30, 1967): 14.

71. George H. Williams, "Karol Wojtyla and Marxism," in Ramet, *Catholicism and Politics,* 361; see also George Hunston Williams, *The Mind of John Paul II: Origins of His Thought and Action* (New York: Seabury, 1981).

72. Many recent biographies of John Paul II discuss his role in the fall of communism in Eastern Europe. See, for example, Jonathan Kwitny, *Man of the Century: The Life and Times of John Paul II* (New York: Henry Holt, 1997); Tad Szulc, *Pope John Paul II: The Biography* (New York: Scribner, 1995); George Weigel, *Witness to Hope: The Biography of Pope John Paul II* (New York: Cliff Street Books, 1999).

73. Arthur F. McGovern, "Catholic Social Teachings: A Brief History," in Ramet, *Catholicism and Politics,* 41–42.

74. On the issue of the market, see Dietmar Mieth and Marciano Vidal, eds., *Outside the Market No Salvation?* (Maryknoll, N.Y.: Orbis, 1997); see especially Hollenbach, "The Market and Catholic Social Teaching," 67–76.

75. Michael Novak, "Tested by Our Own Ideals," in Curran and McCormick, *John Paul II and Moral Theology,* 323.

76. Dorr, *Option for the Poor,* 345–47.

77. David Hollenbach, "The Pope and Capitalism," *America* (June 1, 1991): 591.

CHAPTER 7

Further Political Aspects

In this chapter I discuss further political aspects in Catholic social teaching. In the first section I study the development and meaning of human rights. A more extensive discussion of religious freedom follows in the second section. In the third section I discuss the related question of law and morality.

HUMAN RIGHTS

Nineteenth-century Roman Catholicism strongly opposed the concept of human rights. Human rights were identified with the Enlightenment in the philosophical realm and with the call for democracy in the political realm. Pius IX's *Syllabus of Errors* and Leo XIII's condemnation of modern freedoms illustrate this perspective. The Enlightenment grounded human rights in the freedom and autonomy of the individual person, which Catholicism strongly opposed. The person is not autonomous precisely because human beings are related to God as well as to the world itself. Freedom is not an absolute; it must always be considered in relationship to truth and other values. The concept of rights rests on the shaky foundation of a one-sided individualism that cuts off the individual from God and from all others. Catholic moral theology insisted on duties and not on rights.[1]

Historical Development

In opposition to Enlightenment thought, Leo XIII called for the establishment of Thomism as the Catholic philosophy and theology.[2] This nineteenth-century neoscholasticism proposed its own version of Thomas Aquinas, as illustrated by the issue of private property. There is no doubt, however, that Aquinas himself did not have any place for subjective rights. For us, a right is a claim or something that is due one. In Aquinas, *ius*, the Latin word for right, has an objective sense but not a subjective sense. *Ius* is the just thing or the just ordering.[3] Thus, neoscholasticism rightly appealed to Aquinas against a subjective notion of right as a power or claim of the person.

Michel Villey, writing from a neoscholastic perspective in the 1960s, provides an analysis of the historical overview of the development of rights language (in the subjective sense) within the Catholic approach.[4] In keeping with the neoscholastic approach, Villey strongly opposes the concept of subjective human rights; he insists on an objectively just order in which everyone procures her or his fair share. Thomism had no room for championing one's personal rights. Villey points out that the move to subjective human rights first appeared in the thought of fourteenth-century philosopher William of Ockham.

William of Ockham departed from Aquinas by espousing nominalism, which denies the existence of universal principles and concepts apart from the human mind. Only individual particular things exist. Thus, Villey regarded acceptance of rights in a subjective sense as coming from a decadent scholasticism that had broken away from the true teaching of Aquinas. According to Villey, as a voluntarist (as opposed to Aquinas's rationalism) Ockham gave great importance to God's power and to our power—not to the objective ordering of the world. As a nominalist (as opposed to Aquinas' realism), Ockham insisted that only individuals have real existence, so one must begin with the claims of the individual.[5] Thus, in keeping with the approach of neoscholasticism, Villey concludes that Ockham gave birth to the monstrous infant of *ius* as a subjective power of the individual—a concept that ultimately paved the way for the excesses of the Enlightenment.[6]

Contemporary historical studies paint a somewhat different picture of the relationship of subjective rights to the Catholic tradition. Distinguished medieval historian Brian Tierney and his student Charles Reid have convincingly challenged Villey's historical thesis.[7] Although Aquinas did not have a place for the subjective rights of the person, the thirteenth-century canon lawyers known as the decretalists possessed a well-developed and explicit understanding of subjective rights before Ockham. Thus, the idea of subjective rights was not foreign to the Catholic tradition and did not come from a breakdown in Thomistic philosophy. Everyone recognizes, however, that the full blossoming of subjective human rights came into prominence with the Enlightenment.

In this context of neoscholasticism and its opposition to the Enlightenment, Leo XIII strongly opposed subjective rights (see chapter 2). All modern freedoms espoused by the Enlightenment—such as freedom of religion, speech, the press, and association—fail to give enough importance to objective reality and to truth itself. In the following section I discuss in detail religious freedom that the hierarchical magisterium in the Catholic Church finally accepted only at Vatican II in 1965.

The subjective rights associated with the Enlightenment are political and civil rights that involve immunities and emphasize freedom—understood as "freedom from." Freedom of speech means that no external person, force, or reality outside the individual person can force one to speak in a certain way or prevent one from speaking as one wants. Thus, such rights are immunities; they involve freedom from any outside force or coercion. Such rights are grounded in the freedom and autonomy of the individual.

Change in the Twentieth Century

A dramatic change occurred between the end of the nineteenth century and the middle of the twentieth century, however—in Roman Catholicism in general and papal teaching in particular. Papal teaching not only accepted human rights but the popes became strong champions of human rights throughout the world. Insistence on human rights has become a cornerstone in Catholic social teaching.[8]

Rerum novarum (1891) uses rights language on several occasions. The first paragraph refers to "the relative rights and mutual duties of the wealthy and of the poor" (n. 1, O-S, p. 15). In keeping with the basic thrust of its first part, *Rerum novarum* maintains, "Every human being has by nature the right to possess property as one's own" (n. 5, O-S p. 16). "The rights here spoken of belonging to each individual human being are seen in a much stronger light if they are considered in relation to the individual's social and domestic obligations" (n. 9, O-S, p. 18). "The preservation of life is the bounden duty of each and all. . . . It follows that each one has a right to procure what is required in order to live; and the poor can procure it in no other way than by work and wages" (n. 34, O-S, p. 31). *Rerum novarum* also insists on the right of workers to form associations (n. 38, O-S, p. 33).

Although *Rerum novarum* often uses rights language, its understanding differs from liberalism's understanding of rights. The rights in *Rerum novarum* are not primarily immunities protecting freedom; they are empowerments that give freedom for a particular end or purpose. Notice how duties come first, and rights are the necessary means to fulfill one's duties. The understanding of rights here is objective: It is based on the objective order of things, not simply on subjective aspects of the person. The rights developed here also belong to what are called social and economic rights, as distinguished from political and civil rights. Such rights involve empowerments (e.g., the right to a living wage) rather than immunities.

Rerum novarum does not develop the political and civil rights that are dear to the Enlightenment and liberalism. In fact, Leo XIII opposed such rights. This encyclical does recognize, however, the need to respect the dignity of every human being (n. 16, O-S, p. 21).

A dramatic change occurred in *Pacem in terris* (1963), which contains the first full-blown discussion of human rights in Catholic social teaching. *Pacem in terris* begins its discussion of order among human beings with a consideration of human rights. On the basis of being a person with human dignity, everyone has rights and obligations "flowing directly and simultaneously from one's nature" (n. 9, O-S, p. 132). This discussion of sixteen short paragraphs frequently mentions the natural law basis of these rights (nn. 12–13, O-S, p. 133; n. 18, O-S, p. 134). This encyclical mentions different types of rights: the right to life and a worthy standard of living, rights pertaining to moral and cultural values, the right to worship according to one's conscience, the right to freely chose one's state of life, economic rights, the right of meeting and association, the right to emigrate and immigrate, and political rights. Note that rights are the first topic in dealing with the moral order among persons; duties are treated after rights. Rights include civil and political rights, with special emphasis on religious freedom as well as economic and social rights.

Gaudium et spes (1965) teaches,

> From a keener awareness of human dignity there arises in many parts of the world a desire to establish a political-juridical order in which personal rights can gain better protection. These include the rights of free assembly, of common action, of expressing personal opinions, and of professing a religion both privately and publicly (n. 73, O-S, p. 215).

Centesimus annus (1991) points out,

> [I]t is necessary for peoples in the process of reforming their systems to give democracy an authentic and solid foundation through the explicit recognition of those rights. . . . In a certain sense, the source and synthesis of these rights is religious freedom, understood as the right to live in the truth of one's faith and in conformity with one's transcendent dignity as a person (n. 47, O-S, p. 474–75).

The U.S. bishops' economic pastoral (1986) summarizes the contemporary approach to human rights well: "These fundamental human rights—civil and political as well as social and economic—state the minimum conditions for social institutions that respect human dignity, social solidarity, and justice." Civil and political rights include "rights to freedom of speech, worship, and assembly." Social and economic rights include the "right to life, food, clothing, shelter, rest, medical care, and basic education" as well as "the right to earn a living" and the "right to security in the event of sickness, unemployment, and old age." The document goes on to talk about the differences between the two kinds of rights (n. 80, O-S, p. 598).

These rights are grounded in the dignity of the human person who is called to live in community and solidarity with others. "In Catholic social thought, therefore, respect for human rights and a strong sense of both personal and community responsibility are linked, not opposed." In keeping with the traditional Catholic understanding about the state and the individual, "These rights are bestowed on human beings by God and grounded in the nature and dignity of human persons. They are not created by society. Indeed society has a duty to secure and protect them" (n. 79, O-S, p. 547). In the language of moral theology, these rights are natural and inalienable, given by God—not positive rights conferred by an act of the state or another individual.

This understanding of economic rights coheres with and depends to some degree on what Catholic social teaching has said about the meaning of material goods, the preferential option for the poor, and the demands of distributive justice. Every human being has a right to a minimally human existence.

The U.S. bishops recognize that securing these economic rights in the United States "will be an arduous task":

> There is certainly room for diversity of opinion in the church and in U.S. society on how to protect the human dignity and economic rights of all our brothers and sisters. In our view, however, there can be no legitimate disagreement on the basic moral objectives (n. 84, O-S, pp. 598–99).

The greatest change has occurred in the area of political and civil rights. In opposition to totalitarianism and especially communism and Marxism, Roman Catholicism became a strong defender of political and civil human rights and the freedoms that go along with them. I trace this historical development in chapter 2.

Catholicism and Liberalism

Does this change mean that Catholic social teaching has accepted the principles and approach of philosophical liberalism that in the nineteenth century was associated with the defense of political and civil rights? The answer is no.

First, Catholic social teaching cannot accept an approach that absolutizes human freedom and autonomy. Again, the question of human rights goes to the foundational issue of anthropology. Catholic social teaching denies human autonomy, refuses to absolutize freedom, and sees the human person in relationship with God, other human beings, and the world itself. The section of *Pacem in terris* that develops human rights insists that human society must be grounded in truth, justice, charity, and freedom to be well-ordered (n. 35, O-S, p. 136). Recall that before *Pacem in terris*, freedom was not included in these values. Acceptance of freedom constitutes a significant change in Catholic social teaching, but that freedom can never be absolutized and must be considered together with other values.

Second, Catholic social teaching does not ground these political and civil rights in the freedom and autonomy of the person. God is the ultimate author and giver of these rights. *Pacem in terris* and *Gaudium et spes* ground such rights in natural law. Ultimately these rights are grounded in God's gift and mediately—in keeping with the Catholic emphasis on mediation—in the dignity of the person. An objective moral order is the basis for these rights. Although Catholic social teaching regards rights as based on the dignity of the person, in keeping with its anthropology this dignity is always tied up with human solidarity. *Gaudium et spes* recognizes that "the protection of personal rights is a necessary condition for the active participation of citizens, whether as individuals or collectively, in the life and government of the state" (n. 73, p. 215). Political and civil rights are not based on autonomy and understood only in terms of "freedom from." These rights enable and empower the person to participate in the life of the political community. Political participation also grounds these rights. The economic pastoral also regards participation in the life of the community as a partial grounding of civil rights (nn. 79–84, O-S, pp. 597–99). David Hollenbach maintains that Catholic social teaching has developed a more communitarian grounding of rights, as opposed to the individualistic grounding in liberalism.[9]

Third, Catholic social teaching insists on both rights and duties—unlike many liberal approaches. *Pacem in terris* maintains, "The natural rights with which we have been dealing are, however, inseparably connected in the very person who is their subject, with just as many respective duties . . ." (n. 28, O-S, p. 135). The economic pastoral considers human rights only after it has considered duties that derive from justice. Human rights are important, but they are inextricably connected with duties (nn. 63–84, O-S, pp. 594–99). Liberalism, on the other hand, tends to downplay duties.

Fourth, Catholic social teaching insists on political and civil rights as well as economic and social rights. Communism in the cold war insisted on social and economic rights only.[10] The United States, by contrast, insisted on political and civil rights and only recently and hesitatingly has come to acknowledge some social and economic rights. The United States is one of the few countries in the Western world that does not recognize the right to health care for all its citizens—which Catholic social teaching insists on. The Catholic approach to human rights, even with its acceptance of political rights and immunities, differs sharply from the approach to rights of individualistic liberalism because it also insists on social and economic rights. The major point of contention between Catholic social teaching and the American ethos concerns the Catholic opposition to one-sided individualism. The economic pastoral points to these differences and the need for the United States to do in the economic realm what it has done in the political realm.

> The nation's founders took daring steps to create structures of participation, mutual accountability, and widely distributed power to ensure the political rights and freedom of all. We believe that similar steps are needed today to expand economic participation, broaden the sharing of economic power, and make economic decisions more accountable to the common good (n. 297, O-S, p. 646).

Fifth, the epistemology of Catholic social teaching differs considerably from the epistemology of liberalism. Here, too, however, one must recognize great diversity and difference within the general banner of liberalistic philosophy. I discuss this epistemology in greater detail in the third section of this chapter. Catholic social teaching proposes a comprehensive view of the social order with a very "thick" concept of the good. Most liberals claim it is impossible for a pluralistic human society to agree on such a comprehensive view of the world and argue for a much more limited and at best "thin" concept of the good.[11]

There is no doubt that a very significant change occurred in the twentieth century as Catholic social teaching came to a greater appreciation of the freedom, dignity, and rights of the individual person. Yet although Catholic social teaching did learn from philosophical liberalism and human experience, it cannot and will not accept liberalism's individualistic understanding of the human person.

The nature of Catholic social teaching means that it does not delve into the more systematic and complex questions of ethics—nor does it become too particular and specific in its teaching. These characteristics help to explain two aspects of the human rights debate that are not treated in Catholic social teaching.

First, Catholic social teaching does not enter into the deeper question of the exact relationship between rights and duties. The teaching is content simply to recognize the need for both without further development.

Second, the documents of Catholic social teaching do not address the most pressing practical question of human rights: How does one solve a conflict of rights? Rights language involves the strongest possible moral language precisely because a right involves a claim to something as one's own. The danger is that too great an insistence on rights language can easily become just a battleground of individual claims. Even in the best conditions, however, human rights often conflict. Significant ethical and political issues often depend on the need to adjudicate this conflict of rights. Catholic social teaching—with its more general and less specific approach—generally has avoided this thorny problem.[12]

RELIGIOUS FREEDOM

The changing Catholic approach to religious freedom helps to explain in a more accurate and detailed way the general development in the preceding section. Hierarchical Catholic social teaching never entered a sustained discussion of the theory of human rights; at most it devoted a few paragraphs to human rights (as in *Pacem in terris*). After all, the purpose of these documents is to present church teaching, not to become involved in a theoretical analysis. However, Vatican II devoted an entire document—albeit a relatively short one—to the question of religious freedom. From a theoretical viewpoint, many people assert that religious freedom is the first of the political and civil rights. People who recognize God and the believer's obligation to follow God point out that the state should not interfere in the religious realm between the individual and God. This is the strongest barrier there can be against state interference.[13]

Overview

From a Catholic perspective, religious freedom remained a hotly debated issue up to and during Vatican II. Hierarchical church documents in the nineteenth century, as illustrated in the encyclicals of Leo XIII, strongly opposed religious freedom. In *Longinqua oceani* (1895), Leo XIII praised the progress of the Catholic Church in the United States but then stated that this church would make far greater progress if, in addition to freedom, she were to enjoy the favor of the laws and the patronage of the political power. The situation in the United States is not the most desirable for a church-state relationship.[14]

Hierarchical Catholic teaching prior to Vatican II upheld the union of church and state and denied religious freedom. The state has an obligation to support the one true religion. Religious freedom can be tolerated only as the lesser of two evils, to avoid a greater evil, or to achieve a greater good—which can occur especially in situations where Catholics are not the majority. The ideal situation called for the union of church and state.[15]

Hierarchical church teaching continued to insist on the union of church and state in the twentieth century. Governments in Spain and some South American countries lived in accord with this teaching.[16] The Catholic teaching on religious freedom became a source of Protestant suspicion of U.S. Catholics because the latter could not fully accept the basic principles of the U.S. political order—the separation of church and state and freedom of religion. The issue spilled over in the public political arena when Al Smith ran for president in 1928 and again in John F. Kennedy's successful presidential campaign in 1960.[17] In 1949 Paul Blanshard published his well-read *American Freedom and Catholic Power,* which pointed out the danger of a Catholic takeover of the United States and a change in its political institutions if Catholics were to become the majority.[18] In 1955 John Courtney Murray, who had been arguing for a change in Catholic teaching, was silenced by his Jesuit superiors in Rome as a result of Vatican pressure.[19] Thus, up to and during Vatican II religious freedom was a contentious issue in the Catholic Church; the attitude toward human rights in general was nowhere near as public and prominent an issue.

As Catholic teaching in general and social teaching in particular began to give more emphasis to the dignity, freedom, and rights of the person in its opposition to communism, however, the teaching on religious liberty stood in the way. One can easily see that in light of the newer emphasis in Catholic social teaching on human freedom, the older teaching on religious freedom had to change. And change it did at Vatican II—but even then the change did not come easily.

The primary area of U.S. involvement in Vatican II concerned religious freedom. The U.S. church made comparatively few contributions to the broader issues of revelation, church, church in the world, liturgy, and ecumenism. Intellectual leadership on these issues came primarily from Europe. The U.S. church before Vatican II was not known for its intellectual creativity and depth. Ours was a brick-and-mortar church. Bishops were not intellectuals or scholars; they were primarily pastors and builders. The pragmatic and pastoral bent of the U.S. Catholic bishops made them strong supporters of religious freedom, however, especially in light of attacks by Protestants and others in the United States on this teaching.

John Courtney Murray and Religious Freedom

Not only Catholic practice in the United States but especially Catholic theory—as proposed by John Courtney Murray—had an overriding effect on Vatican II's acceptance of religious freedom. Murray had been the editor of the distinguished Jesuit journal *Theological Studies* since 1941, a frequent contributor to the more popular Jesuit weekly *America,* and a professor of dogmatic theology at the Jesuit theologate at Woodstock, Maryland. (He usually taught courses dealing with God and grace.) He began to address church-state issues in the 1940s. Previously, Murray wrote on the role of the church in the world and on the role of the laity. He ultimately opposed the extremes of a secularism that had no role for religion in the public square and a union of church and state that failed to recognize religious freedom.

Murray developed his position on religious freedom beginning in the late 1940s. In the process, he was involved in a sharp dispute in the United States with Joseph Clifford Fenton and Francis Connell of the Catholic University of America and George Shea of Immaculate Conception Seminary in Darlington, New Jersey, all of whom wrote in the *American Ecclesiastical Review.* Murray's position also was challenged by important people in Rome—including Cardinal Alfredo Ottaviani, who at that time was the head of the Holy Office, the Vatican congregation in charge of matters of faith and doctrine.[20] After developing his position in favor of religious liberty, Murray realized that he also had to come to grips with the teaching of Leo XIII, who had denied religious freedom. From 1952 to 1954, Murray published five articles in *Theological Studies* justifying in great detail the continuity between his position and that of the nineteenth-century pope. (A sixth article was about to be published when Murray was silenced in 1955.)[21]

Murray was "disinvited" from the first session of the council in 1962. In April 1963, however, at the insistence of Cardinal Francis Spellman of New York, the Cardinal Secretary of State invited Murray to the council as a *peritus* (expert).[22] The U.S. church was united in its support of religious freedom. Spellman generally was identified with the conservative side at Vatican II, but he strongly supported religious freedom. Although the preconciliar documents prepared for the council opposed religious freedom, after significant debate Vatican II fully accepted religious freedom in its 1965 declaration.[23] No one played a more significant role in developing and influencing the final document than John Courtney Murray.

To understand the Declaration on Religious Freedom, one must appreciate Murray's thought. The following discussion involves a systematic analysis of his mature thought on religious freedom. To begin, one must appreciate the argument proposed by the older position denying religious freedom.

ARGUMENTS AGAINST RELIGIOUS FREEDOM

The older position denying religious freedom and defending the union of church and state rested on the primacy of truth and the obligation of society as a creature of God to worship the one true God. The primacy of truth illustrates the primacy of the objective order over the subjective. Truth is the all-important reality. In the Catholic understanding, the Catholic Church is the one true church of Jesus Christ, and all people have an obligation to accept that truth. What about the individual person's rights of conscience? Error has no rights. People cannot be free to profess error in society because of all the problems that error creates. One clearly sees here the basic reason for the denial of other freedoms such as freedom of speech and freedom of the press.

The older teaching maintains that the state deals only with the temporal order, but the temporal is subordinate to the spiritual. The state is a creature of God and has an obligation to worship God in the proper way. In this understanding the state has not only a paternal role and an ethical role but even a religious role of bringing people to the truth. A sincere but erroneous conscience (one that holds what is not true, though without any personal fault involved) is endowed with individual, internal, and personal freedom. Such a person can never be forced to change her or his religious belief. Because this conscience is not in objective conformity with the truth, however, it has no right to external social freedom within society.[24]

This position has been understood as representing the thesis or the ideal since the middle of the nineteenth century, in response to the Syllabus of Errors. In accord with the principle of toleration, one can tolerate religious freedom in practice—especially where the Catholic Church is not the majority. The need to achieve a greater good or avoid a greater evil justifies toleration. This hypothesis or historical order falls short of the ideal or the thesis.[25]

TWO DIFFERENT APPROACHES IN DEFENSE OF
RELIGIOUS FREEDOM

In developing Murray's approach to religious freedom, which Vatican II closely followed, the logical starting place is the understanding of religious freedom. The right to religious freedom involves a twofold immunity in civil society. No person can be forced to act against her or his conscience in religious matters, and no one can be coercively restrained from acting in accord with her or his conscience.[26] What is the basis or grounding of such religious freedom? According to Murray, the demand for religious freedom is based on two signs of the times: the growth of human personal consciousness and the growth of political consciousness. The common consciousness of human beings today considers the demand for personal, social, and political freedom to be an exigency arising from the depth of the human person.[27]

Murray explicitly recognized two different approaches for developing the argument for religious freedom on the basis of the growing consciousness of human freedom. One school regards religious freedom primarily as a theological-moral concept that is based on the single abstract demand of the free human person for religious freedom—the freedom of conscience in religious matters.[28] Murray criticizes such a concept for three reasons.[29] First, its methodology is abstract and ahistorical, and it gives insufficient attention to the signs of the times and particular types of states. Second, although it results in an ideal instance of constitutional law, constitutional law by nature never deals with the ideal but with practical necessity. Especially in his arguments before Vatican II, Murray went out of his way to claim that the approach for religious liberty that he was proposing in the United States was not the thesis or ideal for everybody. In other historical circumstances (e.g., Spain), a different approach could be maintained. Throughout his writing before Vatican II, Murray never condemned the situation of religious freedom in Spain.[30] He implies that we are always dealing with changing understandings of the state, and there can be no such thing as an ideal constitutional order.[31] (Note that such a position exposes Murray to a charge of relativism.)[32] Third, Murray maintains that such an approach opens the problem of the erroneous conscience. Here the argument seems to be very much on target. What are the rights of an erroneous conscience? Adolf Eichmann claimed to be following his conscience. Does that mean that the civil law could not punish him for what he did? In light of such an argument, there could be no limits whatsoever on religious freedom. What if your religion calls for you to practice child sacrifice? Must civil society stand by and allow this to happen?

Murray proposed a different argument for religious freedom—a formally juridical or constitutional argument that has moral and theological implications. His approach begins with the constitutional issue of the free human person under a government of limited powers. Murray brings in the juridical role of government at the beginning of his argument because we are dealing primarily with political and civil rights.[33] He also was a forceful advocate of natural law and used natural law arguments in developing his position. Murray strongly insisted on the metaphysical realism of natural law epistemology.[34] In contrast to the older Catholic natural law approach, however, Murray employed a more historically conscious methodology. The other approach started with an ahistorical concept of the state and deduced obligations from it. Murray began with the existing, limited, constitutional government.

FOUR GOVERNING PRINCIPLES

The mature Murray developed his understanding of the state and its role on the basis of four principles or distinctions. The first principle involves the distinction between the sacred and the secular orders of human existence—a distinction that corresponds somewhat to the supernatural-natural distinction. The whole of human excellence is not confined to the realm of the temporal and temporal existence. Using the teleological language of natural law, Murray points out that every human being has a transcendent and supernatural end that transcends the power and competency of the state.[35]

The relationship between church and state builds on this distinction between the spiritual and temporal orders. With regard to church and state, Murray frequently cites Pope Gelasius I (d. 496) and medieval thinker John of Paris to insist that there are two distinct powers—church and state—that cannot be confused. Others in the Catholic tradition had talked about the direct or indirect power of the church over the state, but Murray disagreed with such attempts. "The dyarchy" is one of his favorite expressions—two societies that cannot become confused. There can be no monism from either the church or the state.

The church can wrongly intrude in the realm of the state in many ways. Murray opposes the older forms of direct power according to which church authorities have ultimate power over the civil government. The church also errs, however, by using terrestrial power for its own purposes. The state also can overstep its bounds by allowing no room for the sacred in the temporal sphere. This was the problem with continental liberalism, which insisted on the omnicompetence of the state and reduced religion to the private sphere. The same problem exists with secularism in the United States.[36]

How is it possible to hold onto the autonomy of the state and yet not exclude religion and the church from public life? Murray himself was first interested in the role of the church in social and political life and came to the church-state question in that way.[37] The very existence of Catholic social teaching presupposes that the church or religion has a role to play in forming public life. In light of the transcendence of the spiritual, the church must always be free to carry out its total mission—which also includes a concern for the temporal order. Yet how can one affirm the autonomy of the state and still say that the church has to have the freedom to exercise a mission that includes having some effect on the temporal realm?

Here Murray appeals to modern constitutional governments. In a modern constitutional government, there is no authority such as a king. Constitutional governments generally give power to the people; those who govern are representatives of the people. The link between the spiritual and temporal, between church and state, is *idem civis et Christianus*—the person who is both a citizen and a Christian. Precisely through the mediation of the conscience of the Christian citizen, the purely spiritual power of the church has repercussions in the temporal order. For Murray, the whole system pivots on and respects freedom—the free adherence of Christians to the truth of faith and the free participation of Christian citizens with all other citizens in temporal life. Thus, Murray holds onto both the autonomy of the state and the primacy of the spiritual.[38]

Murray's second principle for a proper understanding of the state, especially in the context of a limited constitutional government, involves the distinction between society and the state. Murray first recognized the important distinction between society and the state in 1948.[39] The state has a limited role within civil society. The state exercises the coercive power of law, limiting freedom for the benefit of society. The state is a limited agency that plays a limited role within society. The purposes of the state are not coextensive with the purposes of society. By definition, a limited constitutional government recognizes a comparatively small and limited role for government. By contrast, a totalitarian government would regard the state as the totality of the temporal society and absorbing all parts of it.[40] Religion and churches are not excluded from a role in the broader society. The church can speak out on issues and try to influence all aspects of life in society. Unlike continental liberalism and some forms of secularism, the constitutional situation in the United States allows a public role for the church in society and does not reduce it to the private sphere. Although religion and the church have no direct role in the state, they can influence the broader society in many different ways.[41]

The third principle, which involves the distinction between common good and public order, follows from the distinction between the society and the state. The common good is the end and purpose of society, whereas public order is the end and purpose of the state. The common good devolves upon all members and institutions of society in accord with the principles of justice and subsidiarity. The common good involves all of the social goods that the human person in solidarity with all others seeks.

The public order is a much narrower concept. The role of the coercive power of the state is determined by the purpose of promoting and protecting public order as a narrower concept than the common good. What is the content of public order? Public order involves three goods: justice, public peace, and public morality. Justice demands that the rights of all citizens be effectively safeguarded and that provision is made for settlement of conflicts. Public peace (the U.S. Constitution's preamble uses the phrase "domestic tranquility") comes not from repressive police action but from meeting the demands of justice and having orderly processes to air and settle grievances. Public morality by definition differs from private morality and involves certain minimal standards of morality that affect public order.[42]

Murray, the natural law theoretician, insists that these three principles belong to the order of political truth. The fourth principle, which is a substantive political truth and the primary rule of political procedure, is "freedom under law." "Let there be as much freedom, personal and social, as is possible; let there be only as much restraint and constraint, personal and social, as may be necessary for the public order."[43]

Religious Freedom at Vatican II

The declaration of Vatican II accepted and incorporated most of the points in Murray's understanding of religious freedom. The document includes the generic grounding in the dignity and freedom of the human person that has been impressing itself more and more deeply on contemporary people (n. 1) and the description of religious freedom as a twofold immunity (n. 2). The four principles for understanding the role of the state appear in the document, as does the role of the state, based on these principles (n. 7). Like Murray, the declaration insists on the freedom of the church to carry out its mission (n. 13), the criterion of public order to justify state intervention, and the principle of as much freedom as possible and as little restraint as necessary (n. 7).

Curiously, in one important area—the precise argument for religious freedom—the document does not follow Murray's insistence on regarding religious freedom as a constitutional question of the juridical order and rejecting the theological-moral argument that begins with the free human person and conscience in religious matters. The first argument in the declaration comes from the human person's obligation to seek religious truth in freedom and responsibility and the consequent obligation to follow one's conscience, free from external coercion. The second reason maintains that no human power can command or prohibit religious acts because such acts are free, voluntary acts that relate the person directly to God. By reason of the Christian person's social nature, acts of religion require external expression that must be freely allowed. Third, the document offers a further consideration that government has no right to coerce or inhibit acts of religion because religious acts transcend the limited power of government (n. 3). This last point was Murray's argument.

How should the difference between Murray and the declaration be assessed? Before and during Vatican II, different arguments for religious liberty were proposed and discussed. The declaration is a pastoral document, not an ethical treatise that proposes detailed argument. In addition, such a document should not necessarily exclude some positions that are legitimate within the church community. Thus, the declaration rightly does not take sides on this disputed matter of the argument for religious liberty. It does clearly accept Murray's position, however, on the role and limits of government with regard to religion.

Thus, at Vatican II the Catholic Church fully accepted religious freedom and proposed its understanding of the role of government. A limited constitutional government recognizes the principle of freedom and limits the coercive use of government to the threefold aspects of public order. Even in religious matters, however, some limitations can be placed on religion by virtue of the demands of public order. The demands of justice, public peace, and public morality can limit religious freedom. For example, if a religion believes in child sacrifice and tries to practice it, the demands of justice require the state to prevent such murder. If a religion calls for 1,000 people to process through a quiet neighborhood with a 100-piece band at 3 o'clock on a Sunday morning, other citizens have a right to call the police to prevent this disturbance of public peace. The U.S. Supreme Court has used the criterion of public morality to limit religious freedom. The court prohibited Mormons from carrying out their religious beliefs in the practice of polygamy.[44] One might disagree with such an approach (if the religion allowed both males and females to have a number of different spouses, it would be easier to defend today), but the courts have followed it in their rulings.

In the process of finally accepting religious freedom, Vatican II also finally accepted the concept of limited constitutional government. The difference between such an understanding and Leo XIII's approach to government is huge. For Leo XIII, the state has an ethical and religious role in leading the untutored multitude to moral and religious truth. Such an approach was authoritarian or paternalistic at best. The limited constitutional state gives a much reduced role to government but still does not divorce the role of government from truth (as I point out in the following section).

Some critical comments arise with regard to the declaration and its teaching, as well as with regard to Murray's approach. First, as I point out in chapter 1, the declaration does not propose an integrated theological approach to religious liberty. The first of the declaration's two chapters proposes a natural law argument that is based on human reason. Recall that Murray himself used such a natural law argument. The second chapter, "Religious Freedom in the Light of Revelation," maintains, "What is more, this doctrine of freedom has roots in divine revelation, and for this reason Christians are bound to respect it all the more conscientiously."[45] Again, this approach illustrates the tension created by the twofold audiences of church members and all people of good will. In addition, developing an integrated theological-philosophical argument for religious freedom is not simple.

Second, I fear that the justice element in the public order concept might be interpreted—especially in the U.S. context—in a very individualistic manner. For that reason, the justice component of public order should be described as "justice and social justice." Catholic social teaching frequently calls for the government to play an important role in these areas. Many people in the United States, including some Catholics, have disagreed with such a role for the government. Social justice is a legitimate concern of government, and its demands can justify the use of the coercive force of law.

Third, Murray opens himself to the charge of relativism (though the declaration does not). He does not want to speak of an ideal instance of constitutional law. Perhaps for political reasons in the 1940s and 1950s he did not condemn the denial of religious freedom in some countries. Religious liberty today should be an absolute right for all people, however.

Explanation of the Change in the Teaching

Murray and the fathers of Vatican II realized that the teaching on religious freedom itself was not the whole issue. In the Catholic understanding, one had to explain how the hierarchical church could teach in the twentieth century what Leo XIII had denied in the nineteenth century. The issue raises the old question of explaining the change or development that occurred in this particular matter—a change that also has occurred in the whole area of human rights and the proper role of the state.

Murray examined the teachings of Leo XIII in five articles published in *Theological Studies* from 1952 to 1954.[46] Murray employed a historical hermeneutic in his interpretation of Leo XIII. Leo XIII was fighting against continental liberalism that espoused a totalitarian democracy. Totalitarian liberalism embodied a thoroughgoing monism—political, social, juridical, and religious. There was one sovereign, one society, one law, and one secular faith. The dyarchy of two societies—the spiritual and the temporal—was denied. Separation of church and state meant removal of the church and religion from public society. The church was reduced to the private sphere. In contrast, Leo XIII insisted on the dyarchy—the two powers and their respective roles.[47]

Murray distinguished the doctrinal, polemical, and historical aspects of Leo's teaching. The doctrinal aspect involves what Murray calls three transtemporal principles. The first principle, the freedom of the church (according to Murray, the phrase appears eighty-one times in sixty Leonine documents) involves the church's right to carry out its own mission and functions. The second principle is the necessary harmony (*concordia*) that should exist between the spiritual and temporal societies. For Leo XIII, as in earlier Catholic approaches, the two societies meet in the conscience of the individual person who is both a citizen and a Christian. Recall that Murray used this approach to show how the church could and should try to influence the temporal order, while still respecting the autonomy of the state. Even in the temporal sphere, there is something sacred in the human person—the *res sacra in temporalibus*. This aspect also explains the third transtemporal principle: the necessary cooperation between the two societies. The contribution of each to the other is indirect but necessary. The church imbues a Christian spirit in the temporal order that helps the temporal society achieve its purpose as such. The state aids the church by creating a temporal structure that is conducive for the church's mission.[48]

These three transtemporal principles in Leo XIII are precisely the principles behind the declaration of Vatican II. Yet Leo XIII did not accept religious liberty and in fact espoused the confessional state and the denial of religious freedom. According to Murray, Leo XIII posed the confessional state not as an ideal (notice how Murray uses his denial of an ideal instance to help explain away Leo's position) but as necessitated by two historical circumstances. First, Leo XIII was involved in a polemic with continental liberalism, which gave no public role to the church and espoused an atheistic society. Second, in the traditional Catholic countries the large number of illiterate masses meant that these very weak people had to be protected in their faith. Leo XIII's position is reasonable and prudent in light of the circumstances of the times.[49]

> Implicit in the statement [of Leo] was a declaration of the freedom of the people, once the people had fulfilled the conditions of freedom, which are the growth of the personal and political consciousness. And implicit in the freedom of the people is religious freedom as a juridical institution correlative with constitutional government as a form of polity.[50]

Thus, Murray explained a development in the teaching on religious freedom that justified Leo XIII's position in the nineteenth century as well as the new position in the twentieth century.

In presenting an early draft supporting religious liberty to the second session of Vatican II, Bishop Émile-Joseph de Smedt of Bruges, Belgium, also realized he had to deal with the issue of development and the earlier teaching of Catholic popes. Although quotations from earlier pontifical documents oppose the conclusion of the schema supporting religious freedom, these quotations must be considered in their doctrinal and historical context. Half of de Smedt's address deals with the issue of these past teachings. He proposes a doctrinal evolution that took place according to a twofold law: the law of continuity and the law of progress. His whole purpose was to show that there was no incompatibility between support for religious freedom in the 1960s and the older teachings denying religious freedom. His approach in this speech to the council essentially follows Murray, without going into the matter in as great detail or depth.[51]

There is no doubt that such an understanding made it much easier for the bishops to accept Vatican II's teaching on religious freedom. It does not contradict the previous teaching. Everything could be explained in terms of continuity, evolution, and historical development. In making this point I do not mean to impugn the good faith of Murray or de Smedt. They obviously were convinced of the truth of their explanations. Nevertheless, it would have been much more difficult to accept religious freedom if its proponents had to admit that the teaching of previous popes was erroneous.

In my judgment there *was* error in the previous teachings. I doubt if Leo XIII would recognize himself in the explanation proposed by Murray. For Leo XIII, denial of religious freedom was a matter of doctrine and not merely an historical or polemical contingency. For Leo XIII, continental liberalism was not the only alternative to the confessional state, even though he was much more familiar with it. The U.S. experiment had been in existence for more than a century. Recall that Leo XIII explicitly condemned the U.S. constitutional system. Any theory of the development of the teaching on religious liberty must recognize some discontinuity and error as well as continuity. In chapter 3 I point out that the Catholic Church must recognize discontinuity in Catholic social teaching to be true to the reality itself, to be credible to people of good will, and to have a proper understanding of the role and limits of the hierarchical magisterium in these issues. The change in teaching on religious freedom illustrates the need for the church on occasion to recognize error in some of its social teaching.

Religious Pluralism

Acceptance of religious freedom not only changed the particular teaching of the church; it also involved a new Catholic understanding of the role of the state. Perhaps even more important, acceptance of religious liberty also marked a significant and deep change in the Catholic Church's understanding of the church and its relationship to the broader culture. Vatican II's acceptance of religious freedom in 1965 finally recognized religious pluralism in the world, with the church as just one of the many moral and religious voices trying to influence society. Leo XIII had a very different understanding of the role of the church in society and culture. As I point out in chapter 3, Leo XIII had a triumphalistic understanding of the church as the kingdom of God on earth and a perfect society that alone offered secure salvation to human beings and had a primary moral leadership role in leading the whole world to truth, justice, and goodness.

Leo XIII's view of the church and of nineteenth-century history greatly influenced his approach. In the nineteenth century, the Roman Catholic Church under the papacy became more centralized and authoritarian than ever before. Unlike his predecessors, however, for Leo XIII the primary role of the church was now spiritual and intellectual. The pope had lost his temporal power. Leo XIII now saw his leadership role as providing truth and values that ultimately would allow the church to triumph over liberalism and modernity. Catholic social teaching was part of this strategy. All other approaches, such as Protestantism in the religious order or liberalism in the intellectual and political order, were deficient. The Catholic Church alone had the answers to the problems confronting the modern world.[52]

Leo XIII's immediate successors continued the same basic approach. The article on Pius XI in the *New Catholic Encyclopedia* succinctly illustrates this approach. "For him [Pius XI], the highest good was the unification of humanity—a humanity seeking true peace and community—under the royal scepter of Christ."[53] Pius XI knew he was the Vicar of Christ on earth. Pius XI also instituted the Feast of Christ the King in 1925 to counteract the errors of the modern world and to affirm the sovereignty of Christ over the whole world.[54] Remnants of this approach persisted to the papacy of John XXIII. Recall that his 1961 encyclical was titled *Mater et magistra* : The church, through the pope, is the mother and teacher of all!

At Vatican II, for many reasons, the approach of the Catholic Church changed from condemnation to dialogue. This change affected the church's approach to other churches and religious groups as well as its relationship to the broader world. The Catholic Church now accepts that the modern world is pluralistic in many ways, including religion. Although the Catholic Church still believes it has a social mission and something to contribute to the world, it now does so in dialogue with many others. The triumphalistic view of the church enshrined in the approach of Leo XIII no longer determines how the church functions in a pluralistic society in which it is one of many actors and voices. At times, however, some vestiges of the older approach remain.

LAW AND MORALITY

In the long process of finally accepting religious freedom, Catholic social teaching also proposed a different understanding of the state as a limited constitutional government. This aspect of the role of the state comes to the fore in the discussion of law and morality in a pluralistic society. The Declaration on Religious Freedom strongly insists on the distinction between temporal society and the state and the corresponding distinction between the common good and public order. The purpose of the limited constitutional state is to provide as much freedom as possible and to use the coercive power of the law only when the public order requires it.

Different Approaches to Law and Morality

One would expect Catholic social teaching to employ and develop this concept of public order as the criterion for state intervention. Such is not the case, however. The post–Vatican II documents of papal social teaching do not develop the concept of public order; in fact, they do not use it at all. The documents continue to speak about the common good with regard to the state. What explains this puzzling and even astounding failure of Catholic social teaching to use the concept of public order? A few reasons might shed some light on this very curious omission, although the problem remains.

Although there is no precise canon of documents belonging to Catholic social teaching, many collections do not include the Declaration on Religious Freedom.[55] The subject matter of the declaration clearly differs from the documents of Catholic social teaching that emphasize economic and social aspects. The documents of Catholic social teaching invariably and often refer back to earlier ones, as illustrated especially by documents written on the occasion of earlier encyclicals. The Declaration on Religious Freedom was never in this loop and has not been cited frequently in subsequent social documents and encyclicals.

One could make the point that the important distinction between common good and public order was not important in matters dealing with economic justice. Because justice is an important component of the public order (recall my insistence on explicitly adding social justice to Murray's understanding of justice), the criterion of public order would justify the same involvement by the state as the appeal to the common good.

In theory, however, the distinction between common good and public order is most important for determining the proper role of the state. One practical area of great importance involving such a distinction concerns the relationship between law and morality when dealing with personal behavior. The documents of Catholic social teaching do not consider this issue in any detail, although there are occasional references to the right to life from conception and the evils of abortion. Other church documents have dealt in some detail with abortion and the life issues. *Evangelium vitae* (1995) calls for civil laws to protect the right to life.[56]

In practice, everyone recognizes the central role that the Catholic Church has played in opposing abortion and insisting on civil laws to protect the right to life from the moment of conception. The popes frequently have spoken out on abortion.[57] In the United States, the bishops seem to have stressed the abortion issue more than any other issue.[58] Although the documents of Catholic social teaching—with their relatively narrow focus on economic issues—occasionally mention abortion in passing,[59] Catholic social teaching understood in a broader and nontechnical sense has put great emphasis on abortion and the need for civil laws to protect the fetus. Because I have written this volume in the U.S. context and the theoretical understanding of the state proposed in the Declaration on Religious Freedom has important ramifications for the law-morality issue, it is appropriate to consider this issue in greater depth.

THOMISTIC APPROACH

The theory of the role of the state and the role of law proposed in the Declaration on Religious Freedom differs greatly from the understanding of civil law that had preceded it in the Catholic tradition. The pre–Vatican II manuals of moral theology developed their understanding of human law in the context of natural law and the teaching of Thomas Aquinas in the *Summa*. The Thomistic approach regards natural law as a participation of eternal law in the rational creature. Eternal law is the plan for the world in the mind of God. Human law is derived from natural law in two different ways. Human law either repeats the natural law (e.g., murder is forbidden) or makes specific what the natural law leaves general or undetermined (e.g., determining the penalties that are applied to particular crimes) The connection with eternal law and natural law explains the obligatory force of human law but also provides a criterion for testing whether a law is just. A law that contravenes natural law is an unjust law and does not oblige in conscience. Aquinas defines human law as the ordering of reason for the common good made by the one who has charge of the community.[60] Such an understanding of human law coheres with a strong ethical and even religious role for the state in guiding and governing the life of all.

Aquinas points out, however, that there is not an exact equation between natural law and civil law or what today we would call morality and law. Law is ordered to the common good. It does not consider all the acts of all the virtues—only those that affect the common good. One sees here a distinction between private and public morality. What does not affect the common good does not pertain to law. Aquinas makes a further move. Human law does not have to prohibit all evils because laws are imposed on actual living people. Most humans are not perfect. Human law should suppress the more grievous vices from which most people are able to abstain—especially those that are harmful to others—because such prohibitions are necessary for the good of society.[61] Although Aquinas sees a connection between law and morality, they are not the same.

In another context, Aquinas approves of Augustine's toleration of legal and public prostitution. Aquinas was discussing directly whether the liturgical rites of infidels should be tolerated by the Catholic state. In the process, he develops the classic defense of toleration in human society on the basis of actions of God. God, all-powerful and good, sometimes permits some evils to occur that he could have prevented to bring about greater good or avoid greater evil. Human beings can and should act in the same way. Aquinas then approvingly cites Augustine on tolerating prostitution.[62] One sees here the theoretical basis for the later toleration of religious freedom in certain circumstances that prevailed before Vatican II. This older approach might rightly be called the Thomistic approach because it depends heavily on Thomas Aquinas.

RELIGIOUS FREEDOM APPROACH

The role of the limited constitutional state outlined in the Declaration on Religious Freedom and developed by Murray forms the basis for a different understanding of the law-morality relationship. The Thomistic approach started with the demands of natural law, even though these demands might not always hold. The religious freedom approach begins with the principle of the free society—as much freedom as possible and as little restraint as necessary.

What are the limits on this freedom in accord with the declaration? The first limit on any freedom is the responsibility of the individual person in the exercise of that freedom. The state can and should intervene with the coercive power of law, however, to protect and promote public order with the goods of justice and social justice, public peace, and public morality.[63]

In addition, good law must be enforceable and equitable. If a law cannot be enforced, it should not be a law. That many people in society are not observing the law is a good indication that it should not be a law. (Think of the U.S. experience with prohibition.) If the law discriminates against poor people or a particular segment of society, it should not be a law because it fails in equity and justice.

Finally, law in a pluralistic society necessarily involves prudential, pragmatic, and feasible aspects. If one judges that the law cannot be passed because of opposition to it, one can decide not to work for such a law. It is not feasible for such a law to come into existence at the present time. Lawmaking often involves compromises. Sometimes half a loaf is better than none. Although it might not be possible to pass a law that bans the sale of some guns, many people who favor strict gun control would support a law that imposes more restrictions on people who purchase guns. Such a law probably could be passed, and from the perspective of gun-control advocates it would be better than the existing law.

Thus, the relationship between morality and law is complex and must be judged in light of four principles: the presumption in favor of as much freedom as possible and as little restraint as necessary, the demands of public order, questions of enforceability and equitableness, and the feasible and prudential aspects of lawmaking.

Probably all Catholics today agree that there should be no law against the sale of contraceptives (presupposing here the teaching of the hierarchical magisterium, with which many disagree). The foregoing criteria argue strongly against such a law. Yet in the 1940s and 1950s, Catholics staunchly defended such laws as properly enshrining and enforcing natural law.[64]

Abortion Law

How does the foregoing approach to civil law deal with abortion legislation? One could very well argue for a civil law against abortion on the basis of these criteria. In this discussion, I presuppose acceptance of the hierarchical teaching about the right to life from the moment of conception. Note, however, that there is legitimate room for difference on this position within Catholicism.[65] The state can and must intervene for the sake of justice. No human right is more basic than the right to life. Government should do everything possible to protect and promote the right to life, especially of the powerless and the helpless. No one is more powerless than a fetus. Thus, government should strongly protect the fetus's right to life.

On the other hand, one could use the criteria of the religious freedom approach to argue in favor of retaining *Roe v. Wade* at the present time—but using the other criteria proposed for the role of law in the state. On the basis of as much freedom as possible and as little restraint as necessary, one can argue that the present division and impasse in this country over abortion means that the freedom of people who believe in the possibility of abortion should be respected. When the civil society is equally divided, the presumption is in favor of freedom. Likewise, there have been and could be problems of enforceability and equity; before *Roe v. Wade*, wealthier people were able to obtain abortions more easily than poor people. Above all, pragmatic aspects of feasibility come to the fore. Experience has shown that pro-life forces have not been able to change the existing laws and probably will not be able to do so. Although these arguments are by no means above criticism and rebuttal, they have some credibility.

Thus, one could use the criteria derived from the religious freedom approach to law and come to different conclusions about abortion laws. In fact, Catholic authors have used the religious freedom approach to come to differing conclusions about abortion laws.[66]

PAPAL TEACHING ON ABORTION LAWS

Despite acceptance of a limited constitutional government in the Declaration on Religious Freedom and the emphasis on freedom and public order, the papal magisterium has not applied this understanding to the abortion issue. The 1974 Declaration on Procured Abortion of the Congregation for the Doctrine of the Faith clearly follows a Thomistic approach and does not adopt the religious freedom approach.[67] In keeping with the Thomistic approach, this document explicitly recognizes that civil law does not have to cover the whole field of morality and often must tolerate a lesser evil (n. 20). It continues, however:

> The law is not obliged to punish everything, but it cannot act contrary to a law which is deeper and more majestic than any human law, the natural law engraved in human hearts by the Creator as a norm which reason clarifies and strives to formulate

properly, and which one must always struggle to understand better, but which it is always wrong to contradict. Human law can abstain from punishment, but it cannot make right what would be opposed to the natural law... (n. 21).

The succeeding paragraph maintains that a Christian cannot take part in a propaganda campaign in favor of a law allowing abortion or vote for it (n. 22).

John Paul II devotes twelve paragraphs of his 1995 encyclical *Evangelium vitae* to abortion law.[68] The encyclical recognizes but does not accept some of the arguments in favor of permissive abortion law—unenforceability, the danger of illegal and medically unsafe abortions, and divisions within society regarding abortion (nn. 68–69). The theory of law proposed in the encyclical follows the Thomistic approach. The moral value of democracy depends "on conformity to the moral law to which it, like every other form of human behavior, must be subject..." (n. 70). "[T]he acknowledgement of an objective moral law which, as the 'natural law' written in the human heart, is the obligatory point of reference for civil law itself" (n. 70). Civil law must protect the fundamental rights of the person, which above all include the right to life of every innocent human being (n. 71). John Paul II explicitly recognizes, "The doctrine on the necessary conformity of civil law with the moral law is in continuity with the whole tradition of the church" (n. 72). He cites "the clear teaching of St. Thomas Aquinas.... 'Every human law can be called law insofar as it derives from the natural law. But if it is somehow opposed to the natural law, then it is not really a law but rather a corruption of the law'" (n. 72).

In this encyclical John Paul II recognizes the problem of conscience for a legislator opposed to abortion in voting for a more restrictive law than the current permissive law, even though this law still sanctions some abortions. He holds that "an elected official whose absolute personal opposition to procured abortion was well known" could support such a more restrictive abortion law (n. 73). However, *Evangelium vitae* repeats the warning of the Declaration on Procured Abortion. "In the case of an intrinsically unjust law, such as a law permitting abortion or euthanasia, it is therefore never licit to obey it or to 'take part in a propaganda campaign in favor of such a law or vote for it'" (n. 73).

In this discussion of abortion, the encyclical never refers to the concept of public order; it always uses the broader term common good. For example, "the purpose of civil law... is that of ensuring the common good" (n. 71). The common good is "the end and criterion regulating political life..." (n. 70). This section of *Evangelium vitae* twice cites paragraph seven of the Declaration on Religious Freedom (fn. 91, 93)—the paragraph that contains the concept of public order, with its threefold goods as the criteria that govern the coercive power of law, and recognizes the need for as much freedom as possible and as little restraint as necessary. *Evangelium vitae* never quotes these central aspects of that paragraph, however. In the first case (fn. 91), although *Evangelium vitae* cites the declaration concerning the threefold goods of fundamental rights, public peace, and public morality, John Paul II explicitly refers to these goods as comprising the common good and not the public order (n. 71).

JOHN PAUL II AND PUBLIC ORDER

Why does John Paul II not use the religious freedom approach in discussing the morality-law relationship? No outsider can respond to that question with certitude, but some considerations come to mind.

First, the Declaration on Religious Freedom often is not included in the papal documents of Catholic social teaching. In a sense, this document is somewhat out of the loop and does not really influence subsequent documents. The primary thrust of the document is the religious freedom question, and the role of the state proposed there remains incidental to the basic thrust of the document. Although John Paul II explicitly cites the declaration's pivotal paragraph seven, he describes the threefold goods as constituting the common good rather than the public order.

Second, the natural law approach had been the Thomistic and traditional way in which Catholic moral theology addressed this issue until Vatican II. John Paul II clearly was accustomed to that approach in his theology and writings.

Third, there is no doubt that John Paul II is very certain about his position on abortion law. The older Thomistic approach logically gives more certitude about the need for a civil law. Natural law is a participation of eternal law in the rational creature. To contravene natural law is to contravene God's law. Once you claim something as a matter of natural law, there can be no doubt that a civil law can never contravene it. On the other hand, the religious freedom approach to law and public policy is more complex, gives more attention to contemporary empirical evidence, and cannot claim absolute certitude. Some Catholic theologians have used this approach even to argue against restrictive abortion laws.

Fourth, John Paul II consistently maintains that freedom is not an absolute. Freedom must always be understood in its relationship to truth. As I point out in chapter 5, this position is very close to that proposed by Leo XIII. The concept of freedom in the words of the Declaration on Religious Freedom—"The freedom of human beings be respected as far as possible, and curtailed only when and insofar as necessary"—is not closely related to truth. Civic freedom is an immunity from external coercion by the state in matters that do not come under the rubric of public order. At minimum, there is an important difference between the relationship of moral freedom to truth and the relationship of civic freedom to truth. John Paul II does not appear to recognize this crucial difference, which is at the heart of the distinction between common good and public order.

Fifth, John Paul II is very certain about the truths he proposes. As a result, he gives very little or no weight to pluralism when such pluralism contradicts his understanding of the truth. Everyone should agree that civil law should not be based only on the existing consensus in a society. Think of all the forms of discrimination that have been present in U.S. society. To bring about peace and justice in a human society, however, civil law cannot simply ignore the existing pluralism. Even the older Thomistic approach in Roman Catholicism recognized some moral pluralism in human society. It did not make its understanding of truth the overriding factor. Aquinas maintained that civil law should prohibit only the more grievous vices from which the greater number of people can abstain—especially those that are harmful to others, such as murder and theft.[69] On the basis of this Thomistic teaching, one could still argue that there should be a law against abortion because it is murder. The theory proposed in Aquinas, however, loosens the bond between truth and freedom on which John Paul II insists. The relationship of freedom to truth is only one aspect of the complex understanding of freedom and human law.

The foregoing five reasons shed some light on the indisputable fact that John Paul II has purposely avoided using the criterion of public order in discussing the role of civil law and the relationship between morality and law. In contrast to John Paul II, Cardinal Joseph Bernardin in the United States explicitly used the religious freedom approach to call for a restrictive civil law to protect the life of the fetus. Bernardin, writing in the U.S. context, obviously was very familiar with and explicitly cited the approach of John Courtney Murray on this question.[70]

The important distinction between common good and public order is akin to the approach of John Rawls, who has written extensively on political philosophy in the United States. Rawls seeks to defend political liberalism by working out an understanding of political justice for a liberal constitutional democratic regime that a plurality of reasonable doctrines—religious and nonreligious, liberal and nonliberal—may endorse for the right reasons. Rawls distinguishes his approach from an Enlightenment liberalism—a comprehensive theory that was liberal and often totally secular. Rawls distinguishes between comprehensive doctrines—Enlightenment liberalism, his own earlier approach to justice, or natural law theory (my example, not his)—and the overlapping consensus of public reason that can be supported by many different comprehensive doctrines.[71] The Catholic notion of common good would be a comprehensive doctrine, whereas the concept of public order corresponds to the overlapping consensus of public reason.

Rawls explicitly indicates in two footnotes that he regards the public order aspect of John Courtney Murray as similar to his approach.[72] Indeed, there are great similarities. Murray's and Vatican II's acceptance of public order is not simply an overlapping consensus, however; it is based on a realist epistemology that maintains there are substantive goods and truths on which all human beings can agree. Rawls could not accept that epistemology.[73] This religious freedom approach is always willing to discuss these positions in the public forum, however, and argue rationally for them in an attempt to arrive at a consensus in a pluralistic society.

John Paul II's failure to use the religious freedom approach to law and morality illustrates the tension within the body of Catholic social teaching as older approaches in the tradition continue to exist with newer approaches, even though they are in some opposition. In my judgment, Catholic social teaching should accept and employ the religious freedom approach in all questions of law and morality.

In this chapter I have discussed further aspects of the political understanding of Catholic social teaching—human rights, religious freedom, law and morality. Significant historical development has occurred in all the areas and some tensions remain.

NOTES

1. See, for example, Robert Reuel Hull, *The Syllabus of Errors of Pope Pius IX, The Scourge of Liberalism* (Huntington, Ind.: Our Sunday Visitor, 1926). For an acclaimed historical overview of the period, see Roger Aubert et al., *The Church in the Age of Liberalism, History of the Church*, vol. 8, ed. Herbert Jedin and John Dolan (New York: Crossroad, 1981).

2. James Hennesey, "Leo XIII's Thomistic Revival: A Political and Philosophical Event," in *Celebrating the Medieval Heritage: A Colloquy on the Thought of Aquinas and Bonaventure*, ed. David Tracy, *Journal of Religion* 58 (Supplement, 1978): 85–197; Victor B. Brezik, ed., *One Hundred Years of Thomism: Aeterni Patris and Afterwards, A Symposium* (Houston: Center for Thomistic Studies, University of St. Thomas, 1981).

3. John M. Finnis, *Natural Law and Natural Rights* (Oxford: Clarendon, 1980), 205–10.

4. Michel Villey, *Leçons d'histoire de la philosophie du droit*, rev. ed. (Paris: Dalloz, 1977).

5. For an opposing and more positive evaluation of Ockham, see Marylin McCord Adams, *William Ockham*, 2 vols. (Notre Dame Ind.: University of Notre Dame Press, 1987).

6. Michel Villey, "La genèse du droit subjectif chez Gillaume d'Occam," *Archives de philosophie du droit* 9 (1964): 97–127.

7. Brian Tierney, *The Idea of Natural Rights: Studies on Natural Rights, Natural Law, and Church Law* (Atlanta: Scholars, 1997), 1–203; Charles J. Reid, Jr., "The Canonistic Contribution to the Western Rights Tradition: An Historical Inquiry," *Boston College Law Review* 33 (1991): 37–92.

8. For a Catholic objection to the contemporary emphasis on human rights in Catholic thought, see Ernest L. Fortin, "The New Rights Theory and Natural Law," *Review of Politics* 44 (1982): 590–612.

9. David Hollenbach, "A Communitarian Reconstruction of Human Rights: Contributions from Catholic Tradition," in Douglass and Hollenbach, *Catholicism and Liberalism*, 127–50.

10. Theo Tschuy, "Human Rights: Moving beyond the Cold War," *Christian Century* 100 (July 20–27, 1983): 683–89; see also David Hollenbach, *Claims in Conflict: Retrieving and Renewing the Catholic Human Rights Tradition* (New York: Paulist, 1979), 7–38.

11. Hollenbach, "A Communitarian Reconstruction of Human Rights," 132–38.

12. Hollenbach, *Claims in Conflict*, 141–85.

13. George Weigel, "Religious Freedom, the First American Right," *This World*, no. 21 (spring 1988): 31–45; Stephen L. Carter, *The Culture of Disbelief: How American Law and Politics Trivialize Religious Devotion* (New York: Basic Books, 1993).

14. Pope Leo XIII, *Longinqua oceani*, n. 6, in *The Papal Encyclicals 1878–1903*, ed. Claudia Carlen (Wilmington, N.C.: McGrath, 1981), 364–65.

15. For affirmations of this position by U.S. Catholic theologians in the mid-twentieth century, see Francis J. Connell, "The Theory of the 'Lay State,'" *American Ecclesiastical Review* 125 (July 1951): 7–18; Joseph Clifford Fenton, "Principles Underlying Traditional Church-State Doctrine," *American Ecclesiastical Review* 126 (June 1952): 452–62; Joseph Clifford Fenton, "Toleration and the Church-State Controversy," *American Ecclesiastical Review* 130 (May 1954): 330–43.

16. For a Protestant perspective, see John David Hughey, *Religious Freedom in Spain* (Nashville: Broadman, 1955); George P. Howard, *Religious Liberty in Latin America?* (Philadelphia: Westminster, 1944).

17. Edmund Moore, *A Catholic Runs for President: The Campaign of 1928* (Gloucester, Mass.: P. Smith, 1968); Mark S. Massa, "A Catholic for President? John F. Kennedy and the 'Secular' Theology of the Houston Speech, 1960," *Journal of Church and State* 39 (spring 1997): 297–317.

18. Paul Blanshard, *American Freedom and Catholic Power* (Boston: Beacon, 1949). For a Catholic response to Blanshard, see James M. O'Neill, *Catholicism and American Freedom* (New York: Harper, 1952).

19. Donald E. Pelotte, *John Courtney Murray: Theologian in Conflict* (New York: Paulist, 1975), 51–54.

20. For a biography of Murray, see Pellote, *John Courtney Murray*. For an in-depth discussion of the controversy between Murray and other Catholic theologians and his own development, see Thomas T. Love, *John Courtney Murray: Contemporary Church-State Theory* (Garden City, N.Y.: Doubleday, 1965). For my appraisal of Murray, see Curran, *American Catholic Social Ethics*, 172–232.

21. The five published articles by Murray are "The Church and Totalitarian Democracy," *Theological Studies* 13 (1952): 525–63; "Leo XIII on Church and State: The General Structure of the Controversy," *Theological Studies* 14 (1953): 1–30; "Leo XIII: Separation of Church and State," *Theological Studies* 14 (1953): 145–214; "Leo XIII: Two Concepts of Government," *Theological Studies* 14 (1953): 551–67; and "Leo XIII: Two Concepts of Government, II: Government and the Order of Culture," *Theological Studies* 15 (1954): 1–33. A sixth article, "Leo XIII and Pius XII: Government and the Order of Religion," existed in galley proofs but was not allowed to be published in *Theological Studies*. This article has been published in John Courtney Murray, *Religious Liberty: Catholic Struggles with Pluralism*, ed. J. Leon Hooper (Louisville, Ky.: Westminster/John Knox, 1993), 49–125.

22. Pelotte, *John Courtney Murray*, 77–82.

23. For the historical development of the Document on Religious Freedom at Vatican II, see Richard J. Regan, *Conflict and Consensus: Religious Freedom in the Second Vatican Council* (New York: Macmillan, 1967).

24. See notes 20 and 21. For Murray's description of the older position, see Murray, *The Problem of Religious Freedom*, 7–17.

25. Roger Aubert, "Mgr. Dupanloup et le Syllabus," *Revue d'histoire ecclésiastique* 51 (1956): 79–142, 471–512, 837–915.

26. John Courtney Murray, "The Declaration on Religious Freedom," in *Vatican II: An Interfaith Appraisal*, ed. John H. Miller (Notre Dame, Ind.: University of Notre Dame Press, 1966), 565–76.

27. Murray, *The Problem of Religious Freedom*, 17–18.

28. Murray contends that the first two drafts or schemas on religious freedom presented to Vatican II in November 1963 and September 1964 follow this approach; see Murray, "The Declaration on Religious Freedom: A Moment in Its Legislative History," in *Religious Liberty: An End and a Beginning*, ed. John Courtney Murray (New York: Macmillan, 1966), 16–27.

29. Murray, *The Problem of Religious Freedom*, 20–22.

30. John Courtney Murray, "The Problem of State Religion," *Theological Studies* 12 (1951): 160–61.

31. Murray, *The Problem of Religious Freedom*, 31.

32. Edward A. Goerner, *Peter and Caesar: The Catholic Church and Political Authority* (New York: Herder and Herder, 1965), 186–91; A. F. Carillo de Albornoz, "Religious Freedom: Intrinsic or Fortuitous? A Critique of a Treatise by John Courtney Murray," *Christian Century* 82 (September 15, 1965): 1122–26.

33. Murray, *The Problem of Religious Freedom*, 23–28. Without mentioning his own role as first scribe, Murray sees this approach in the third draft or schema discussed at Vatican II in November 1964; see Murray, *Religious Liberty, an End and a Beginning*, 27–42.

34. Murray, *We Hold These Truths*, 275–336.

35. Murray, *The Problem of Religious Freedom*, 28.

36. See note 21.

37. Curran, *American Catholic Social Ethics*, 187–92.

38. John Courtney Murray, "Contemporary Orientations of Catholic Thought," *Theological Studies* 10 (1949): 211–27.

39. John Courtney Murray, "Governmental Repression of Heresy," *Proceedings of the Catholic Theological Society of America* 3 (1948): 26–98.

40. Murray, *The Problem of Religious Freedom*, 28–29.

41. Murray, *We Hold These Truths*, 63–78.

42. Murray, *The Problem of Religious Freedom*, 29–30.

43. Ibid., 30–31.

44. Richard P. McBrien, *Caesar's Coin: Religion and Politics in America* (New York: Macmillan, 1987), 73–79.

45. Declaration on Religious Freedom, n. 9, in Abbott, *Documents of Vatican II*, 688.

46. See note 21.

47. Murray, "The Church and Totalitarian Democracy," 525*ff.*

48. Murray, "Leo XIII: Separation of Church and State," 206-209.

49. John Courtney Murray, "Vers une intelligence du dévelopment de la doctrine de l'Église sur la liberté religieuse," in *Vatican II: La liberté religieuse, declaration 'Dignitatis humanae personae'*, ed. Jérôme Hamer and Yves Congar (Paris: Cerf, 1967), 127–28.

50. Murray, *The Problem of Religious Freedom*, 60.

51. Émile-Joseph de Smedt, "Religious Freedom," in *Council Speeches of Vatican II*, ed. Yves Congar, Hans Küng, and Daniel O'Hanlon (London: Sheed and Ward, 1964), 161–68. For

commentaries on this speech see Regan, *Conflict and Consensus*, 41–46; Xavier Rynne, *The Second Session: The Debates and Decrees of Vatican Council II, September 29–December 4, 1963* (New York: Farrar, Straus, 1964), 223–34.

52. Émile Poulat, "L'Église romaine, le savoir et le pouvoir," *Archives de sciences sociales des religions* 37 (1974): 5–21; Hennesey, *Celebrating the Medieval Heritage*, 185–97. For more general evaluations of Leo XIII's pontificate that include this aspect, see Owen Chadwick, *A History of the Popes 1830–1914* (Oxford: Clarendon, 1998), 273–331; Oskar Köhler, "The World Plan of Leo XIII: Goals and Methods," in *The Church in the Industrial Age, History of the Church*, vol. 8, ed. Herbert Jedin and John Dolan (New York: Crossroad, 1981), 3–25.

53. G. Schwaiger, "Pius XI, Pope," in *New Catholic Encyclopedia*, vol. 11, 412.

54. Mary Collins, "On Becoming a Sacramental Church Again," in *Open Catholicism: The Tradition at Its Best: Essays in Honor of Gerard S. Sloyan*, ed. David Efroymson and John Raines (Collegeville, Minn.: Liturgical, 1997), 115.

55. See, e.g., O'Brien and Shannon, eds., *Catholic Social Thought*; Walsh and Davies, *Proclaiming Justice and Peace*.

56. Pope John Paul II, *Evangelium vitae*, nn. 68–74, in *Origins* 24 (1995): 713–16.

57. James J. McCartney, *Unborn Persons: Pope John Paul II and the Abortion Debate* (New York: Peter Lang, 1987).

58. Timothy A. Byrnes and Mary C. Segers, eds., *The Catholic Church and the Politics of Abortion: A View from the States* (Boulder, Colo.: Westview, 1992).

59. E.g., *Centesimus annus*, n. 47, in O'Brien and Shannon, *Catholic Social Thought*, 474, calls for laws to protect the right to life from conception.

60. Zalba, *Theologiae Moralis Summa*, vol. 1, 340–595.

61. Aquinas, *IaIIae*, q. 95–96.

62. Aquinas, *IIaIIae*, q. 10, a. 11.

63. Declaration on Religious Freedom, n. 7, in Abbott, *Documents of Vatican II*, 686–87.

64. William J. Kenealy, "Contraception: A Violation of God's Law," *Catholic Mind* 46 (1948): 552–64.

65. See Curran, *Catholic Moral Theology Today*, 222–26.

66. Mary C. Segers, "Murray, American Pluralism, and the Abortion Controversy," in *John Courtney Murray and the American Civil Conversation*, ed. Robert P. Hunt and Kenneth L. Grasso (Grand Rapids, Mich.: Eerdmans, 1992), 241–48; Todd David Whitmore, "What Would John Courtney Murray Say on Abortion and Euthanasia?" *Commonweal* (October 7, 1994): 16–22. For my position, see Charles E. Curran, *Ongoing Revision in Moral Theology* (Notre Dame, Ind.: Fides/Claretian, 1975), 107–43.

67. Congregation for the Doctrine of the Faith, *Declaration on Procured Abortion* (Vatican City: Vatican Polyglot, 1974).

68. John Paul II, *Evangelium vitae*, *Origins* 24 (1995): 691–727.

69. Aquinas, *IaIIae*, q. 96, a. 2.

70. Joseph Cardinal Bernardin et al., *Consistent Ethic of Life*, ed. Thomas G. Fuechtmann (Kansas City, Mo.: Sheed and Ward, 1988), 91–93.

71. John Rawls, *Political Liberalism*, rev. ed. (New York: Columbia University Press, 1996), xl–xli.

72. Ibid., lvi–lvii, fn. 32–33.

73. For a critique of Rawls' notion of public reason from a strong natural law perspective, see Robert P. George and Christopher Wolfe, eds., *Natural Law and Public Reason* (Washington, D.C.: Georgetown University Press, 2000).

Afterword

The United States constitutes the social milieu in which I have written this volume. Along the way, the text and notes make references to other writings on the U.S. scene. Volumes have been written about the public life of the Catholic Church in the United States. In this afterword I very briefly sketch the landscape in which Catholic social teaching finds itself. In the first section I describe the landscape within U.S. Catholicism; in the second section I relate Catholic social teaching to the broader scene of political and social thinking and writing in the United States.

U.S. CATHOLIC LANDSCAPE

First, there are many different interpretations of Catholic social teaching on the U.S. Catholic scene. There probably are as many different interpretations as there are interpreters and commentators. The major discussion today is between two different groups: a movement whose members consciously call themselves neoconservatives and another movement that often is called—at least by the neoconservatives—liberal or progressive. One should always keep in mind the caveat that there also is much diversity under these two umbrellas. My approach belongs to the progressive or liberal rubric. Many of the authors I cite in this book belong under this same general umbrella. The neoconservative movement includes especially Michael Novak, Richard John Neuhaus, and George Weigel, who have claimed for themselves the name neoconservative.[1]

The neoconservatives believe that the current crisis in the church derives not from a crisis of authority but from a crisis of faith. Responding to this crisis, the neoconservative project carries on an ecumenical and interreligious dialogue, especially with conservative evangelical Protestants who previously had not been in dialogue with Catholicism. Neoconservative thinkers employ a theological method that challenges the dominant ways of thinking in the academy today and specifically opposes the claims of race/class/gender political correctness. Finally, they call for a social, cultural, and political transformation of American society with a religiously grounded public philosophy that is capable of informing and disciplining the public moral argument that is the lifeblood of democracy. Neoconservatives see themselves in the middle within the Catholic Church—between restorationists on the right and progressives on the left.[2]

The liberal or progressive movement and the neoconservative movement share many basic outlooks. They both accept Catholic social teaching; they both call for a religious voice in American public life; they both recognize that at times the church can learn from the world and that at other times it must criticize it; and they both claim the mantle and legacy of John Courtney Murray.

Neoconservatives disagree with many of the positions I take in this volume. Neoconservatives object to the general tone and approach of the two pastoral letters of the U.S. bishops and consider them to be in opposition to the approach of John Paul II, whereas in this volume I regard the pastoral letters of the U.S. bishops as making papal social teaching more specific on the United States scene. Neoconservatives maintain that liberals are too critical of U.S. capitalism and give too great a role to the state. They strongly support antiabortion legislation and believe that the bishops' support for a consistent ethic of life downplays the abortion issue. Neoconservatives strongly identify themselves with all that John Paul II has proposed and do not dissent from papal teaching in any way. Many Catholics who are associated with the liberal or progressive movement, including myself, disagree with some of the papal sexual teaching and, as this volume indicates, also are critical of some aspects of John Paul II's social teaching.[3]

Catholic social teaching and its commentators are not the only Catholic players on the U.S. landscape. In *Public Catholicism* David O'Brien has traced the historical development of the public presence of the Catholic Church in the United States. With regard to the public presence of Catholicism and its attempts to work for political and social change, O'Brien identifies three different approaches in the historical development of Catholicism in the United States that are still evident on the contemporary scene: republican, evangelical, and immigrant.[4]

The republican approach—as exemplified in the writings of John A. Ryan and John Courtney Murray, as well as the public policy statements of the U.S. bishops—seeks to influence the broader society through reasonable discussion and discourse. Catholic social teaching in general, as well as progressives and neoconservatives, belong to this category. This movement tends to be more academic and theoretical.

The evangelical approach emphasizes conversion, some detachment from a corrupt society, and a commitment to a community of faith. Perhaps the best-known example of such an approach in the United States is the Catholic Worker Movement founded by Dorothy Day, with its commitment to voluntary poverty.[5] Evangelical approaches rely much less on Catholic social teaching and appeal primarily to a scriptural and personalist approach.

The immigrant approach seeks to mobilize support for a particular goal of the group. This approach is more practical than theoretical and relies on political power and organized efforts rather than primarily on reason and discussion. Examples of such an approach include Catholics working for specific Catholic issues such as aid to schools; the organizing approach of labor unions, which often had strong Catholic support; and, on the contemporary scene, community organizing—especially among Hispanics and people on the margins of society.

Thus, Catholic social teaching—with its basic republican approach—does not exhaust public Catholicism in its relationship to the good of society. In this volume I have occasionally mentioned the evangelical and immigrant approaches proposed by O'Brien. A further question involves the relationship among these different approaches, but that issue lies beyond the pale of this volume. In a sense, these three approaches are somewhat abstract; in practice they often are intermingled with one another. In the eyes of many observers, the Catholic approach to abortion in the United States is not so much a matter of reasoning and discussion as it is a mobilizing of pro-life forces to work for the cause.[6]

Broader U.S. Landscape

I now turn to the broader landscape of theological, philosophical, and political thought in the United States that shares the general republican approach of persuasion through reasoned discussion.

With regard to the broader landscape, Catholic social thought or the republican approach (in O'Brien's terminology) plays a limited role. On a more popular level, the U.S. bishops' pastoral letters on peace and the economy evoked a major response when they were first written. On the theological and ecumenical scenes, Catholics and Protestants are in serious dialogue with one another on social issues and social theory; the literature is substantial. There also have been less-extensive Catholic-Jewish dialogues on issues facing society.

Catholic social teaching has little or no visibility in the wider philosophical or political science discussions and writings in the United States. Two examples illustrate this point. I have frequently cited *Catholicism and Liberalism*, edited by R. Bruce Douglass and David Hollenbach. This significant book is subtitled *Contributions to American Public Philosophy*. The book is entirely one-sided, however: The authors are all Catholics or speaking from the Christian tradition. There are no proponents of liberalism contributing to the volume. There is no dialogue from the side of philosophical liberalism with regard to Catholic social teaching.

A second illustration comes from the work of John Rawls—probably the most respected proponent of philosophical liberalism in the United States today. Rawls has attempted to develop a liberal approach that recognizes the importance of justice and social justice in society. Although he starts from principles of liberalism, he develops in his major work a theory of justice that is not individualistic.[7] In his major writings, I have found only two footnote references to the Catholic republican tradition. These footnotes appear in the new introduction to the paperback version of *Political Liberalism*, which was published in 1996. These two footnotes refer to positions of Cardinal Joseph Bernardin and John Courtney Murray on the concept of public order, which Rawls regards as similar to his understanding of public reason as the basis for an overlapping consensus in a pluralistic society. In a footnote, he credits two Catholics who have worked with him—Leslie Griffin, a theological ethicist and lawyer from Santa Clara University, and Paul Weithman, a philosopher from Notre Dame—for introducing him to the thought of John Courtney Murray.[8] The most renowned political philosopher in the United States (now retired) did not mention until recently the social thought of the most renowned Catholic writer on political theory. Catholic social thought has played almost no role in the wider philosophical and political science community in the academy in this country, except for communitarians such as Robert Bellah.[9]

What explains the isolation of Catholic social teaching from the purview and interest of secular social ethicists and political scientists? Several factors come to mind. Secular disciplines have always kept religious thought at a distance. In addition, a disciplinary structure dominates the academic scene, sealing off one discipline from another. Some of the problem lies with Catholic authors, who tend to write for members of their own community and do not make attempts to address a wider community. (This book constitutes a good illustration of such an approach!)

One other factor deserves attention. The general impression in the popular mind in the United States is that the Catholic Church primarily is a pressure group (the immigrant approach of O'Brien), working and mobilizing for its own purposes and teachings, not a voice trying to persuade through reason and deliberation. The ethos of the culture wars in this country in the past few decades has contributed to the polarization of religious groups and the role of religion as a political force.[10] There is an inevitable tension between the republican and the immigrant approaches. Rational discourse and political pressure do not easily fit together. The fact that Catholic teaching regards itself as authoritative church teaching also downplays the rational and deliberative nature of that teaching.

I have frequently pointed out what the Catholic Church has learned from the experience of history in general and the U.S. experience in particular. The learning and teaching dialogue goes both ways, however. I also have pointed out that Catholic social teaching can contribute a great deal to a better public life in this country.

In *The First Liberty* William Lee Miller wrote about the Catholic contribution to public life in the United States. The older Protestant hegemony and the anti-Catholicism of an earlier period are now gone. Miller sees two important contributions that Catholicism can make to the public life of the United States today:

> Something like such a personalistic communitarianism is the necessary base for a true republic in the interdependent world of the third century of this nation's existence. And the Roman Catholic community is the most likely single source for it—the largest and intellectually and spiritually most potent institution that is the bearer of such ideas.[11]

Miller, who is Protestant, goes on to point out a second contribution that Catholicism can make to American public discourse and life: "the tradition of reason as applied to complex matters of collective life." Pietism and romanticism unfortunately have triumphed over intellect in much of American Protestantism. In moral matters, however, we need reason rather than just feeling or heart or conscience.[12]

I agree with Miller about these two important contributions that the tradition of Catholic social thought can make to the United States public ethos. In this volume, I have tried to develop these two contributions in depth.

NOTES

1. For descriptions of Catholic neoconservatism from its own adherents, see Michael Novak, "Neoconservatives," in Dwyer, *New Dictionary of Catholic Social Thought*, 678–82; George Weigel, "The Neoconservative Difference: A Proposal for the Renewal of Church and Society," in *Being Right: Conservative Catholics in America*, ed. Mary Jo Weaver and R. Scott Appelby (Bloomington: Indiana University Press, 1995), 138–62.

2. Weigel, "The Neoconservative Difference," 147–57.

3. Ibid., 138–62.

4. David O'Brien, *Public Catholicism* (New York: Macmillan, 1989), 242–52.

5. See William D. Miller, *A Harsh and Dreadful Love: Dorothy Day and the Catholic Worker Movement* (Garden City, N.Y.: Image, 1974); June O'Connor, *The Moral Vision of Dorothy Day: A Feminist Perspective* (New York: Crossroad, 1991). For somewhat similar contemporary approaches, see Michel L. Budde and Robert W. Brimlow, eds., *The Church as Counterculture* (Albany: State University of New York Press, 2000).

6. For contrasting criticisms of the position of the U.S. bishops on abortion from a liberal and a neoconservative perspective, see Margaret A. Farley, "The Church in the Public Forum: Scandal or Prophetic Witness?" *Proceedings of the Catholic Theological Society of America* 55 (2000): 87–101, and Michael Pakaluk, "A Cardinal Error: Does the 'Seamless Garment' Make Sense?" *Crisis* 6 (November 1988): 10–14.

7. John Rawls, *A Theory of Justice* (Cambridge, Mass.: Belknap Press of Harvard University Press, 1971).

8. Rawls, *Political Liberalism*, rev. ed., lvi–lvii, fn. 32 and 33. In a 1963 symposium, Murray criticized Rawls's approach to justice from a natural law perspective; see John Courtney Murray, "The Problem of Mr. Rawls's Problem," in *Law and Philosophy: A Symposium*, ed. Sidney Hook (New York: New York University Press, 1964), 29–34.

9. Bellah et al., *The Good Society*, 182–83, 281–83, 299–304.

10. James Davison Hunter, *Culture Wars: The Struggle to Define America* (New York: Basic Books, 1991).

11. William Lee Miller, *The First Liberty: Religion and the American Republic* (New York: Knopf, 1986), 288–89.

12. Ibid., 289.

Index

Curran, Charles: cited on, 17 n.26; 50 n.7; 51
nn.34, 35, 40; 98 n.25; 100 nn.66, 70; 123
nn.21, 23, 28, 30, 36; 169 nn.31, 33;
170–71 n.52; 210 n.16; 213 n.75; 244
n.20; 245 n.37; 246 nn.65, 66

Davies, Brian, 17 n.18; 246 n.55

Davis, Thomas, 210 n.22

DeBerri, Edward, 16 n.1

Declaration on Religious Freedom. *See*
Dignitatis humanae

Decree on Training of Priests. *See Optatam*
totius

Dei verbum (Constitution on Divine Revelation,
1965), 50 n.22; 123 n.27

Delhaye, Philippe, 50 n.5; 96 n.3

Derr, Thomas Sieger, 122 n.14

Deschamps, Ivan, 99 n.61

Destro, Robert A., 97 n.15

Diez-Alegría, J., 209 n.9; 210 n.14

Dignitatis humanae (Declaration on Religious
Freedom, 1965), 7, 11, 35, 48, 75, 83,
117–18, 222; and church and state, 106,
229–30, 235–36, 237–38, 241–42; and
conscience, 76–77, 105, 225–26, 229, 232;
and historical consciousness, 58, 76, 226;
and public peace, 76–77, 147, 157, 229–30,
235–36, 239–41; and religious freedom, 39,
76–77, 105, 106, 154, 224–35; cited on, 99
nn.46–49, 50, 55; 245 n.45; 246 n.63

Dogmatic Constitution on the Church. *See*
Lumen gentium

Dolan, John, 16 n.10; 243 n.1; 246 n.52

Donahue, James, 169 n.34

Donovan, John Timothy, 212 n.63

Donovan, Mary Ann, 136 n.1

Dorr, Donal, 14, 183, 208; cited on,16 n.2; 17
n.27; 98 n.24; 210 n.21; 213 n.76

Douglas, Mary, 98 n.21

Douglass, R. Bruce, 250; cited on, 99 nn.43, 53;
169 n.30; 244 n.9

Droulers, Paul, 123 n.30

Duffy, Stephen, 50 n.25

Dunn, James D. G., 16 n.4

Dwyer, Judith, 85, 189; cited on, 99 n.56; 171
n.54; 211 n.41; 252 n.1

Eagleson, John, 213 n.65

ecclesiology, 89, 95, 101, 105, 121; and
hierarchical teaching office, 106–9,
109–22; and juridical institution, 102, 104;
and methodology, 101–22; and pilgrim
church, 103–4, 121; and tensions with
authoritative teaching, 114–21

Economic Justice for All (U.S. Catholic Bishops'
economics pastoral, 1986), 1, 7, 14, 42,
44–45, 138, 149, 186, 248, 250; and
common good, 14, 144–45, 150, 221; and
justice, 190–92, 197, 219; and mediation,
110–11; and poor, 183–84, 187–88,
218–19; and rights, 218–19, 221; and
specificity, 111, 113–14, 118

Efroymson, David, 246 n.54

Eichmann, Adolf, 226

Elizondo, Virgil, 211 n.23

Ellacuría, Ignacio, 51 n.31; 98 n.23; 210 n.22;
211 nn.23, 26, 34

Elsbernd, Mary, 97 n.13

Engel, Lawrence J., 99 n.60; 211 n.35

Engelen, William J., 16 n.13

Enlightenment, 4, 5, 6, 9, 69, 215, 216, 218

epistemology, 95, 221; and certitude, 96, 105,
113–14; and impartiality, 94–95, 184, 186–
87; and moral truth, 91–96; and realism,
91, 226; and universalism, 92–93, 119–20

Eschmann, I. Th., 170 n.36

Evangelii nuntiandi, 36, 49, 162; and
conversion, 46–47

Evangelium vitae (The Gospel of Life, 1995),
120, 236, 240–41; cited in, 246 nn.66, 68

Farley, Margaret, 98 n.25; 252 n.6

feminist theology, 66–67, 92, 94, 120

Fenton, Joseph Clifford, 244 n.15

Feree, William, 211 n.39

Ferrari, Liliana, 50 n.18

Finn, Daniel R., 210 n.20

Finnis, John, 167; cited on, 171 n.55; 243 n.3